THE SOVIET UNION AND REVOLUTIONARY IRAN

THE SOVIET UNION
·AND·
REVOLUTIONARY
IRAN

ARYEH Y· YODFAT

CROOM HELM
London & Canberra

ST MARTIN'S PRESS
New York

© 1984 Aryeh Y. Yodfat
Croom Helm Ltd, Provident House, Burrell Row,
Beckenham, Kent BR3 1AT

Croom Helm Australia Pty Ltd,
28 Kembla Street, Fyshwick,
ACT 2609, Australia

British Library Cataloguing in Publication Data

Yodfat, Aryeh Y.
    The USSR and revolutionary Iran.
    1. Soviet Union–Foreign relations–Iran
    2. Soviet Union–Foreign relations–1945-
    3. Iran–Foreign relations–Soviet Union
    4. Iran–Foreign relations–1945-
    I. Title
    327.47055   DK68.7.I55
    ISBN 0-7099-2905-6

Library of Congress Cataloging in Publication Data

Yodfat, Aryeh, 1923-
    The Soviet Union and the Iranian Revolution.
    Bibliography, p. 150
    1. Iran–Foreign relations–Soviet Union. 2. Soviet
Union–Foreign relations–Iran. I. Title.
DS274.2.S65Y62 1983 327.47055   83-3130
ISBN 0-312-74910-4 (St. Martin's)

CONTENTS

PREFACE

This book reviews and analyses relations between the Soviet Union and Iran, from the time of the overthrow of the Shah's regime and the establishment of the Islamic Republic up to mid 1983. It begins with a brief survey of earlier periods in Russian-Persian relations, with a focus on the developments which served as a background to the current events.

While much has been written about Iran during the Shah's regime, very little has been published about the period since 1979, and almost nothing about the USSR and Iran — what relations were actually like between them and how these relations were viewed by either side. Here the subject is dealt with extensively in an attempt to present both facets, together with views and a commentary.

Extensive background material is given on both internal Iranian developments and wider Middle Eastern politics. Emphasis has been placed on matters which attracted the Soviets' attention, and to which they attached considerable importance. These influenced their policy and views in regard to Iran. Both Iran's 'neither East nor West' policy, and the Soviet attempts to attract Iran and influence it, are examined in depth.

The term 'Russia' is used when dealing with the period of Russia's old regime. The expression 'Soviet Russia' represents the country during the first years of the Soviet regime; and the terms 'Union of Soviet Socialist Republics' (USSR), 'the Soviet Union' or 'the Soviets' refer to the same country after the adoption of the Soviet constitution in 1924. The term 'Iran' became current in Western usage after 1927. In this book the term 'Persia' is generally used until the late 1920s and from that time onwards the country has been referred to as 'Iran'.

The author would like to express his thanks to the documentation centres and libraries of the Shiloah Centre for Middle Eastern and African Studies, Tel Aviv University; and of the Harry S. Truman Research Institute, Jerusalem, and to their staff — whose help has been of inestimable value.

Aryeh Y. Yodfat

ABBREVIATIONS

ADP	Azerbaijani Democratic Party
AFP	Agence France Presse, Paris
AIOC	Anglo-Iranian Oil Company
BBC	British Broadcasting Corporation
CENTO	Central Treaty Organization
CIA	Central Intelligence Agency, USA
Cong.	Congress
CPSU	Communist Party of the Soviet Union
DPK	Democratic Party of Kordestan, Iran
	Democratic Party of Kurdistan, Iraq
FBIS	Foreign Broadcast Information Service, USA
FRG	Federal Republic of Germany
GCC	Gulf Co-operation Council
GDR	German Democratic Republic
ICP	Iraqi Communist Party
IRNA	Islamic Republic News Agency (formerly PARS)
IRP	Islamic Republican Party, Iran
KGB	Komitet Gosudarstvennoy Bezopasnosti, Committee for State Security, USSR
ME	Middle East
NIOC	National Iranian Oil Company
NVOI	National Voice of Iran
NY	New York
OPEC	Organization of Petroleum Exporting Countries
PDPA	People's Democratic Party of Afghanistan
PDRY	People's Democratic Republic of Yemen (South Yemen)
PRC	People's Republic of China
PUK	Patriotic Union of Kurdistan, Iraq
Sess.	Session
Supp.	Supplement
TASS	Telegraph Agency of the Soviet Union
UAE	United Arab Emirates
UN	United Nations
US, USA	United States, United States of America
USSR	Union of Soviet Socialist Republics

1 RUSSIA'S OLD REGIME – PERSIA 'SLIPPED OUT OF RUSSIAN HANDS'

Russia's Moving Frontier

Russian history has been characterized by constant expansion – from the principality of Moscow to an empire. The movement was in all directions: east and west, north and south. The frontier was a moving one similar to that of pioneering America, a frontier of the hunter, fisherman, trader, miner, bandit, freebooter, military conqueror and colonizer.

The conquest of Transcaucasia by Russian forces began in the late eighteenth century. Its western part, the Black Sea coast, and its hinterland were at that time in the sphere of influence of the Ottoman Empire. Armenia, Azerbaijan and Eastern Georgia (Gruzia) in the east were under Persian control. The rivalry between Persians and Ottomans was much to Russia's advantage and facilitated its conquests. Generally, the Russians had to fight only one of these powers at a time; only from 1806-12 did they fight Persia and Turkey simultaneously. Tbilisi, the capital of Gruzia, was captured by the Russians in 1801, Baku in 1806, Yerevan, the capital of Armenia, in 1828. The Russian frontier advanced to the river Araxes, where it has remained. The occupation of the Caucasus was accomplished only in 1864.

The conquest of Central Asia by Russia was similar to the colonial history of West European powers in Africa. In both cases trade came before the flag and traders before soldiers. Deserts played the same role for the Russians as the sea for the West Europeans in separating metropolis from colony. The remoteness and the unfamiliar climate made Central Asia a place more for exploitation than for colonization. The Russians (adopting a strategy similar to that of the British in India) made the weaker states of Kokand and Khorezm a part of their empire. The more productive areas, such as the Fergana Valley and Samarkand, were put directly under Russian control with the intention of growing cotton. Bukhara and Khiva were left as native states, nominally independent, with the freedom to control their own affairs.[1]

The advances in Central Asia brought the Russians close to the sphere of British interests. The Russian occupation in 1844 of Merv, from which a road was open to Herat and further south to India, led to British

1

reactions described at the time as 'mervousness'. A period of Anglo-Russian tension followed, and negotiations concerning Afghanistan: the British attempted to define the northern frontier of Afghanistan as the southern limit of the Russian sphere of influence. Afghanistan was declared to be a neutral buffer state, separating the Russian and British areas.[2]

In Persia, the Russian presence and influence steadily increased. The Treaty of Turkmenchai in 1828 ceded the provinces of Erevan and Nakhichevan to Russia, imposed a heavy indemnity on Persia, and forced it to grant commercial privileges and extraterritorial rights to Russian subjects. This was the beginning of the Russian economic and political penetration of Persia, and it was particularly predominant in Russian-controlled territory in the north.

Towards the Persian Gulf

To consolidate their gains in Central Asia, the Russians built a number of railways. The first was officially opened in 1888, commencing at the Caspian Sea eastward, from Krasnovodsk, via Ashkhabad to Merv, Samarkand and Tashkent, continuing to Kokand and Andizhan. Plans were made to continue Russian railroads through Persia to the Persian Gulf, facilitating Russian access to the Indian Ocean. However, the plans never got beyond the discussion stage. At a Russian government meeting on the subject, on 4 February 1890, the head of the Asian Department in the Foreign Ministry claimed that a railroad from the Russian border through Persia to the Gulf would necessitate complete security and un-disturbed movement. The situation in Persia did not meet this require-ment, and the further one went from the Russian frontier, the harder it would be to achieve this. In the Persian Gulf, he said, 'we do not have any point of support, while the British have their agents and navy there'. He further stated that there was a need to establish a Russian military naval station in the Gulf, strong enough not to fear British rivalry, and able to command the respect of the littoral population.[3] However, no decision was taken.

The Persian Gulf at that time was still quite distant from the Russian border and Russian control. However, there was a constant Russian advance in that direction. Northern Persia was almost completely under Russian control and the Caspian Sea became a 'Russian lake'. The Trans-Caspian railway enabled the Russians to transfer troops close to the Persian border and Russian steamers were available in the Caspian Sea for the transfer of troops to northern Persia. The Russian and British forces were at some distance from each other, and Britain proposed to maintain the situation by declaring Persia a buffer state — like Afghanistan — between the Russian and British spheres of influence. Such proposals were viewed with disfavour in Russia since they would mean an end to Russian advances southwards.

Tsar Nicholai II said in 1897 that he did not believe in buffer states 'unless they were strong and independent, and Persia . . . was too weak to play the role of such a state with advantage'. As regards British-Russian relations, he remarked to a British diplomat that they 'would be far more friendly and satisfactory were there no Persia between us'.[4] This statement could have meant a proposal to divide Persia between Britain and Russia, but generally the Tsar and most of his advisers rejected such proposals since they were interested in controlling *all* of Persia.

On 25 November 1899 the Ottoman Porte granted Germany the right to construct what came to be known as the Baghdad railway, from Konia to Baghdad.[5] This plan gave rise to much concern in Russia. It was believed that the railway would extend through southern Persia to Baluchistan, thus impeding Russian access to the Persian Gulf.[6] The Russian press published opinions stating that, since the Germans were building a railway to the Persian Gulf from the west, Russia should immediately commence construction of a road to the Gulf from the north. Plans existed to construct a Russian railway which would reach Bandar Abbas in the Strait of Hormuz, Bushire (further north, opposite Kuwait), or Chahbahar (eastwards, in the Arabian Sea). Russian plans included either having a port there or the use of existing naval facilities, particularly in Bandar Abbas.

In a memorandum to the Tsar in January 1900 the Foreign Minister, Count M.N. Muravyov, stated that the Russian government had decided to forgo these plans, for both political and financial reasons. First, it would have opened northern Persia to British commerce, whereas at present the Persians were purchasing mostly Russian goods. Secondly, it might also have brought about the construction of a British railway from southern to northern Persia.

On the question of Russian occupation of a port in the Persian Gulf, Foreign Minister Muravyov said he saw no reason to occupy ports

whose defence could not be fully guaranteed. In addition, the building of strategic positions and coaling stations at great distances from the operational base disperses the country's forces and is so costly that, in most cases, the strategic advantages are outweighed by the material sacrifices.

A declaration that Russia would not tolerate any violation of Persia's territorial integrity, Muravyov stated, would 'to some extent moderate England's expansionist designs'. A Russian promise 'to come to the defence of Persia's territorial rights at any moment' had some disadvantages, however. It would 'place upon us the fairly heavy necessity of maintaining troops in perpetual war readiness on our borders ... deprive us of freedom of action in the north of Persia, where we are at present the only and complete masters'.

The Tsar was advised to oppose an agreement with Britain to divide Persia into Russian and British spheres of influence. Such a division would grant Russia the north and Britain the south, but:

> the north of Persia is in Russian hands anyway, and is completely inaccessible to foreigners; by officially acknowledging England's right to act unilaterally in the south ... we thereby ... voluntarily block any further movement by us beyond the limits of Persia's northern provinces.[7]

Commenting on the above, Naval Minister P. Tyrtov said he fully agreed 'about the usefulness of our acquiring coaling stations or any bases outside the Empire's borders which do not justify the expenses of strengthening and maintaining a fleet there, without which they would become easy prey for the enemy'. He did not mention the Persian Gulf by name, but that was his intention. His preferences lay in the Far East.

For War Minister General A. Kuropatkin the Bosphorus was more important. He stated his opinion that its occupation was 'the most important task for Russia. Until this came about, all the other tasks had relatively small significance.' He agreed in general to what was said about Persia, but insisted that sooner or later Russia would have to reach an agreement with England on this question. He was bound to add that as long as a railway connecting European Russia with Central Asia was not completed, the military would refuse to support negotiations with England regarding Persia.

Finance Minister S. Witte said that an implementation of the Muravyov proposals would cost a great deal. Strengthening Russian military forces in Turkestan and the Transcaucasus required sums of money which the army and the country needed elsewhere. It would force Britain to increase its armaments, putting Russia in a financially inconvenient position, competing with a much richer England, without bringing about a commensurate increase in power. As regards Persia, the Finance Minister was considering building highways and assisting the development of Russian enterprises.[8]

All the above recommendations were made to the Tsar, who was, however, unable to decide either way and left most of the options open. This meant, in fact, that nothing was done. Efforts were concentrated in other directions. A Trans-Persian railway or any other extensive investments in that country would divert resources from the expansion and further development of the Trans-Siberian railway and other Far Eastern projects. Persia and the Persian Gulf were not at the top of the list of St Petersburg's priorities. But there were also some less influential and lower ranking officials who allotted Persia and the Gulf a much higher priority.

In February 1900, at the same time as the Naval Minister was speaking about the 'uselessness' of Russia's acquiring distant coaling stations or bases, a small Russian gunboat anchored off Bandar Abbas. Its commander had ordered coal from Bombay; when it arrived, he took part of it, intending to leave the remainder. This would require Russian guards to watch over it, but the local governor refused permission. 'Thus the attempt failed to create a nucleus store from which a coaling station might develop.'[9] In the following years Russian warships toured the Gulf but they made no attempt to acquire a foothold there.[10] This incident was probably an exception, perhaps an attempt to test local, and perhaps even more, British, reactions.

British naval supremacy in fact made the Gulf a British preserve and blocked Russian attempts to establish a presence there. In the House of Lords on 15 May 1903, the British Foreign Minister Lord Lansdowne gave what might be taken as a warning to Russia and Germany, a sort of 'Monroe Doctrine' for the Gulf:

> We should regard the establishment of a naval base, or of a fortified port, in the Persian Gulf by any other power as a grave menace to British interests, and we should certainly resist it with all the means at our disposal.[11]

The Division of Persia into Russian and British Spheres of Influence

British influence predominated in the Persian Gulf but in Persia itself the situation was different. Britain, even if it could bring naval forces to the Gulf, was far away. So was British India. Russia, however, was much closer, thus increasing its power and influence inside Persia.

One of Russia's instruments in Persia were the Cossack units. Trained by Russian officers, they dealt directly with the Ministry of War in St Petersburg, and during the 1880s became the most efficient military force in Persia. Russian Cossacks were selected by the Shah in 1878 as a model for the Persian cavalry. A Persian Cossack brigade was organized in 1879,[12] soon growing to three regiments. They became 'a powerful instrument for furthering Russian influence in Persia'.[13] According to George N. Curzon:

> The only Persian troops of any value in the capital are the so-called Cossack regiments, under Russian officers, and in the event of political convulsion it is doubtful whether they would not prefer the country of their uniform to the country of their birth.[14]

The situation which developed, and Russian aims in regard to Persia, were summed up on 30 September (13 October) 1904 in instructions from Russia's Foreign Minister, Count V.N. Lamsdorf, to his Minister in Persia, A.N. Shteyer. Lamsdorf said:

> Our principal aim, which we have pursued by various ways and means during the long years of our relations with Persia, can be defined in the following manner: to preserve the integrity and inviolability of the possessions of the Shah, without seeking for ourselves territorial acquisitions, and not permitting the hegemony of a third power. We have tried gradually to subject Persia to our dominant influence, without violating the external symbols of its independence or its internal regime. In other words, our task is to make Persia politically obedient and useful, i.e., a sufficiently powerful instrument in our hands. Economically — to keep for ourselves a wide Persian market using Russian work and capital freely therein . . .[15]

Russia's defeat by Japan in the war of 1905 made it reconsider relations with Britain. Domestic instability, the 1905 revolution, limited resources, increasing German influence in the Near East — all these were contributing factors.

Japan's increasing strength checked Russian advances in the Far East and the Anglo-Japanese alliance covered India, provided for joint action in its defence and made Britain less fearful of Russian advances in that direction. British control of Egypt guaranteed its domination of the

Eastern Mediterranean. Although Britain had for years tried to contain Russian advances in the Near East, Britian now began to change its mind and even saw certain advantages in the Russian presence. It might bring about a deterioration in Russia's relations with Austro-Hungary and Germany, restricting their expansion in the Balkans and eastwards.

As Britain and Russia moved closer together, the British made another attempt to define the two spheres of influence in Persia. The subject came up on 1 February 1907 at a meeting of Russian ministers. Most of the speakers, especially Foreign Minister A.P. Izvolsky, connected it with the German Baghdad railway project which was seen to threaten Russian interests. As to the British proposal, Izvolsky said:

> until now that idea has not received much understanding from Russian public opinion. In leading circles the conviction prevailed that Persia must fall entirely under Russian influence and that we must aim for a free exit to the Persian Gulf, building a railway across all Persia and establishing a fortified point on that Gulf. Events of the last years have, however, made clear the infeasibility of such a plan.

The Minister of Trade and Commerce said that the Baghdad railway would harm Russian interests. A branch line to Persia would harm those interests still further, leading to the development of a transit trade from Europe to the Persian Gulf, 'bypassing Russia'. Such a branch to northern Persia would endanger exclusive Russian economic interests there. In talks with England and Germany, the Minister requested assurances that no such branch lines would be built and that the prohibition on the construction of a railway in northern Persia would be extended for an additional ten years. He also demanded that any such lines be built only with Russia's consent and in keeping with its interests.[16]

The Russian-British *rapprochement* reached its peak with the signing of the convention of 31 August 1907 between the two countries. Among its provisions was the division of Persia into British and Russian spheres of influence, with a neutral zone between them. The richer northern part was in the Russian sphere and Bandar Abbas was east of it, while Afghanistan was in the British sphere. The Gulf area to the west was in the neutral zone.[17]

The convention was criticized both in Britain and in Russia. Count Witte, the Russian Finance Minister during the period 1892-1903 and Premier until 1906, said in his memoirs that in the division of Persia, Russia received what she already possessed. 'The northern part of Persia was naturally destined, so to speak, to become a part of the Russian

Empire.' Russia renounced 'all claims to the southern Persian parts. In a word, Persia has slipped out of our hands'.[18]

The erstwhile Russian sphere of influence came in fact under full Russian control and was only nominally ruled by the Shah and his Persian authorities. Since the capital city and the centres of power were in the Russian sphere it meant, to a certain extent, Russian control of the Persian government, and through it, of the whole country (as far as the government by itself exercised such control).

This situation was described to the Tsar in June 1914 by George Buchanan, the British ambassador, as follows:

> Northern Persia was now to all intents and purposes a Russian province . . . Little by little, the whole machinery of administration had been placed in the hands of the Russian consuls. The Governor-General of Azerbaijan was a mere puppet who received and carried out the orders of the Russian Consul-General and the same might be said of the Governors at Rasht, Kazvin and Julfa. They were one and all agents of the Russian government and acted in entire independence of the central government in Tehran. Vast tracts of land in north Persia were being acquired by illegal methods. Large numbers of Persians were being converted into Russian-protected subjects, and the taxes were being collected by the Russian consuls to the exclusion of the agents of the Persian financial administration. The above system was being extended to Isfahan and even to the neutral zone.

The Tsar proposed to partition the neutral zone and offered to appoint a committee on behalf of the Ministry of Foreign Affairs to investigate the activities of his consuls.[19] Nothing was done, however.

The First World War brought Britain and Russia into the same camp. During the war Russia raised the question of the annexation of Constantinople and on 15 March 1915 the matter was discussed between the Tsar and Ambassador Buchanan. It was agreed to transfer the neutral zone in Persia to Britain in exchange for Russian annexation of Constantinople and the Turkish Straits.[20] The agreement was later repudiated by the Soviet regime.

Notes

1. Seymour Becker, *Russia's Protectorates in Central Asia: Bukhara and Khiva, 1865-1924* (Harvard University Press, Cambridge, Mass., 1968); Richard A. Pierce,

Russian Central Asia, 1867-1917 (University of California Press, Berkeley, Calif., 1960).

2. William Habberton, *Anglo-Russian Relations Concerning Afghanistan* (University of Illinois, Urbana, 1937). Illinois Studies in the Social Sciences, vol. XXI, no. 4).

3. 'Anglo-Russkoe sopernichestvo v Persii 1890-1906 godov' (Anglo-Russian Rivalry in Persia in 1890-1906), *Krasnyi Arkhiv* (Moscow) (1933), no. 1 (56), p. 46.

4. George Buchanan, *My Mission to Russia and other Diplomatic Memoirs* (Little, Brown & Co., Boston, 1923), vol. 1, p. 169.

5. Edward Mead Earle, *Turkey, the Great Powers and the Baghdad Railway. A Study in Imperialism* (Macmillan, New York, 1935).

6. For Russian concern over the German Baghdad railway, see: *The Times,* 12 January 1902, giving the views of the Russian Finance Ministry's *Financial Messenger.*

7. 'Tsarskaya Diplomatiya o Zadachakh Rossii na Vostoke V 1900 Godu' (Tsarist Diplomacy on Russia's Tasks in the East in 1900), *Krasnyi Arkhiv* (1926), no. 5 (18), pp. 11-14.

8. Ibid., pp. 18-25.

9. A.W. Ward and G.P. Gooch (eds), *The Cambridge History of British Foreign Policy* (Macmillan, New York, 1922-1923), vol. 3, 1866-1919, p. 320.

10. For the first Russian incursions in the Persian Gulf area and British reactions to them, see: Firuz Kazemzadeh, *Russia and Britain in Persia, 1864-1914. A Study in Imperialism* (Yale University Press, New Haven and London, 1968); Ravinder Kumar, *India and the Persian Gulf Region, 1858-1909. A Study in British Imperial Policy* (Asia Publishing House, London, 1965), pp. 216-39.

11. *Parliamentary Debates* (London), 4th series, vol. CXXI (1903), p. 1348.

12. F. Kazemzadeh, 'The Origin and Early Development of the Persian Cossack Brigade', *The American Slavic and East European Review* (Seattle, October 1956), pp. 351-63.

13. A. Lobanov-Rostovsky, *Russia and Asia* (George Wahr Publishing Co., Ann Arbor, Mich., 1965), pp. 197-8.

14. George N. Curzon, *Persia and the Persian Question* (Longman, Green & Co., London, 1892), vol. II, p. 593.

15. 'Tsarskaya Rossiya i Persya v Epoku Russko-Yaponskoy Voyni' (Tsarist Russia and Persia at the Time of the Russian-Japanese War), *Krasnyi Arkhiv* (1932), no. 4 (53), p. 14.

16. 'Historii Anglo-Ruskogo Soglasheniya 1907 Goda' (The History of the 1907 Anglo-Russian Agreement), *Krasnyi Arkhiv* (1935), nos. 2-3 (69-70), pp. 19, 21.

17. On the 1907 Anglo-Russian agreement, see: ibid., pp. 3-39; 'The 1907 Anglo-Russian Convention and the Division of Afghanistan', *Krasnyi Arkhiv* (1927), no. 3 (10), pp. 54-66; R.P. Churchill, *The Anglo-Russian Convention of 1907* (Iowa, 1939). For the part of the convention relating to Persia, see: J.C. Hurewitz (ed.), *Diplomacy in the Near and Middle East; A Documentary Record, 1914-1956* (Van Nostrand, Princeton, N.J., 1956), vol. 1, pp. 266-7.

18. *The Memoirs of Count Witte,* translated and edited by Abraham Yarmolinsky (Howard Fertig, New York, 1967), pp. 433-4.

19. Buchanan, *My Mission to Russia,* vol. 1, pp. 114-18.

20. Ibid., pp. 224-7.

2 THE SOVIET REGIME – BETWEEN GOOD NEIGHBOURLINESS AND INTERVENTION (1917-1953)

The End of Russian Influence

The Soviet regime which came to power in Russia in November 1917 gave first priority to its own survival and to keeping all, or at least most, of the areas that had belonged to Russia prior to the revolution. In its foreign relations, primary attention was focused on Europe. Any dealings with the 'East' were undertaken in such a way as to influence developments in Europe and create difficulties for the colonial powers, thus distracting them from fighting Soviet Russia.

One of the first measures taken by the new regime was to publish the secret agreements made by the Tsar's government, which included the British-Russian agreements of 1907 concerning Persia. All claims of the old regime pertaining to Persia were renounced.

On 3 December 1917 the Soviet government appealed to all Muslim toilers of Russia and the East, proclaiming 'the treaty on the partition of Persia' null and void. This appeal stated, *inter alia*, that 'as soon as military activities cease, troops will be withdrawn from Persia and the Persians will be guaranteed the right freely to determine their own destiny'.[1] The immediate aim of this appeal was to create difficulties for Britain, thus diverting its attention from any military intervention in Russia itself.

A Soviet note on 26 June 1919 to the Persian government proclaimed:

(1) All Persian debts to the Tsarist government were annulled.
(2) Russian interference in Persia's income from customs, post and telegraph was at an end.
(3) All Russian official and private concessions in Persia were void.
(4) The Russian bank in Persia, with all its inventory, branches, land, etc., was declared the property of the Persian people.
(5) All the roads, electricity stations, port equipment, railway lines, etc. built and owned by Russia were transferred to the Persian nation.
(6) Capitulations ceased to exist.[2]

Persia, however, was in no position to reply to this gesture. The country had been occupied by Britain and a Tsarist consul was still in Tehran.

Russia too was able to devote little attention to Persia, being primarily preoccupied with internal affairs. Almost all of Transcaucasia and Central Asia were at that time outside Soviet control. The former was taken over by the 'Reds' around 1920. In Central Asia, local Muslim nationalists, the Basmachi, were finally crushed only in 1928. (In some areas, resistance lingered on until 1936.)[3]

This situation was exploited by Britain, which occupied all of Persia, using it as a base of operations against the Bolsheviks in Transcaucasia and Turkestan.[4] An Anglo-Persian treaty was signed in 1919, reaffirming Persia's independence and territorial integrity and revoking the 1907 Anglo-Persian convention. In fact it made Persia dependent on Britain, giving the latter a considerable number of privileges in the organization of military forces, and especially in the handling of state finances.[5]

The new Soviet regime tried to attract the Persian government, to win its confidence and goodwill, but it also provided aid to those who opposed that government and acted against it.

The Republic of Gilan

A Persian communist party was organized among Persian workers in the Baku oilfields after the November 1917 Bolshevik revolution. Originally named 'Adalet' (Justice), it attracted Persians both in Turkestan and in Persia itself. Later, the Party Congress at Enzeli (renamed Pahlevi) changed its name in July 1920 to the Iranian Communist Party.[6]

The communists, however, had little power and influence in Persia. The Soviets saw more chances in a nationalist Islamic reform movement established in the Gilan province in northern Persia in 1915. This group was headed by Kuchuk Khan, Ehsanullah Khan and others. Their revolt, beginning in 1917, fought Persian troops, but in 1919, finding themselves in a difficult situation, they appealed to the Soviets for help.

On 28 April 1920 Red forces occupied Baku and proclaimed the establishment of an Azerbaijani Soviet Republic. Some of the retreating Whites fled to the Persian port of Enzeli seeking British protection. They were pursued by Soviet Caspian Sea naval units who forced the British to withdraw. The Soviet Caspian fleet landed a force at Enzeli on 18 May 1920, and assisted the forces of Kuchuk Khan in bringing all the Gilan region under their control. That same year, on 4 June, a

Persian Soviet Socialist Republic was proclaimed in the Gilan province, with Rasht as its capital.

This came during a time of Persian-Soviet negotiations to establish diplomatic and trade relations. To Persian protests the Russians replied that there were no Russian troops involved, only those of the Azerbaijani Soviet Republic. Moscow expressed its readiness to try to influence the Azerbaijani Republic to withdraw its forces from Persia on condition that Britain would do likewise. Britain's weakening position prevented it from controlling all of Persia. It was therefore ready to divide the country, as in 1907, into zones of British and Soviet military presence. The British minister in Tehran made hints to this effect to the Soviet envoy, Theodore Rothstein, but the latter ignored the offer.[7] British forces were evacuated during May 1921. Afterwards the Soviets gradually withdrew, completing the move on 8 September 1921. Persian forces, headed by Reza Khan, then entered Gilan. There were some in Baku and Moscow who opposed the withdrawal and called for a 'Sovietization' of Persia. Their opinions, however, were not accepted. Lenin and the Commissariat for Foreign Affairs were opposed. So was the Soviet envoy in Tehran.[8] If the Soviets remained in Gilan, the British would continue to occupy the south.

There existed in Tehran a strong anti-British nationalist movement which the Soviets tried to strengthen still further. The Kuchuk Khan movement was far from communist. It was against Britain and in favour of reforms, but was seen by the Soviets to have a 'bourgeois-democratic' character, being to some extent similar to certain anti-Soviet 'Whites'. With the establishment of relations with Persia, the signing of a friendship treaty between the two countries and the evacuation of British troops, the Soviets found it more advantageous to end their military presence in Gilan, whereupon the Gilan republic came to an end.[9]

The Treaties of 1921 and 1927

A Soviet-Persian friendship treaty was signed on 26 February 1921. It was on the same day that the 1919 treaty with Britain was formally renounced, and only a few days after the Cossack Brigade headed by Reza Khan took control of Tehran (on 21 February 1921). Reza Khan became War Minister in April 1921, and Prime Minister as well as *de facto* ruler of Iran in October 1923. He was crowned Shah on 26 April 1926. In the 1921 treaty Soviet Russia renounced all Tsarist privileges and concessions, recognized Persia's sovereignty and agreed to evacuate its troops. All Persian debts were cancelled, and the Russian Bank, railways, roads and ports were handed over to Iran. Capitulations were abolished.

Article V stipulated that the parties would undertake to prohibit the formation and presence within their territories of organizations, groups, persons, troops or armies 'whose object is to engage in acts of hostility' against Persia or Russia. They undertook: 'not to permit a third party or any organization . . . which is hostile to the other Contracting Party, to import or to convey in transit across their countries, material which could be used against the other Party'. They also agreed to prevent the presence within their territories 'of all armies or forces of a third party in cases in which the presence of such forces would be regarded as a menace to the frontiers, interests or safety of the other contracting parties'.

Article VI declared that in case a third party intended to pursue an armed intervention in Persia, 'to use Persian territory as a base of operations against Russia', and if thereby a danger threatened the frontiers of Soviet Russia or its federated associates, and if the Persian government, having been notified by the Soviet government, was unable to remove that danger itself, the Soviet government 'shall have the right to advance its troops into the Persian interior for the purpose of carrying out the military operations necessary for its defence'. Russia undertook to withdraw its troops after 'the danger has been removed'.

Article XIII stated that the Persian government would not place under the possession, authority or use of any third government, the concessions and properties transferred to Persia according to this treaty.[10] This made any West European or American economic activities in northern Iran very difficult, if not impossible.

A note from a Russian diplomatic representative in Tehran on 12 December 1921 specified that Articles V and VI were intended: 'to apply only in cases in which preparations have been made for a considerable armed attack upon Russia or the Soviet Republics allied to it, by the partisans of the regime which has been overthrown or by its supporters'.[11]

On 1 October 1927 a non-aggression and neutrality Soviet-Persian treaty was signed. Article II stated that:

> Each of the High Contracting Parties undertakes to refrain from any aggression or from any hostile acts directed against the other Party, and not to introduce its military forces into the territory of the other Party.

Should one of the parties be attacked by another power or powers, the other contracting party was obliged to remain neutral throughout that conflict.

Article III stated that both parties agreed to:

> take no part, whether *de facto* or *de jure*, in political alliances or agreements directed against the safety of the territory or territorial waters of the other Contracting Party or against its integrity, independence or sovereignty.

Each party contracted not to take part in any economic boycott or blockade together with another power or powers against the other contracting party.

Article IV said:

> Should the citizens of either of the Contracting Parties in the territory of the other Party engage in any propaganda or campaign prohibited by the authorities of the latter Party, the government of that territory shall have the right to put a stop to the activities of such citizens and to impose the statutory penalties.[12]

This was originally directed against the activities of 'White' Russians in Persia. However, the Soviets later invoked this clause, saying that the ties established in the 1950s-70s with the USA were in violation of this and the 1921 treaty.

Iran as a Buffer State

It was Soviet policy to try to attract Iran and bring the two countries closer. Soviet Russia worked hard to improve relations, showing that it was not against Iran, but on the contrary, was both ready to help it and prepared to refrain from interfering in Iranian internal affairs. All this effort had as its main objective the elimination of British influence there, making Iran (and Afghanistan) a buffer state between the USSR and British India.[13]

The rise of Reza Khan to be *de facto* ruler and Shah was generally seen in Soviet Russia as representing the rise of a national liberation movement having 'an anti-imperialist character'. It was also seen to characterize a turn from feudalism to capitalism, representing a nationalism primarily directed against Britain.

A large part of Iran's foreign trade was conducted with the USSR. Extensive commercial relations existed, particularly between Iran's northern provinces and the Soviets, since no other transport facilities were available to turn trade away from north Iran. The situation was changed only as a result of the construction of the Trans-Iranian railway. During the 1930s the USSR occupied first place in Iran's foreign trade, with Soviet-Iranian trade comprising a third of the total. In the late 1930s Iran's trade with the Soviet Union declined while, on the other hand, its trade with Germany increased. Reza Shah tried to offset the dominance of the USSR and Britain by introducing Germany as a third and balancing power.

The rise of Nazi Germany brought changes in Soviet policy. Soviet attention came to be focused even more than before on developments in Europe, and less on the more distant areas. The Soviets, however, viewed with disfavour the strengthening of Iranian ties with Germany and the increasing German presence there.[14]

The Second World War

Nazi-Soviet agreements were concluded in 1939, based on a Soviet assumption that there would be a prolonged German-Western war with no quick victory on either side. The early German victories changed the situation and led to Nazi-Soviet rivalry, especially in the Balkan states. In the negotiations conducted in late 1940 between Soviet and German representatives, the German side tried to turn Soviet attention and interest to the area 'south of the national territory of the Soviet Union in the direction of the Indian Ocean', thus distracting the Soviets from claiming territories in Europe which the Nazis themselves wanted to occupy.

In a conversation between Hitler and Molotov (at the time Soviet Premier and Foreign Minister) in Berlin on 13 November 1940, Hitler said that after the German conquest of England and the division of the British Empire, 'there would be for Russia an access to the ice-free and really open ocean' and that 'even now' Germany recognized the 'Asiatic area' to the south of the Soviet Union as 'Russia's sphere of influence'. Molotov replied that 'he was in agreement with everything that he had understood', but he preferred to talk about Bulgaria, the Turkish straits and more immediate issues.[15] This was reiterated at a meeting the same day between German Foreign Minister von Ribbentrop and Molotov.[16]

A secret protocol of a draft agreement between Germany, Italy, Japan and the Soviet Union, prepared by the Germans, defined the proposed spheres of the territorial aspirations of each 'apart from the territorial revisions in Europe to be carried out at the conclusion of peace'. Germany's 'territorial aspirations' were said to centre on Central Africa. 'The Soviet Union declares that its territorial aspirations lie south of the national territory of the Soviet Union in the direction of the Indian Ocean.'[17]

The above draft apparently formed the basis of a conversation on 26 November 1940 between Molotov and the German ambassador in Moscow, Schulenburg. As reported by Schulenburg to the German Foreign Office, Molotov stated that the Soviet government was prepared 'to accept the draft of the Four Power Pact' under certain conditions. One of them was the following: 'Provided that the area south of Batum and Baku in the general direction of the Persian Gulf is recognized as the centre of the aspirations of the Soviet Union'.[18]

No agreement was reached and a month later, on 18 December 1940, Hitler issued his 'Operation Barbarossa' order to attack the Soviet Union.[19] The German attack began on 22 June 1941. Reza Shah declared his country's neutrality but tended to favour Germany, refusing requests to permit Iran to be used as a route for the transport of Western aid to the Soviet Union. The large number of Germans and the German influence in Iran were seen as a danger both to the USSR and to Britain, which became allies in a common war against a common enemy. On 25 August 1941, after the Iranian government had rejected an ultimatum to expel all Germans from its territory and allow the transportation of Allied war materials for the USSR over its roads and railways, Soviet and British troops entered Iran.[20] The pro-German Reza Shah was forced to abdicate and was succeeded by his son, Muhammad Reza Pahlavi.

Iran became important as a corridor of US military supplies to the USSR. The Trans-Iranian railway, completed in 1938 from Bandar Shahpur on the Persian Gulf to Bandar Shah on the Caspian Sea, became the main line of that route.[21] This was the very same line that had been planned by Russia many years earlier, to the Persian Gulf.

The British-Soviet occupation was formalized by a treaty of alliance between the United Kingdom, the Soviet Union and Iran. It was signed in Tehran on 29 January 1942. The Allied Powers undertook 'to respect the territorial integrity, sovereignty and political independence of Iran'. It was declared (Article IV) that this did not constitute occupation of Iran, but rather co-operation between the three governments in a common aim to defeat the Nazis.

Article V stated:

> The forces of the Allied Powers shall be withdrawn from Iranian
> territory not later than six months after all hostilities between the
> Allied Powers and Germany and her associates have been suspended
> by the conclusion of an armistice or armistices, or on the conclusion
> of peace between them, whichever date is the earlier. The expression
> 'associates' of Germany means all other Powers which have engaged
> or may in the future engage in hostilities against either of the Allied
> Powers.[22]

Iran declared war on Germany on 9 September 1943. On numerous
occasions the United States and Britain pressed for an additional Allied
declaration regarding the withdrawal of troops from Iran. The Soviets
were not interested in this and used every possible excuse to delay such
declarations. At the Tehran Conference between Roosevelt, Churchill
and Stalin from 28 November-1 December 1943, the Soviets could find
no excuses for further delay and signed a declaration that:

(a) recognized 'the assistance which Iran has given to the prosecu-
tion of the war . . . particularly by facilitating the transportation of
supplies from overseas to the Soviet Union';
(b) promised Iran economic assistance; and
(c) said that the USA, USSR and the UK 'are at one with the Government of Iran in their desire for the maintenance of the independence,
sovereignty and territorial integrity of Iran'.[23]

The Soviets, however, with the changing war situation, took an increasing interest in Iranian politics, with a view to furthering their own
interests.

The Autonomous Republic of Azerbaijan and the Kurdish People's Republic

After the end of the war Soviet military forces remained in Iran. In
the Soviet-occupied areas, two autonomous republics were established
with Soviet backing: the Autonomous Republic of Azerbaijan, on 12
December 1945, and a Kurdish People's Republic, three days later,
on 15 December 1945. The Soviet military authorities supported
their establishment and forestalled any action by the central Iranian

authorities against them. For example, they prevented Iranian officials and troops from moving into the Soviet-controlled northern provinces.[24] It appeared that the Soviets planned to have northern Iran under their control; to dismember Iran, weaken it and make it dependent on them. To secure the evacuation of Soviet troops, Prime Minister Ghavam al-Sultaneh made concessions to the Soviets. He signed an agreement establishing a joint Soviet-Iranian company to exploit northern Iran's oil resources in which 51 per cent of the stock belonged to the Soviets. He instructed Iran's delegate at the UN to withdraw Iran's complaints against the Soviet Union (which the delegate did not do), gave the Tudeh Party three places in his cabinet and promised to enter into negotiations with the Azerbaijani Democratic Party, recognizing it as the legal principal government.

While such Iranian steps did help to influence the USSR's decision to withdraw its troops, the withdrawal came primarily as a result of sharp American protests and pressure. Soviet troops were withdrawn on 9 May 1946. The Azerbaijani and Kurdish republics collapsed a few months later.

The Soviet-Iranian oil concession agreement included a reservation that it would take effect only after ratification by the Majlis (the Iranian parliament). Thus Iran meanwhile gained time. In the newly elected Majlis Mohammad Mossadeq, head of the National Front coalition, strongly urged rejection of the concession. On 22 October 1947 the Majlis refused to ratify the agreement. Ghavam al-Sultaneh resigned as Prime Minister in December 1947 and a pro-Western cabinet came into office. The Soviet plans had failed for the time being, but the Soviets still saw many opportunities to change the situation.[25]

The Tudeh Party and the Azerbaijani Democratic Party

The occupation of Iran by Allied forces was followed by a weakening of the regime and the release from prison of communists and other political prisoners. On 30 January 1942 a group of communists established the Tudeh (Masses) Party, initially more of a front organization than a communist party. It was left-wing, nationalist and anti-Western, having in its ranks some members who had earlier been pro-German — not because of pro-Nazi leanings but rather because they wished to demonstrate their anti-British feelings. The party was particularly strong in the Soviet-occupied north of Iran, not only because of Soviet influence there, but also because these areas were more industrialized. In the elections to the Majlis held in the spring of 1944, the Soviet-occupied zone had 50 seats out of a total of 130 in the entire country. Of these 50, the Tudeh gained eight mandates. This was the only organized party in the Majlis. The others were not really parties in the European sense, with programmes, platforms and organizations. Rather, the various groups each supported one or other popular leader.[26]

Azerbaijan was one of the Tudeh centres of power, but the party was weakened by the establishment of an Azerbaijani Democratic Party (ADP) on 3 September 1945, with the Soviets giving it a more influential role in that area. Local branches of the Tudeh in Azerbaijan were dissolved and its members joined the new organization.

Both parties were leftist, Marxist and pro-Soviet. There were, however, considerable differences between them:

> the Tudeh Party reflected the predominant influence of the Persian-speaking community. The Party was formed and led primarily by persons who were Marxist members of the Persian and the Persianized intelligentsia residing in Tehran and who tended to underestimate the regional conflicts between the capital and the provinces. As such, they viewed their society through a class perspective, scorned the communal dimension, and ignored linguistic and regional issues. In contrast such issues constituted the core of the grievances held by the Democratic Party of Azerbaijan.[27]

The ADP came to power in Azerbaijan at the end of 1945. It was weakened after the withdrawal of Soviet troops from Iran in May 1946, followed by the collapse of the Autonomous Republic of Azerbaijan. A few years later it was dissolved and its members joined the Tudeh.

In time, the Tudeh changed from a party striving for a mass following to one restricted to a small group of dedicated, well-trained, militant revolutionaries. This was especially so after it was outlawed in 1949. The Tudeh, however, continued to keep a relatively large membership, estimated in 1953 at between 15,000 and 20,000, half of whom were in Tehran.[28] It had an officers' organization, comprising over 600 members, including a number of army colonels.

> Since the organization had its members in courts, prisons and the police, it was not hard to have a comrade's dossier 'cleaned' of most of its incriminating material, or else simply stolen. Warning members of impending arrests was a regular service.[29]

The Tudeh Party adhered to rigid, dogmatic Stalinist positions. The changes that took place in the USSR after Stalin's death in 1953 influenced the Tudeh leadership, making it more flexible and ready to co-operate with nationalist, anti-Western forces. In practice, however, little could be done as the party became subjected to persecutions and was weakened and isolated. In 1951-3 a situation prevailed whereby the group could have come to power, but they missed their chance.

The 1951-1953 Crisis

At the end of the Second World War and later, Iranian nationalists refused to grant an oil concession to the Soviet Union. They also called for a take-over of the oil concession held by the British-owned Anglo-Iranian Oil Company (AIOC). In March 1951 the Majlis passed a bill nationalizing the AIOC and in April that same year Mohammad Mossadeq, head of the National Front, became Prime Minister. By the end of 1951 most foreign buyers refused to purchase oil from the Iranian nationalized enterprise. In August 1952 Mossadeq was voted full powers, broke off diplomatic relations with Britain and dissolved the Majlis.

The Soviet media strongly supported the Iranian stance during this crisis and attacked Britain and the Americans, even though the latter pressed Britain to reach a compromise. Soviet representatives indicated a readiness to provide Iran with markets and technicians to overcome the Western boycott.

The situation in Iran appealed to the Soviets but came at a most inconvenient time for them. They were in the midst of the Korean war and could not afford another confrontation with the Western powers. Painful memories were still fresh in their minds from previous unsuccessful attempts to interfere in Iranian internal affairs. They were not entirely sure that Dr Mossadeq would replace the British with the Americans. It appeared to the Soviets that Britain was a declining power while the USA was a rising one; they did not wish to assist in removing a weakened Britain and subsequently replacing it by the much stronger USA.[30] Mossadeq was a millionaire and a landlord – a 'bourgeois nationalist' – and Stalin trusted only communists who were obedient to him.

Mossadeq was anti-British but he also had a long record of strong opposition to the granting of oil concessions to the Soviets. Since 1927 a Soviet fishing concession, Iranryba, had been granted to the Soviets, giving them a fishing monopoly in the southern Caspian, the locale of one of the best types of caviar. It was due to expire on 31 January 1953, and shortly before that date Mossadeq informed the Soviets that the concession would not be renewed.[31] In accordance with the 1927 Soviet-Iranian agreement, he undertook not to award the concession to any foreign government or citizen for a period of 25 years, so the Soviets had no choice but to accept this. Stalin's suspicion of Mossadeq increased and contributed to his decision not to support him directly, but rather to act through the Tudeh Party and communist 'front organizations'.

Stalin's death in March 1953 brought about changes in the Soviet position towards nationalist anti-Western movements and leaders. The changes, however, were slow and the Soviet leadership was hesitant, being preoccupied with internal power struggles. On 27 July 1953 an armistice was signed in Korea. The Soviets wanted to improve relations with the USA and tried to become more neighbourly with Turkey. They did not wish to risk an intervention in Iran. Soviet relations with Mossadeq did, however, improve, while the USA moved closer to Britain.

References to Iran in Premier Georgi Malenkov's speech to the USSR Supreme Soviet on 8 August 1953 reflected Soviet expectations of developments in Iran. Malenkov said:

Our neighbour in the south is Iran. The experience of three and a half decades has shown that mutual friendship and co-operation are in the interests of the Soviet Union and Iran. Hence, there is a firm basis for Soviet-Iranian relations, which makes it possible to settle issues arising between the two parties to their mutual satisfaction. Negotiations begun on the initiative of the Soviet Union are now in progress — for the settlement of certain frontier problems, and also of mutual financial claims. We hope that the negotiations will be successful. An agreement to increase trade between the two countries was recently achieved on a mutually advantageous basis. Whether Soviet-Iranian relations will develop on good-neighbourly lines, on the lines of extension of commercial and cultural intercourse, depends on the Iranian government.[32]

In mid-August 1953 the Shah was forced to leave his country. The nationalist forces supporting Dr Mossadeq were confused and disunited. The Tudeh widened its role and if the monarchy had been overthrown, it would undoubtedly have played a major, if not a leading role in this. From April to mid-August 1953 the Tudeh was close to seizing power. Tehran was in their hands for a day or two. They could have wielded power if they had tried, but they hesitated and so lost out. It seems that they were awaiting instructions from Moscow but nothing was forthcoming. A coup staged by General Fazlollah Zahedi with American assistance on 19 August 1953 defeated Mossadeq, who was subsequently arrested. The Shah returned on 21 August. Soviet caution during the events of August 1953 made it possible to continue correct Soviet-Iranian relations. A trade agreement was signed on 3 September 1953. An agreement of 2 December 1954 provided for an exchange of certain border areas, and the turning over of World War debts to Iran. The Soviet press attacked Iran for moving closer to the West but the Soviets could do little to prevent this.

Notes

1. USSR, Ministry of Foreign Affairs, *SSSR i Arabskie Strany, 1917-1960, Dokumenty i Materyaly* (The USSR and Arab Countries, 1917-1960, Documents and Records) (Moscow, 1961), pp. 57-9.

2. Louis Fischer, *The Soviets in World Affairs . . . 1917-1929*, 2nd edn (Princeton University Press, Princeton, N.J., 1951), vol. I, p. 289.

3. Firuz Kazemzadeh, *The Struggle for Transcaucasia (1917-1921)* (Philosophical Library, New York, and George Ronald, Oxford, 1951); Joseph Castagne, *Les Basmatchis: le Mouvement National des Indigènes d'Asie Centrale* (Leroux, Paris, 1925); Alexandre Bennigsen, 'The Bolshevik Conquest of the Moslem Borderlands', *Studies on the Soviet Union* (Munich), vol. XI, no. 4 (1971), pp. 61-70.

4. 'The end of the Russian influence', *The Times*, 24 September 1918.

5. 'Anglo-Persian Agreement of 9 August 1919', ibid., 16 August 1919.

6. 'Pervyi Syezd Persidskikh Kommunistov "Adalet"' (The First Congress of Persian Communists 'Adalet'), *Kommunisticheskii Internatsional*, no. 14 (1920), pp. 2889-92.

7. Fischer, *The Soviets in World Affairs*, p. 429.

8. Ibid., pp. 429-30.

9. Nasrollah S. Fatemi, *Diplomatic History of Persia, 1917-1923; Anglo-Russian Power Politics in Iran* (Moore, New York, 1952); Avetis S. Sultan-Zade, *Persia* (Gosizdat, Moscow, 1924). The author was an old Persian communist, also known as Pishevari.

10. Leonard Shapiro (ed.), *Soviet Treaty Series: A Collection of Bi-lateral Treaties, Agreements and Conventions, etc., concluded between the Soviet Union and Foreign Powers* (Georgetown University Press, Washington, D.C., 1950-1955), vol. I, 1917-1928, pp. 92-4; J.C. Hurewitz (ed.), *Diplomacy in the Near and Middle East: A Documentary Record, 1914-1956* (Van Nostrand, Princeton, N.J., 1956), vol. II, pp. 90-4.

11. Hurewitz, *Diplomacy in the Near and Middle East*, p. 94.

12. Shapiro, *Soviet Treaty Series*, pp. 340-1.

13. George Lenczowski, *Russia and the West in Iran, 1918-1948. A Study of Big-Power Rivalry* (Cornell University Press, Ithaca, New York, 1949); Harish Kapur, *Soviet Russia and Asia, 1917-1927* (Michael Joseph, Geneva, 1966), pp. 143-241; S.L. Agayev, *Iran V Peryod Politicheskogo Krizisa 1920-1925 Godov*

(Voprosy Vneshney Politiki) (Iran in a Period of Political Crisis during the Years 1920-1925 – Foreign Policy Problems) (Nauka, Moscow, 1970).

14. S.L. Agayev, *Germansky Imperializm V Irane (Veymarskaya Republika, Tretyi Reikh)* (German Imperialism in Iran – The Weimar Republic and the Third Reich) (Nauka, Moscow, 1969).

15. Raymond J. Sontag and James S. Beddie (eds.), *Nazi-Soviet Relations, 1939-1941. Documents from the Archives of the German Foreign Office* (Department of State, Washington, D.C., 1948), pp. 242-3.

16. Ibid., pp. 247-54.

17. Ibid., p. 257.

18. Ibid., pp. 258-9. The other conditions related to the Turkish Straits, Finland and Japan.

19. Ibid., pp. 260-4.

20. For Soviet and British notes, see: Leland M. Goodrich (ed.), *Documents on American Foreign Relations* (World Peace Foundation, Boston, 1942), IV (July 1941-July 1942), pp. 674-81.

21. T.H. Vail Matter, *The Persian Corridor and Aid to Russia* (US Department of the Army, Office of Military History, US Army in World War II, The Middle East, Washington, D.C., 1952).

22. Goodrich, *Documents*, pp. 681-6.

23. *Foreign Relations of the US, Diplomatic Papers. The Conferences at Cairo and Tehran 1943* (US Government Printing Office, Washington, D.C., 1961), pp. 646-7.

24. William Eagleton, Jr., *The Kurdish Republic of 1946* (Oxford University Press, London, 1963); Archie Roosevelt, Jr., 'The Kurdish Republic of Mahabad', *Middle East Journal*, vol. 1, no. 3 (July 1947), pp. 247-69; Robert Rossow, 'The Battle for Azerbaijzan, 1946', ibid., vol. 10, no. 1 (Winter, 1956), pp. 17-32 (the author was in charge of the US consulate in Tabriz from December 1945 to June 1946); Rouhollah K. Ramazani, 'The Autonomous Republic of Azerbaijan and the Kurdish People's Republic: The Rise and Fall', *Studies on the Soviet Union*, vol. 11, no. 4 (1971), pp. 401-27.

25. George Lenczowski, 'United States' Support for Iran's Independence and Integrity, 1945-1959', *The Annals of the American Academy of Political and Social Science*, vol. 401 (May 1972), pp. 45-55; Harry S. Truman, *Memoirs, Vol. 1, 1945: Year of Decisions* (New York, 1955), p. 523; idem, *New York Times*, 25 August 1957; George Lenczowski, *Russia and the West in Iran, 1918-1948* (Cornell University, Ithaca, N.Y., 1949); Richard W. Van Wagenen, *The Iranian Case, 1946* (Carnegie Endowment, New York, 1952).

26. George Lenczowski, 'The Communist Movement in Iran', *Middle East Journal*, vol. 1, no. 1 (January 1947), pp. 29-45; L.P. Elwell-Sutton, 'Political Parties in Iran, 1941-1948', ibid., vol. 3, no. 1 (January 1949), pp. 45-62; Sepher Zabih, 'Communism in Iran', *Problems of Communism*, vol. 14, no. 5 (September-October 1965), pp. 46-55; idem, *The Communist Movement in Iran* (University of California Press, Los Angeles, 1966).

27. Ramazani, 'The Autonomous Republic of Azerbaijan', p. 411. Some Western commentators argue that the Tudeh and the Azeri parties were 'two sides of the same coin'. This was not so.

On the contrary, they were separated from each other by contrasting social bases, conflicting interests and, at times, clashing policies. The former [Tudeh] was organized by Persian intellectuals who had come to communism through the Marxism of Western Europe. The latter [Azerbaijani Democratic Party] was formed by Azeri patriots who had reached the same destination through Leninism [and] the Bolshevik Party in the Caucasus.

(Ervand Abrahamian, 'Communism and Communalism in Iran: The Tudeh and the Firqah-e-Dimukrat', *International Journal of Middle East Studies* (London), vol. 1, no. 4 (1970), p. 315. Cited in ibid.)

28. *New York Times*, 6 September 1953.

29. Isaac Don Levine, 'The Anatomy of a Red Spy Ring', *Life* (21 November 1955).

30. The Soviets treated the 23 July 1952 revolution in Egypt in a similar way, viewing it as the result of 'Anglo-American contradictions' and as replacing the British by the Americans.

31. *New York Times*, 1 February 1953.

32. *Soviet News*, Supp., 15 August 1953. Cited from: *Documents on International Affairs* (Oxford University Press, London, 1953), pp. 25-6.

3 THE SOVIET UNION AND THE SHAH'S REGIME — ATTEMPTS TO WIN AND INFLUENCE (1953-1978)

Iran Joins the Western Alliance

In the mid-1950s Soviet policy towards the Afro-Asian states underwent a complete change. The former doctrinaire attitude of 'whoever is not with us is against us' was replaced by a far more pragmatic approach of 'whoever is not against us is with us'.[1] Changes also took place in American policy. When President Eisenhower assumed office in January 1953 his chief spokesman on foreign policy, Secretary of State John Foster Dulles, advocated a more vigorous approach in relations with the Soviets. A chain of bases located in American-allied states around the USSR came into being. On 24 February 1955 a Western-sponsored mutual defence treaty, known as the Baghdad Pact, was signed between Turkey and Iraq. On 23 September Pakistan joined in, and on 11 October Iran announced its intention to do likewise, formally signing on 3 November. Iran was late in becoming a signatory, due, *inter alia*, to strong Soviet pressure. Britain also entered, and the United States joined the alliance 'in all but name'.[2] The USA entered the pact's main bodies, the economic committee and the committee to fight subversion, on 16 April 1956, but did not officially become a member of the alliance. Iran's entry into the pact ended its officially proclaimed policy of neutrality and even-handedness between East and West, and it now became integrated into the Western camp. The Shah's decision to do so was based on a conviction that only massive American aid would enable his regime to survive.

The Baghdad Pact evoked considerable anxiety in the USSR. The Soviets felt that it endangered vital parts of their country and they sought ways of enticing pact members both by threats and by offers of generous technical and other aid. When this proved unsuccessful, they tried to circumvent the pact by establishing a presence to the south. The Soviet-Egyptian arms deal announced in September 1955 was a step in the circumvention process.[3] This was soon followed by a similar Soviet-Syrian deal, and after the July 1958 revolution in Iraq, an Iraqi-Soviet deal. Iraq then withdrew from the Baghdad Pact, which changed its name to the Central Treaty Organization (CENTO).

A bilateral Iran-USA security pact was signed on 5 March 1959, and similar pacts were signed with the US by other CENTO members, Turkey and Pakistan. The Soviets, on learning of Iran's intention to sign the security pact, tried to stop Iran by promising a long-term non-aggression pact and considerable economic aid. The Soviets felt that their plan had a good chance of succeeding, because there were those among the Shah's advisers who counselled against outright rejection of the Soviet proposals. So Iran entered into negotiations with the USSR on a non-aggression treaty.[4]

An analysis by William B. Ballis described Iran's dilemma in its policy towards the Soviet Union:

> It wanted to have its cake and eat it: it wanted to receive Soviet economic aid and at the same time be a fully-fledged member of the Central Treaty Organization, receiving via this organization and its patron, the United States, adequate defence assistance; it wanted to obtain United States' economic aid and at the same time conclude a non-aggression pact with the Soviet Union; it wanted, in a word, to get the maximum returns from a policy of friendly relations with both the USSR and the USA. As far as Iran was concerned, the same comment might well be applied to the USSR: it wanted Iran to withdraw from any alliance with the East while itself not giving it the same economic and defence assistance as the West could offer.[5]

A Soviet mission headed by Deputy Foreign Minister Semenov arrived in Tehran in early February 1959.[6] The Soviets, however, as the Shah described it, 'made the mistake of delaying two weeks before sending a mission here'.[7] They asked Iran to withdraw from the Baghdad Pact and to refuse to sign a bilateral treaty with the USA, promising a Soviet-Iranian non-aggression treaty and economic aid. They were even ready to renounce their right, under the 1921 treaty, to send troops to Iran. The Soviet mission failed to achieve its aims and returned to Moscow on 11 February 1959.[8]

Meanwhile the USA, Britain, West Germany, Turkey and Pakistan appealed to Iran to resist the Soviet proposals. The Shah reconsidered the matter and on 5 March 1959 the American-Iranian treaty was signed. The Soviets sharply protested at the move, considering it inconsistent with the 1921 and 1927 Soviet-Iranian treaties. A strong Soviet propaganda campaign against Iran was initiated which Iran, for the most part, ignored.

The Shah saw himself as containing Soviet advances in the region, thus serving Western interests, and in particular those of the USA. He considered that he was doing what the Americans would otherwise have to do by themselves, and therefore deserved assistance in shouldering a burden too heavy to manage alone. To this end, he requested American assistance, both economic and military — modern American arms in great quantities to be supplied on convenient terms. These would serve to counter the massive Soviet arms supplies to Iraq, Syria, Egypt and Afghanistan and enable Iran to defend its long frontier with the Soviet Union if the need arose — at least until the Americans could come to its assistance.

This was the way the situation was presented to the US administration, but many tended to see it otherwise. According to Walter Lippmann:

> the problem of Iranian security . . . is essentially an internal problem . . . the problem of stability and durability of the Shah's government . . . The principal cause of [US] support to Iran is not to prepare for a world war, but to uphold the Shah's government which is aligned with us.[9]

Soviet-Iranian Rapprochement

Positions of this kind — divergent from those of the Eisenhower-Dulles cold war view — became prevalent in Washington when the J.F. Kennedy administration took office in early 1961. The latter realized that support of any anti-communist regime meant that America was backing feudal rulers whose days were numbered. Local reform movements aiming to overthrow hated corrupt regimes were described in the USA as communist or pro-communist, even when they were far from being so. But such a change of policy appeared paradoxical. It took into account not only strategic considerations, but moral ones as well. It supported those regimes which it considered righteous and just. Often it attempted to persuade certain governments, friendly to America, to introduce internal reforms, changing their policies and sometimes even their leaders. Thus the USA would sometimes find itself supporting anti-American, pro-Soviet governments at the expense of its relations with friends and allies. These allies often came to conclude that one could never completely rely on the USA, which treated both friends and enemies alike. They began to feel that it might be more advantageous to improve relations with the USSR, which knew how to help its friends when they needed it.

Pakistan was an American ally but the USA adopted a neutral position in the Indian-Pakistani conflict and refrained from supporting its
ally. On the Cyprus problem, the USA was closer to the Greek position
than to the Turkish one. Egypt's President Gamal abd Al-Nasir, who
served Soviet interests, tried to overthrow pro-American regimes, but
the Kennedy administration wooed him, even at the expense of the
Shah – who was pro-American and anti-Soviet.

The Shah pointed out this situation to President Kennedy during his
American visit from 10-18 April 1962. The Shah was worried that the
USSR was working hard to get control of Iran, and he requested more
arms and economic aid.[10] The reply he received was that American aid
would emphasize long-term economic development rather than military
power, and that Iran was to receive even less aid in future. Kennedy felt
that Iran could well afford to take care of itself.[11]

This American position was influenced by technological developments which diminished the strategic value of the Middle East for the
USA. By 1962 American intermediate range ballistic missiles (IRBM)
were withdrawn from Turkey. At the time it was made to look as if
this was an American response to the Soviet withdrawal of missiles
from Cuba, but it was no less because the IRBMs' presence there was
no longer necessary. Conventional military bases near an adversary's
border became less valuable with the development of inter-continental
ballistic missiles (ICBM) and nuclear-powered missile-carrying Polaris
submarines. The USSR, however, continued to consider this area important both because of its proximity to Soviet borders and because of
its oil resources.

The USA initiated a process of withdrawal from the region. The Shah
was against this and feared it, although there was little he could do to
prevent it. He therefore decided to terminate Iran's sole dependence
on the USA and try to improve relations with the USSR. He tried to
persuade the Soviets that the American withdrawal had come about as
a result of Iranian pressure. He was hoping that by this, his country
could get something out of the Soviets.

Even at the peak of Iran's exclusive reliance on the USA, there were
no American military bases there, as existed, for example, in Turkey.
Because missiles were becoming obsolete and superfluous, the Americans had no intention of stationing them in this area. Thus it was easy
for the Shah to pledge to the Soviets that he would never allow such
missiles to be based in Iran. This promise was given by his government
on 15 September 1962. According to *Pravda*, an exchange of notes took
place between the two governments on:

Iran's pledge not to permit the establishment of foreign missile bases of any sort on its territory . . . The official statement of the Iranian government to the effect that it will never permit Iran to become a tool of aggression against the Soviet Union has also been taken into account.

It was welcomed as 'an important step in the path of improving relations between the two neighbours'.[12]

On 19 December 1962 a Soviet delegation headed by Deputy Foreign Minister Sergey Lapin arrived in Tehran, discussed economic, cultural and technical co-operation, and signed an agreement providing for the reopening to Iran of the land route to Western Europe across the Soviet Union.[13] According to *Izvestia*, 'the conclusion of the transit agreement shortens the route to Europe no more, no less, than 5,000 kilometres', and 65 per cent of Iran's exports went to Europe.

Now, goods will take only two weeks to reach their destination, instead of the three or four months that they took by sea. The agreement is particularly advantageous for the northern regions of the country, which are the most developed. It will not any longer be necessary to spend money on carrying goods to the ports in the south.[14]

The USSR-Iranian *rapprochement* brought an end to anti-Iranian Soviet radio and press propaganda and led to favourable appraisals of developments in Iran. The 26 January 1963 referendum on the reforms proposed by the Iranian government received favourable Soviet comments, stressing that a majority of the Iranians favoured the Shah's proposals. 'The reactionary forces — the large landholders, supported by the reactionary clergy — violently opposed the land reform.' The referendum 'dealt a blow to their hopes and those of the Western colonialists who supported the Iranian feudalists.'[15] This tone was repeated in almost all Soviet comments. Soviet commentators saw the reform as an advance from feudalism to capitalism, a strengthening of the proletarian element in rural society, an acceleration of polarization of the classes, and an undermining of the political influence of the big landlords. As such, it was welcomed by them.[16]

There was considerable opposition from religious leaders and landlords who were threatened by the 'white revolution' reforms. This led to riots in Tehran in June 1963, which were used by the Shah to neutralize overt opposition. He emerged internally much strengthened, and this influenced his pursuit of an independent foreign policy. In the USSR it was viewed favourably at the time, as a sign of progress and advancement, to suppress feudalism and reaction.[17]

The remnants of the Tudeh Party, which continued to be active outside Iran (mainly in East Germany) had to adapt themselves to the changed Soviet policy towards Iran, and to moderate the party's image. Tudeh representatives continued to appear at Soviet Communist Party forums and to use the Soviet press to attack Iran's regime. The Soviets, however, were careful to distinguish between themselves and the Tudeh, pointing out that the latter did not represent them or their views and that the Soviets had nothing to do with them. Soviet experts coming to Iran were careful not to indulge in communist propaganda.

Economic and technical co-operation between the USSR and Iran intensified. An agreement signed on 27 June 1963 provided for the construction of hydro-electric power stations on the river Araxes near the border, and co-operation in dredging work at Bandar Pahlavi. The construction of grain silos and research at Caspian Sea fisheries were also provided for, and Soviet credit for up to 35 million roubles, to be repaid in 'traditional Iranian export goods', was granted.[18]

The June 1963 accord was the first of a number of Soviet-Iranian agreements on economic and technical co-operation, and reciprocal high-level visits. The Chairman of the USSR Supreme Soviet, Leonid Brezhnev, visited Iran in November 1963. This was the first time that a Soviet head of state had come to Iran, and by itself exemplified the vast improvement in relations.

The Shah visited the USSR from 21 June to 3 July 1965.[19] It had been agreed that the Soviet Union would render technical assistance to Iran in the construction of a metallurgical plant, a machine-building plant and a trans-Iranian pipeline for delivering gas to the USSR. An agreement was also signed on the delivery of natural gas from Iran to the USSR and of machinery and equipment from the USSR to Iran during 1970-85.[20]

The Soviets were interested in the establishment of close economic relations and were even prepared to yield on certain points, to make the deals more advantageous for Iran. By this they hoped that its political relations would be influenced and ties with Western countries would be weakened, in favour of ties with the USSR which would be difficult for Iran to break. This would create a certain dependence on the Soviet Union.[21]

On 13 July 1966 the US State Department admitted having received reports that Iran was requesting Soviet missiles. In February 1967 it became known that Iran and the USSR had signed a secret $110 million arms agreement. The Shah explained that he had turned to the Soviets for arms because their terms were reasonable. The US wanted payment in hard cash. The Soviets, on the other hand, offered an eight-year repayment plan at 2½ per cent interest, with repayment in Iranian products and later in natural gas, which would be piped to the Soviet Union. The Shah later disclosed that Iran had already received shipments of trucks and armoured personnel carriers from the Soviet Union. He played down the political significance of acquiring Soviet armaments, saying, 'It is the man who manipulates the weapons who counts.'[22]

The arms deals with the Soviets were explained in Tehran, *inter alia*, as attempts to meet the designs of Egypt's President Nasir in the Persian Gulf. The Iranians believed that the USSR, having improved relations with Iran, would restrain Nasir who had close ties with the Soviets and had received most of his arms from them. The Shah hoped that the USSR could prevent Nasir from acting against Iran and its regime.

The fear of Arab radicalism greatly influenced the Shah's policy. He did not believe that Soviet troops would enter Iran directly and this made him station fewer forces on the Soviet border. However, he was of the opinion that the Soviets were acting against him indirectly, attempting to encircle him by using the radical forces in the region as proxies. He saw a danger to himself in Egypt's heavy involvement, until mid-1967, in the civil war in Yemen, and in the Soviet's strengthening of Iraq and Afghanistan. Also, the revolt in the Dhofar province of Oman was, in his view, an attempt to start overthrowing regimes in the west of the Gulf and then turn against him. He was afraid that the British withdrawal from Aden and the planned withdrawal from Eastern Arabia would leave a vacuum, with radical Arab forces backed by Soviet aid trying to fill it. This made him decide to strengthen Iran, making it a strong regional power able to defend itself against any combination of local forces.

Looking to Moscow – and then Back to Washington

The Arab-Israeli war in June 1967 changed the strategic situation not only in the eastern Mediterranean, but also in the Persian Gulf region. The Shah saw a danger to his regime from radical Arab forces. These forces, which had been defeated in the war, now had to concentrate their efforts on their own immediate affairs and could less afford an involvement in distant places. Egypt was forced to withdraw its expeditionary forces from Yemen. It now received financial aid from the same

conservative Arab rulers whom it had earlier tried to overthrow. The
Shah thus became freer to act in the Gulf region, which Britain was
planning to vacate.

The situation in the Gulf region was also of great interest to the
USSR. It was one of the subjects discussed between the Shah and the
Soviet Premier Alexei Kosygin during the latter's visit to Iran from 2-7
April 1968.[23] The Soviets wished to forestall the creation of a Western-
oriented defence organization of Gulf countries as well as preventing
ties between these countries and CENTO, or the conclusion of bilateral
treaties with the Western powers. Iran was against the establishment of a
federation of Gulf countries as a successor to British rule in the Gulf.[24]
The Soviets too were against a federation because they considered the
independence granted to the Gulf countries to be nothing but a farce
justifying a continued British presence, or Britain being replaced by the
USA.[25]

Kosygin and the Shah also discussed bilateral matters and, in particular, ways of strengthening economic ties. It looked as if Iran was going
to follow an independent foreign policy. However, the Shah had no
intention of turning away from Washington. The most that he desired
was to pursue some kind of equilibrium in his relations with both West
and East — while leaning Westward — and to utilize his negotiations
with the East as bargaining points with the West. The Soviet invasion
of Czechoslovakia in August 1968 slowed that trend and once more
made Iran suspicious of Soviet intentions. Iran also started to be concerned about the first appearance since 1968 of Soviet naval vessels in
the Indian Ocean.[26]

A short time after the invasion of Czechoslovakia the Shah visited
the USSR between 24 September and 4 October 1968. The statement
describing the visit was short, and dealt mainly with bilateral economic
relations. There were no long references, as was customary, to international affairs. It was not termed a joint statement, having apparently
been drafted by the Soviet side with no Iranian approval of the text.[27]

A few months later, from 5-6 December 1968, the Iranian Prime
Minister Amir Abbas Hoveyda went to Washington where he conferred
with President Lyndon B. Johnson.[28] The following year a change of
American administration took place. The Shah visited Washington from
21-23 October 1969, and conferred with President Richard Nixon. The
visit came at a time when he again turned closer to the USA. The Soviet
media ignored this, continuing to write about improvements in Soviet-
Iranian relations. However, parallel to this, a different language was used
in the Soviet-controlled international communist *Problems of Peace*

and Socialism. It spoke of 'terror in Iran', 'the ruling clique of Iran' and its 'evil deeds'.[29]

The Chairman of the USSR Supreme Soviet, N. Podgorny, visited Iran between 25-31 March 1970. The joint communiqué on the visit said that 'the talks were held in an atmosphere of friendship and mutual understanding'. It spoke about friendship, good-neighbourly relations, and economic and other forms of co-operation. Both sides had had 'a frank and useful exchange of opinions on important international problems'. On some issues they had 'close or identical positions'.[30] Podgorny and the Shah met again at Astara on the Soviet-Iranian border on 28 October 1970 at the inauguration of the natural gas pipeline from southeast Iran to the Soviet border, marking the beginning of Iranian gas shipments to the USSR. In return for its gas, Iran received machinery and equipment.[31]

Podgorny arrived in Iran together with other heads of state in October 1971 for the celebrations of the 2,500th anniversary of the founding of the Persian Empire.[32] There were indications that on this occasion, the Soviets proposed to the Shah that the two countries review the old friendship agreements in the light of the evacuation of the Gulf by the British. However, the Shah refused the Soviet offer. He saw the Soviets as the main threat to Iran's achieving predominance in the region, while the Western powers were ready to accept such a situation.

Ties with the Soviet Union were a part of the Shah's attempts to diversify Iran's foreign relations and avoid complete dependence on the USA. His main arms supplies came from the latter, but he made it known in October 1971 that Iran was getting artillery, jeeps, trucks and armoured personnel carriers from the Soviet Union, phantom planes from the USA and Chieftain tanks from Britain.[33]

The announcement about receiving arms from the USSR followed the disclosure on 18 August 1971 that Iran and the People's Republic of China (PRC) were establishing diplomatic relations at ambassadorial level.[34] This announcement came a short time after the signing of a Soviet-Indian treaty of friendship and co-operation on 9 August 1971[35] in which the PRC and Iran saw a danger both to themselves and to their interests.[36]

The Indo-Pakistani war at the end of December 1971 brought the PRC and Iran even closer, both having ties with Pakistan. In the war the USSR supported India, while the USA, Pakistan's formal ally, was passive, trying to appear even-handed and neutral. It imposed an embargo on arms supplies to Pakistan and did not permit Iran to transfer American-made arms to Pakistan. The partition of Pakistan and the

establishment of Bangladesh made Iran fear attempts of yet another
partition of Pakistan – perhaps a secession of Baluchistan which would
later claim Iranian Baluchistan.

The Soviet-Iraqi friendship treaty of 9 April 1972[37] increased Iran's
fears. Iran saw Iraq as a tool of Soviet policy, a 'proxy' through which
the Soviets tried to provoke instability in the Gulf region in order to
enter it directly at a later stage. Baghdad was the headquarters of a
movement with the declared aim of detaching Khuzestan (which the
Iraqis called Arabistan) province from Iran.

Iran's feeling of insecurity increased as a result of a series of develop-
ments that evolved in proximity to it: Britain's evacuation of the Gulf;
Iraqi claims to Kuwait; the independence of Bahrain, Qatar and the
United Arab Emirates (UAE); the revolt in the Dhofar province of
Oman which was supported by the radical People's Democratic Re-
public of Yemen (PDRY) regime, whose relations with the USSR were
growing stronger. It looked as if the Soviets were trying to replace
Britain in the Gulf area.

This led the Shah to move even closer to the USA, but at the same
time, in an attempt to strike some sort of balance, he attempted to
strengthen his ties with the USSR. From 10-21 October 1972 he visited
the Soviet Union and a treaty was signed setting out the development
of economic and technical co-operation for a term of 15 years. The
Soviets agreed to enlarge the capacity of the Isfahan metallurgical
works to 4 million tons of steel a year and undertook to construct and
study more projects.[38]

No agreement was reached concerning the situation in the Gulf region, although for the time being both the USSR and Iran wanted the
Gulf left to its littoral states, without the presence of foreign powers.
The USSR meant to prevent America from replacing Britain there. Iran,
as the strongest local power, would then assume the predominant position in the region.

The American Connection

The Shah's increasing fears of Soviet advancement in the region came at
a time when the Nixon administration, too, wished to stop that advancement and was looking for a surrogate local power ready to perform the
function of 'regional policeman'. Only Iran and Saudi Arabia could
play such a role in the Persian Gulf and it was planned that they would
co-operate and divide the functions between themselves. In fact, Saudi

Arabia, without a navy and with only a small army, was incapable of such a role.

In May 1972, a few weeks after the signing of the Soviet-Iraqi friendship treaty, President Nixon and his Assistant, Henry Kissinger, visited Tehran. The President informed the Shah that the US would sell Iran F-14 and F-15 aircraft, and that 'in the future the US would, in general, sell Iran any conventional weapon systems that it wanted'.[39] During the years 1972-8 Iran ordered about $20 billion worth of US arms. American reconnaissance stations were also established near the Soviet border.[40] The assimilation of large amounts of modern American arms required the employment of a great number of foreign instructors, mainly Americans. It made the Shah dependent not only on continuing American supplies, but also on the availability of American specialists.

These arms supplies to Iran were soon to become more a solution to American problems than to Iranian ones. Rising oil prices and the negative American balance of payments meant that the USA had an economic interest in the sale of arms to Iran. American companies competed among themselves to sell as much as possible. Their efforts to persuade Iranian officials to buy exclusively from them were often accompanied by corruption and bribery, and this included high military officials as well as members of the royal family. Not only weapons manufacturers, but also branches of the US armed forces — the army, navy and air force — all had vested interests in selling various weapon systems to Iran.

To the Americans Iran's regime looked strong, powerful and stable,[41] contributing to stability in the region, and performing 'police' functions which the USA would have had to do itself. Little was known about the opposition to the regime and few expected that it could constitute a challenge to the Shah and to his power.[42]

President Jimmy Carter said during his Tehran visit on 31 December 1977:

> Iran, because of the great leadership of the Shah, is an island of stability in one of the more troubled areas of the world.
>
> This is a great tribute to you, Your Majesty, and to your leadership and to the respect and the admiration and love which your people give to you.
>
> The transformation that has taken place in this nation is indeed remarkable under your leadership . . . I was profoundly impressed again not only with your wisdom and your judgment and your sensitivity and insight but also with the close compatibility that we found.[43]

This was a time when opposition forces began to come out openly against the Shah's regime, a situation that had been made possible by the liberalization measures advised by President Carter. This time the Shah did not act against the opposition forces (as he had done in 1963). This was in no small measure because he took into consideration Carter's expected opposition.

The Soviet media criticized the strengthening of US-Iranian co-operation. They were, however, careful not to say anything directly against Iran or the Shah, preferring to criticize the USA. These criticisms, too, were mild and indirect.

Iran's Role as 'Regional Policeman'

The improvement in relations with the USSR enabled Iran to turn its attention to the region around it. The increasing oil prices gave it the means to increase its power and intervention capabilities. The first step in this direction was to expand the Iranian navy and shift its centre from the Shatt al-Arab river area further southward. On 30 November 1971, in order to control the Gulf entrances, Iran occupied three islands (the two Tunbs and Abu Musa) at the entrance to the Strait of Hormuz. At the same time, it abandoned its claims to Bahrain and tried to improve relations with the Arab states in the Gulf region.

Iran's aims were:

(1) To maintain the *status quo* in the Gulf region; to prevent changes due to external threats or internal revolts. In fact, Iran saw both these as being closely interconnected — as in Oman, where foreign support was the main source of power for an internal revolution.

(2) To secure free navigation in the Gulf, the Strait of Hormuz and the north-west Indian Ocean.

(3) To oppose foreign intervention in or near the region; to close down foreign bases and military facilities; to bring about a withdrawal of foreign navies. The local powers would then take responsibility for the region's security, thereby granting Iran a major role as the region's strongest power.[44]

The Strait of Hormuz is controlled by Iran and Oman. Both countries extended the limits of their territorial waters to twelve nautical miles — giving them control of most of the Strait. Iranian forces intervened in

Oman to support the Sultan against a local revolt that was backed by the neighbouring PDRY and indirectly by the USSR.[45] From time to time these actions were criticized by Soviet commentators. For example, in November 1978, one said:

It is 'inconvenient' for the United States itself to carry out 'delicate' operations, involving the suppression of the national liberation movement in the Near East. Iran has agreed to this role and in the course of several years has sent 30,000 of its soldiers to Oman to suppress the uprising in the south of the country in Dhofar. These and other operations have been carried out under the flag of the defence of 'freedom of navigation' in the Persian Gulf . . . and although no one here is threatening freedom of navigation, Iran continues to act as 'sentry' over Near East oil.[46]

Relations between Iran and Egypt improved and a so-called Tehran-Cairo (or Tehran-Riyadh-Cairo) axis evolved (although it was rather short-lived), having a clear anti-Soviet character and being directed at diminishing, as much as possible, the Soviet presence and activity in the region. The Shah acted to prevent Egypt's return to the Soviet sphere of influence.

In the conflict between Iran and Iraq, the USSR supported Iraq but attempted not to be directly involved. The Soviets advised both sides to settle their differences by negotiation. Thus, the Chairman of the USSR Supreme Soviet, N. Podgorny, said to the Shah, during the latter's visit to Moscow on 18 November 1974:

We must say outright that the tension existing in relations between Iran and Iraq is not in the interests of peace and we have declared and declare in favour of Iranian-Iraqi differences being settled by these countries themselves at a conference table on the basis of the principle of peaceful co-existence and good-neighbourliness. We shall be welcoming constructive steps which, we hope, will be made by the sides in quest of the ways for a peaceful settlement of the questions in dispute.[47]

An agreement on 6 March 1975 between Iran and Iraq brought an end, for the time being, to the conflict between the two countries. It settled complex questions, defined navigation rights in the Shatt al-Arab and brought an end to Iranian support for the Kurdish revolt in Iraq. The agreement was welcomed by the Soviets, who had called for it all along, and who were relieved of the possibility of becoming involved in a conflict in which they had no interest. After the end of the Kurdish revolt, however, and when the threat from Iran had been removed, Iraq became less dependent on Soviet aid and protection; it could now more easily afford to follow an independent policy and was less prone to accept Soviet advice.

The Soviets viewed with disfavour the establishment of close Iranian-PRC ties. Chairman Hua Guofeng visited Iran from 29 August to 1 September 1978.[48] The visit was interpreted by the Soviets as being directed against them. However, they preferred to attack the PRC about it and to pretend that friendly and 'good-neighbourly' relations existed between the USSR and Iran.

Improving Soviet-Iranian Bilateral Relations

Two parallel but opposing trends characterized Soviet-Iranian relations. On the one hand there was an apparent improvement in bilateral relations, declarations of friendship, the strengthening of economic ties, and high-level visits. Iran became part of non-Western combinations or blocs, sometimes even anti-Western and Soviet-supported. Iran was part of the Third World, of the bloc of Muslim countries and a leading member of OPEC. On the other hand, from the Soviet point of view, the trend was just the opposite. Iran served as a barrier to Soviet advances in the region. It had close ties with the USA and ties with the PRC, and helped to preserve conservative Arab regimes. Iranian forces acted in Oman against radical pro-Soviet guerrillas, and from 1977 Iran helped Somalia against Ethiopia, contributing to Somalia's departure from its previous pro-Soviet orientation and its abrogation, in November 1977, of its friendship treaty with the USSR.

Soviet declarations talked of friendship and good relations with Iran. This was perhaps so, compared to earlier years, but there was also much wishful thinking. The Shah too pretended friendship with the Soviets, often visiting the USSR. He used to flatter the Soviets, praising their good-neighbourly relations and stressing his wish to strengthen relations still further by increasing trade and economic co-operation. He attempted to reassure the Soviets that Iran's military increases were for the country's defence, and were not directed against any other power.

The Soviets tried to attract Iran by economic inducements. The USSR became Iran's largest customer for gas. The Iranians were permitted to make use of transit trade to Western Europe via Soviet land routes and from the Iranian Caspian Sea ports via the Volga-Baltic network and the Volga-Don canal. The development, with Soviet aid, of the port of Pahlavi on the Caspian contributed to this transit trade. Joint development projects were undertaken in the border areas. The Soviets assisted in the establishment of industrial enterprises. They made concessions to Iran on subjects which were of little importance to them, or related only to bilateral relations, and were not in conflict with their relations with other countries.

On 16 March 1973, the Soviet Premier Kosygin was present at the opening ceremony of the Isfahan iron and steel works, Iran's largest industrial project (outside of the oil industry).[49] Both sides used the visit for talks on the situation in the Gulf region, but no agreement was reached. Immediately prior to this, Iraq had directed threats towards Kuwait, and the Iranians suspected that Iraq had been encouraged by the USSR. There was believed to be a connection between this and the Soviet use of the Iraqi naval facilities at Umm Qasr.

A few days later, on 21 March 1973, Iran nationalized its oil industry, a step that was praised by the Soviet media. A Soviet broadcast to Iran said that 'the Soviet people are approving with pleasure Iran's latest success' and that 'Iran is not alone in this struggle, which is actively joined by the rest of the OPEC oil-producers'.[50]

The Shah visited the USSR from 18-20 November 1974.[51] Podgorny, Chairman of the USSR Supreme Soviet, said at a dinner in his honour on 18 November:

> relations between the USSR and Iran continue to develop and strengthen steadily. The Soviet-Iranian co-operation is built on the solid foundation of mutual respect, equality, non-interference in the affairs of each other, mutually advantageous economic relations ... The policy of friendship and good neighbourliness pursued by our countries in their relations is that of peaceful co-existence in action.

Podgorny referred to the importance of 'personal contacts' between the leaders of both countries, and their contribution to Soviet-Iranian relations:

> Personal contacts between the statesmen of the two countries play an important role in the development of relations between the USSR and Iran, and in this connection we note with satisfaction that the preceding talks and meetings between the Soviet leaders and your-

selves were of a constructive nature and contributed to a further
development of Soviet-Iranian relations.[52]

Soviet comments generally praised Iran's economic policy: 'The
Soviet people note with satisfaction the economic successes scored by
Iran. Soviet workers, technicians and engineers have in some measure
contributed to these successes jointly with their Iranian counterparts.'[53]
At the same time Iran was criticized for strengthening its armed forces
and stepping up its arms purchases.

A description of Soviet-Iranian economic relations, published in
Pravda a few months after the Shah's downfall, summed up the situation at the end of the era of the Shah's rule:

> In terms of the level of trade exchange Iran has recently ranked
> second or third among the USSR's customers from the developing
> states. In turn the Soviet Union has ranked first in Iranian exports
> (excluding oil).
>
> Economic and technical co-operation has assumed considerable
> scope. In all, Soviet organizations have taken part in the building of
> 147 installations: commitments for 88 of them have already been ful-
> filled. To a considerable extent this co-operation is being effected on
> the basis of Soviet credits granted to Iran under preferential terms.
>
> . . . among the largest installations . . . the Isfahan metallurgical
> plant — the largest enterprise in the country, employing 10,000
> people; the machine-building plant in Arak . . . grain elevators . . . a
> hydro-electric system and water supply dam on the Araks [Araxes]
> river . . .
>
> The Soviet Union has constructed the northern sector of the 487-
> kilometre trans-Iranian main gas pipeline, through which gas extracted
> in southern Iran is supplied to Soviet Transcaucasus. In the first eight
> years of this pipeline's operation almost 70 billion cubic metres of
> gas have been supplied . . . Revenue from the sale of natural gas is
> used to pay for Soviet services in construction of the various enter-
> prises . . . Construction workers are already laying the second section
> of the gas pipeline.[54]

At the end of 1975 contracts were signed concerning the sale of
gas to the Federal Republic of Germany (FRG), France, Austria and
Czechoslovakia on the Soviet-Iranian border. However, the Soviet Union
itself planned to consume this gas in its own southern regions, while
supplying these countries with an equivalent quantity from other Soviet

deposits.[55] The deal was delayed indefinitely after the downfall of the Shah.

Bilateral economic relations strengthened and the Soviets hoped that this would in turn influence political relations.

Notes

1. For the changes in Soviet policy, as expressed in changing Soviet appraisals of the Arab world, see: Aryeh Yodfat, *Arab Politics in the Soviet Mirror* (Halsted Press, John Wiley & Sons, New York and Toronto, 1973); Jaan Pennar, *The USSR and the Arabs. The Ideological Dimension* (C. Hurst & Co., London, 1973).
2. *New York Times*, 22 April 1956.
3. On the Soviet-Egyptian arms deal and its background, see: Uri Ra'anan, *The USSR Arms the Third World* (MIT Press, Cambridge, Mass., and London, 1969), pp. 13-72.
4. Mohammed Reza Shah Pahlavi, *Mission For My Country* (McGraw Hill, New York, 1961), p. 122; George Lenczowski, *The Middle East*, 3rd edn. (Cornell University Press, Ithaca, N.Y., 1962), p. 221.
5. William B. Ballis, 'Soviet-Iranian Relations During the Decade 1953-1964', *Bulletin, Institute for the Study of the USSR* (Munich), vol. 12, no. 11 (November 1965), p. 15.
6. *New York Times*, 9 February 1959.
7. Pahlavi, *Mission For My Country*, p. 122.
8. *New York Times*, 12 February 1959.
9. Walter Lippmann, *New York Herald Tribune*, 15 December 1959.
10. *US News & World Report*, 23 April 1962.
11. According to *The Economist* (21 July 1962), the USA cut off military aid to Iran. Presidential Counsel Theodore C. Sorenson commented on the Kennedy administration's position:

> in Iran the Shah insisted on our supporting an expensive army too large for border incidents and internal security and of no use in an all-out war. His army . . . resembled the proverbial man who was too heavy to do any light work and too light to do any heavy work.

(Theodore C. Sorenson, *Kennedy* (Harper & Row, New York, 1965), p. 628).
12. *Pravda*, 17 September 1962.
13. *The Times*, 21 December 1962.
14. V. Lednev, *Izvestia*, 19 December 1962.
15. K. Ivanovsky, 'Blow at Feudalism', *International Affairs* (Moscow), no. 3 (March 1963), p. 88.
16. 'The feudal system in Iran will be liquidated', said a *Pravda* heading that reported the Shah's speech (*Pravda*, 28 February 1963). *Bakinskiy Rabochiy* (V. Medvedev, 22 February 1963) stated that the January 1963 referendum 'convincingly demonstrated that the reform has the whole-hearted support of the people'. *Izvestia* (V. Lednev, 16 February 1963) was similarly approving of the reform. See also: D.L. Morison, 'From Feudal to Bourgeois: The Soviet View of Iran Today', *Mizan*, vol. XI, no. 5 (September-October 1969), pp. 248-51; D.L. Morison – W.E.R., 'Soviet Comment on Iran's Land Reform', ibid., pp. 252-4; M.S. Ivanov, 'The Land Reform and the Development of Capitalist Relations in the Agriculture of Iran', *Narody Azii i Afriki*, no. 4 (1969), pp. 26-33.

17. From 1979-82 the Soviet media reported the opposite of what they had said in 1963 and afterwards, listing the suppression of these riots among 'the Shah's crimes'.
18. *Pravda*, 28 July 1963; *New Times*, no. 47, 27 November 1963, p. 3.
19. Joint communiqué on visit, *Pravda*, 4 July 1965. See also: *Washington Post*, 3 July 1965; *Neue Zurcher Zeitung* (Zurich), 17 July 1965.
20. *Pravda*, 14 January 1966.
21. Manoucher Parvin, 'Political Economy of Soviet-Iranian Trade: An Overview of Theory and Practice', *Middle East Journal*, vol. 31, no. 1 (Winter 1977), pp. 31-44; Christopher D. Lee, 'The Soviet Contribution to Iran's Fourth Development Plan', *Mizan*, vol. XI, no. 5 (September-October 1969), pp. 237-47.
22. *New York Times*, 14 July 1966, 21 February and 14 September 1967; *Le Monde*, 21 February 1967.
23. Statement on visit, *Pravda*, 8 April 1968.
24. *New York Times*, 8 April 1968.
25. *Pravda*, 17 July 1968; G. Drambyants, *New Times*, no. 11, 19 March 1969, p. 19; A. Yodfat and M. Abir, *In the Direction of the Gulf: The Soviet Union and the Persian Gulf* (Frank Cass, London, 1977), pp. 70-1.
26. Geoffrey Jukes, *The Indian Ocean in Soviet Naval Policy* (International Institute for Strategic Studies (IISS), London, Adelphi Papers no. 87, May 1972).
27. *Pravda*, 5 October 1968.
28. *Le Monde*, 19 December 1968.
29. In January 1969, under a heading 'Terror in Iran', the international communist journal, *Problems of Peace and Socialism*, published an article about 'crimes of the Iranian rulers' such as arrests and executions. (*World Marxist Review* (Prague), vol. 12, no. 1 (January 1969), pp. 46-7). 'Iran Atrocities' was the heading of another report in the same journal two months later (ibid., no. 3 (March 1969), pp. 39-40). No articles of this kind appeared in the Soviet press at the time.
30. *Pravda*, 1 April 1970.
31. V. Ivanenko, ibid., 1 June 1979.
32. Ibid., 17 October 1971.
33. *New York Times*, 24 October 1971.
34. *The Times*, 18 August 1971; *Peking Review*, vol. 14, no. 35 (27 August 1971), p. 16.
35. *Pravda*, 10 August 1971.
36. Aryeh Y. Yodfat, *Between Revolutionary Slogans and Pragmatism: The PRC and the Middle East* (Centre d'Etudes du Sud-Est Asiatique et de l'Extrême Orient, Brussels, 1979), pp. 59-61.
37. *Pravda*, 10 April 1972.
38. Ibid., 22 October 1972.
39. US Congress, 94th Cong., 2nd Sess., US Senate, Committee on Foreign Relations, Subcommittee on Foreign Assistance, *US Military Sales to Iran*, A Staff Report . . ., July 1976 (US Government Printing Office, Washington, D.C., 1976), p. 5.
40. The Soviet media generally ignored this at the time of the Shah but described it after his downfall. According to *Za Rubezhom* (Moscow), no. 16, 12 April 1979, pp. 12-13:

Super-sensitive US electronic reconnaissance stations were installed in regions directly adjacent to the Soviet border, near Bandar Shah on the shores of the Caspian and in Kabkam, an uninhabited spot in the mountains 130 kilometres south of Mashad. The Kabkam station, known as the 'Big Ear', was technically equipped 'to next century's standards'.

41. 'Nobody Can Overthrow Me – I Have the Power. Interview with the Shah of Iran', *US News & World Report*, 26 June 1978.
42. James A. Bill, 'Iran and the Crisis of '78', *Foreign Affairs*, vol. 57, no. 2 (Winter 1978-9), pp. 323-42.
43. President Carter toast in Tehran, 31 December 1977, *Weekly Compilation of Presidential Documents*, vol. 13, no. 53 (2 January 1978), p. 1975.
44. Shahram Chubin, 'Iran: Between the Arab West and the Asian East', *Survival* (July-August 1974), pp. 173-82.
45. Penelope Tremayne, 'End of Ten Years' War', *RUSI* (Journal of the Royal United Services Institute for Defence Studies, London), vol. 122, no. 1 (March 1977), pp. 44-8; D.L. Price, *Oman: Insurgency and Development, Conflict Studies* (London), no. 53 (January 1975), pp. 3-17.
46. T. Gamkrelidze, *Zarya Vostoka* (Tbilisi), 14 November 1978.
47. TASS, 18 November 1974. In FBIS, USSR, 19 November 1974, p. F3; *Pravda*, 19 November 1974.
48. Yodfat, *Between Revolutionary Slogans*, pp. 100-3.
49. Joint communiqué on visit, *Pravda*, 18 March 1973.
50. V. Lebedeva, Moscow radio in Persian to Iran, 20 March 1973. In FBIS, USSR, 21 March 1973, pp. B4-B6.
51. Statement on visit, *Pravda*, 21 November 1974.
52. Ibid., 19 November 1974; TASS, 18 November 1974. In FBIS, USSR, 19 November 1974, pp. F1-F4.
53. Pavel Mezentsev, 'Petrodollars and Politics', *New Times*, no. 5 (January 1978), p. 12.
For a Soviet account of the economic, social and military evolution of Iran, see: *Mirovaya Ekonomika i Mezhdunarodnyye Otnosheniya*, no. 6 (1976), pp. 121-31. Translation in: *USSR and Third World*, special issue, no. 1 (1976). See also: 'Soviet-Iranian Energy Relations' in Arthur Jay Klinghoffer, *The Soviet Union and International Oil Politics* (Columbia University Press, New York, 1977), pp. 122-34.
54. P. Demchenko, *Pravda*, 6 April 1979.
55. V. Ivanenko, ibid., 1 June 1979.

4 THE SOVIETS AND THE FALL OF THE SHAH'S REGIME (1978-January 1979)

The Soviets' Wait and See Policy

The opposition to the Shah and his regime grew stronger in 1978. During the years 1971-6 the Shah's internal policy had been a hard-line one. The prisons filled up and hundreds of people were executed. The religious establishment was severely attacked. Early 1977 saw the start of a policy of liberalization, coinciding with the beginning of Jimmy Carter's presidency in the USA. Political prisoners were released and more freedom of the press was allowed, bringing in its wake calls for still more liberalization.

The extreme left tried to reorganize itself but for the time being it was virtually non-existent. Little remained of the Tudeh Party, which had lived underground for many years and whose headquarters were in East Berlin. The Shah declared in the mid-1970s that there were only 3,000 communists in Iran, and all or practically all of them were in prison.[1] They drew their support from a very small segment of the population, mainly the intellectuals. The Tudeh's appeals to peasants and workers were generally unsuccessful because its approach to problems was on a very theoretical basis which did not say much to ordinary people who could not understand the analysis.

Clandestine Tudeh Party broadcasts from *Peyk-e-Iran* (Radio Iran Courier) began around the end of 1957, initially from East Germany and later from Bulgaria. They used to present party statements and quote the party paper *Mardom* (The People). Most statements were in the name of the Tudeh Party Central Committee and names of members were rarely given, because of the regime's repressive measures against them and their families. The broadcasts sharply attacked the Shah, his regime and his ties with the USA. They did so even at times when the Soviet media were saying the opposite. While the Soviet media were praising the reforms introduced by the Shah in 1963, *Peyk-e-Iran* continued to attack them. The station was reported closed by Bulgaria at the end of 1976.

In 1959, a clandestine radio station commenced operations, broadcasting in Persian from Soviet Transcaucasia. It called itself the National Voice of Iran (NVOI), and is still on the air up to the time of writing.

Its attitude on many issues is more flexible than that of the Tudeh, and
it has been able to adapt itself to the many changes in Soviet positions
regarding Iran.

The Soviet media avoided any references that might appear to be
criticizing the Shah's regime. Only in mid-1978 did they begin to report
the existence of an opposition in Iran, and even then, they preferred to
give only news, to cite others, and to avoid all comment. A comment
in August 1978 said that the 'anti-government demonstrations' had
assumed large proportions, 'the popular struggle continued to gain
momentum and by spring had spread practically to the whole country'.
The authorities 'blamed the unrest on "Islamic Marxists"'. Many foreign
news analysts said that the events were a result of an aggravation 'of the
confrontation between the religious opposition and the regime'. But
'most observers believe' that the clashes 'have their roots in the serious
economic and social difficulties Iran is experiencing'.[2] Few, if any, statements by government spokesmen were reported. Some were presented
in such a way as to prove that the authorities themselves 'admitted their
guilt', since they were not prepared to introduce reforms or change their
policy as demanded by the people.

Great care was taken by the Soviets not to support the Tudeh Party
directly or officially. On 6 September 1978 a statement by the Tudeh
Central Committee, published in the Paris communist *L'Humanité*,
called on 'all forces and groups in opposition to the Shah's regime to
form a national coalition front'. Its aim should be 'to overthrow the
Shah's dictatorial regime, to abolish the monarchy and to set up a
national coalition government . . . this new regime can only be a republic'.

The statement was quoted in part in *Pravda*, omitting any direct call
for the overthrow of the regime. This was in order to prevent Iranian
accusations that the Soviets endorsed such calls. But the next day
Pravda quoted Tudeh First Secretary Iraj Iskandari, who defined the
opposition movement as 'popular, democratic and revolutionary' and
stressed that the crisis had come because of the people's 'general dissatisfaction with the existing regime'.[3] The Tudeh's role was, however,
marginal and its appeals received no response from other opposition
forces. Two months later its leaders were forced to admit that:

> Up until now, the mosques have been almost the only meeting place;
> hence the religious influence over the [opposition] movement. How-
> ever, this is definitely a deeply political movement . . . clergy . . .
> positions reflect the people's will . . . we have proposed, for several

months now, the creation of a united front, incorporating all opposition forces. But we have received no response to our appeal to date, which we regret.[4]

The Soviets continued to distinguish between, on the one hand, their official relations with Iran, which they presented as normal, 'correct' and neighbourly, and, on the other hand, 'the Soviet people's' interest in what was going on in a friendly country. On 31 October 1978 *Pravda* published Brezhnev's greetings to the Shah, on the occasion of the Iranian national holiday. He wished 'the friendly Iranian people progress and success'. The Shah's greetings to Brezhnev on the occasion of the anniversary of the revolution included personal greetings to Brezhnev and 'to the friendly people of the USSR', and a wish for 'a still greater development of relations of friendship and fruitful co-operation between our countries'.[5]

Reports occasionally appeared describing temporary stoppages in the flow of natural gas sold to the USSR. They were purported to be part of the general strike of oil workers – but these breaks were only temporary and the gas continued to flow. The work of the few hundreds of Soviet technicians and advisers continued more or less regularly in the iron and steel works in Isfahan, and in the hydro-electric and other projects, mainly in the border areas. According to a later Soviet description, 'during the struggle against the monarchy, the Iranians displayed touching concern for Soviet specialists and their families, supplying them with goods and ensuring their safety'.[6] Although there were reports of incidents directed against Soviet specialists in Isfahan, they were part of general outbursts against foreigners.

By November 1978 Soviet comments began to appear about the situation in Iran. The media now began to express opinions as well. A *Pravda* comment, rather than supporting the role of the religious establishment, tried hard to minimize it. The commentator denied any truth in the 'official propaganda' which 'tried to interpret the disorder as the intrigues of "communists" and "Islamic Marxists"'. He considered that those who saw 'the cause of the mass disturbances only in the clash of interests between the religious opposition, which enjoys great influence, and the ruling secular elite' were taking 'a superficial view'. The roots of the crisis, he said, 'lie in the serious economic and social difficulties Iran is experiencing'.[7]

Western press reports of possible Soviet involvement in the events in Iran were denied by the Soviet media, which spoke with increasing frequency about possible American intervention. A Moscow radio broadcast to North America stated that 'Washington is making no secret of the possibility of a military dictatorship in Iran'. To cover up their intentions, 'certain American quarters are falsely charging Moscow with interference in Iran'. The broadcast referred to a London *Daily Telegraph* report that 'the Soviet Union had a secret division ready on the Soviet-Iranian border and that all their officers and soldiers could speak Iranian'. The commentator considered this report a 'deliberate lie'.[8]

The long official Soviet silence on developments in Iran came to an end in Brezhnev's statement in *Pravda* on 19 November 1978. He said:

> The Soviet Union, which maintains traditional good-neighbourly relations with Iran, emphatically declares that it is against outside interference in Iran's internal affairs by anyone, in any form and under any pretext. What is happening in Iran is a purely internal affair and the issues involved must be solved by the Iranians themselves. All states should adhere in this matter to the principles laid down in the UN Charter and a number of other fundamental international documents, and should respect the sovereignty and independence of Iran and the Iranian people.
>
> It should also be clear that any, particularly military, interference in the affairs of Iran, a state directly bordering on the Soviet Union, would be regarded by the Soviet Union as affecting its security interests.[9]

The Soviets See 'Disturbances' as Engineered by America to Pressure the Shah

The Brezhnev statement of 19 November 1978 was meant to create the impression of a warning regarding American intentions to intervene in Iran; the Soviets would then claim the credit for preventing it by means of the warnings. They had used such tactics on numerous occasions. For example, they spread reports about Turkey's plans (with American backing) of invading Syria in 1957, and also about similar Israeli plans on the eve of the June 1967 Arab-Israeli war. When such an 'invasion' did not occur, the Soviets were able to claim that they had prevented it.[10] The Soviet aim was to direct the dissatisfaction and xenophobia existing in Iran against the Americans, thus weakening American positions. They believed that this would facilitate the penetration of Soviet influence in the region. Reports appeared in the Soviet media about Pentagon and CIA preparations to intervene in Iran. It was stated that there were about 80,000 Americans in Iran, a large number of whom were connected in some way with the US military or intelligence and, according to these Soviet statements, more American military advisers and CIA agents were still arriving.[11]

The frequent Soviet references to possible American intervention were not only for the purpose of inciting the Iranian opposition groups against the Americans – the Soviets were even accusing the USA of trying to woo this very opposition.[12] They genuinely believed that American intervention was imminent. They expected it and prepared their own public for it. Brezhnev's 19 November 1978 warning was repeated almost daily by the Soviet media, but no such further statements were issued by Soviet leaders. They anticipated an American intervention and were greatly surprised when it did not come.

The Soviet media denied reports about the Soviets' own plans to intervene in Iran, the rumours that strikes were being organized by Soviet agents and that 'caches of Soviet weapons have been discovered'.[13] Such reports, the Soviets said, were a cover-up for American plans for an intervention and were intended to damage the image of the opposition by claiming that it was unable to act by itself and needed foreign aid.

The opposition's religious leadership was viewed unfavourably by the USSR. 'The demonstrations are mostly of a political character . . . although Tehran radio tries to portray them as religious processions,' TASS said.[14] Moscow radio denied descriptions of the opposition as 're-actionaries' attempting 'to take the country back to the Middle Ages'.[15] This was an indirect expression of Soviet hopes that if the opposition did come to power, it would not be dominated by the religious leadership. Their experience in the past had been that Muslim political and social movements tended, after victory, to assume an anti-Soviet character, even if they had previously appeared to be sympathetic to the Soviets.

The Soviets foresaw a scenario whereby, if the Shah and his generals were to do to the opposition what the opposition would have liked to do to them – and, in fact, did do later on – his regime could be saved. Had the Soviets found themselves in such a situation they would undoubtedly have done the same. They interpreted American advice to the Shah to avoid bloodshed as an attempt to weaken him, with the intention of controlling him even more.[16] The Americans and the Shah had, for the time being, lost control of the situation, but in the Soviet view they could regain control.

An interpretation of this situation in Iran was made in mid-December 1978 by Leonid Zamyatin, Head of the International Information

Department of the CPSU Central Committee. He felt that it was the Americans who were behind events in Iran, manipulating the opposition and the 'reactionary' clergy, and using the situation for their own aims. Over Moscow television, Zamyatin listed the reasons for the events in Iran. There were several, he said: 'the social and material inequality . . . a corrupt group of people belonging to the government, or previous governments . . . to the Shah's family . . . injustices'. In his view the USA had also played a role in events, by encouraging the opposition to the Shah in its initial stages:

> the United States itself, seeing the strengthening of the Shah . . . and his independent policy on the setting of prices in the framework of OPEC . . . when this independent policy did not please the Americans, it was decided to remind him in this way that it is necessary to look closely at what is happening in his country. They have also allowed the build-up of this opposition to occur in Iran . . . The Americans thought that this would not damage the Shah's regime and at the same time would make him more compliant, since there are more than 80,000 Americans in Iran . . . who also wanted to grab their money in even larger amounts and were prevented by the Shah's regime.

According to Zamyatin, events had not developed as the Americans had expected. Although they had lost control of the situation, they were hoping to come to an agreement with whoever was to rule Iran.

> When these events were in progress, several forces joined in . . . the entire movement was suddenly headed by the Shi'ite priesthood, because it itself had suffered because of the land reform carried out by the Shah at one time. It stood at the head of this movement — although it is actually a reactionary movement . . .
>
> Now the situation is practically out of the control of those who attempted to exercise various pressures . . . It seems that the question for the Americans — since they have contacts with the opposition — is not who rules Iran, but what will Iran be for the United States?[17]

This was the position which seemed to prevail among the Soviet leadership, which considered that the opposition could only restrict the Shah's rule, or replace him with others, more obedient to the USA.

The Soviets Cry 'Wolf', and Speak of American Meddling

In the last months of 1978, the Soviets still saw a possibility of the Shah staying in power. The Soviet media were generally sympathetic to the demonstrations, but said so only indirectly, by judicious selection of published Western reports. A slight shift away from the Shah was noticeable by mid-December, but this was more a manoeuvre to keep pace with events in case the Shah fell, and was hardly felt. There were no attacks on the Shah such as one would expect from the Soviets if they were desirous of his downfall. Neither were there predictions that it was imminent. Reports about calls to overthrow the Shah started to appear, but not in the main press.[18]

There were no apparent signs of Soviet support or encouragement for the opponents of the Shah. However, some events, such as the oil workers' strike, seem to have been organized or at least encouraged by Soviet-supported forces.[19] In general, the Soviets preferred stability along their borders, and an uninterrupted flow of gas.[20] They wanted an authoritative Iranian regime with which they would be able to maintain correct relations.

After a studied silence on the subject for quite some time, an article appeared in *Izvestia* on 6 January 1979, claiming that Soviet-Iranian relations were still governed by the Russian-Persian treaty of 26 February 1921.[21] This was said not as a warning or a threat of intervention, but more to remind those concerned that the USSR had interests in Iran and that Iran had certain obligations toward her northern neighbour.

In demonstrations during late January 1979 a Soviet correspondent noticed some slogans calling for better relations with the Soviet Union. He reviewed Soviet-Iranian economic relations, saying that 'the potential of our economic and trading ties is far from exhausted and there are good prospects for their further development'.[22] An *Izvestia* comment took issue with former US Secretary of State Henry Kissinger and others who wished 'to blame the Soviet Union for the "disorders" in Iran'. It denied any Soviet involvement, claiming that 'American and not Soviet interference is an undisputable fact'.[23] A Moscow broadcast to Iran denied 'rumours about the concentration of Soviet military forces, and of a complete army division in the Iranian border area all of whose soldiers and members speak Persian'.[24]

'US intervention in Iranian affairs' was an almost daily theme in the Soviet media. 'The United States is obviously either seeking ways of saving the regime or replacing it with one more acceptable to the Iranian people and the United States itself, or it is gambling on interference.'[25]

According to a Soviet commentator, 'the extremist group in the army leadership, and the Iranian special services under the leadership of American special services, have already prepared for a coup and are seeking a convenient pretext for rapidly suppressing the anti-Shah and anti-American movement'.[26] 'A military coup, on the Chile model, is by no means inconceivable,' said *Pravda*.[27]

The Tehran visit of General Robert Huyser, Deputy Commander of US Forces in Europe, was frequently referred to in the Soviet media. A comment after the Shah's departure said that General Huyser was 'successfully acting as a substitute for the Shah', and was 'ensuring that the "advice coming in from Washington"' was implemented by the military leadership, with which he had established 'effective relations'. It further stated that 'a kind of "creeping military coup" is already being effected as a result of the crude and overt US interference in Iran's internal affairs'.[28]

The Bakhtiar Government and the Shah are Ousted

On 4 January 1979 the Shah appointed Shahpur Bakhtiar to the post of Prime Minister. Bakhtiar had formerly been a minister in the Mossadeq government and leader of the Iran Party, which formed part of the opposition National Front. The latter, which had opposed his moves, dissociated itself from Bakhtiar and expelled him from its ranks. The Soviets looked upon Bakhtiar as a tool of the Shah, the military and the USA. But until late January 1979 they sat on the fence as far as he was concerned, being unable to decide where events in Iran were leading and whom to back. By the end of January they had concluded that the key leader would be Khomeyni rather than Bakhtiar, so they now began speaking favourably of Khomeyni and against Bakhtiar.[29]

On 16 January 1979 the Shah left Iran. The Soviet reaction was not immediate. The next day, *Pravda* published only a short TASS report from New York about this. The 21 January *Pravda* 'international review' started off the new policy of attacking the Shah. The review included a positive appraisal of the religious leadership and an attempt to explain these leaders' heading the revolution:

the Shi'ites have found themselves on the crest of events, for they have given expression to the protest which has developed among the people against the Shah's despotism and US dominance.

The social outburst has also acquired a religious colouring, because radical opposition in Iran was so drained by repression that at the time of the crisis, there was no political organization capable of leading the masses.[30]

A few days later a *Pravda* comment said that 'a large proportion of [Iran's] population is linked with the tradition of Shi'ism, whose slogans are of an objectively progressive nature in the situation that has taken shape'.[31] The term 'objectively progressive' was much used in the Soviet Union during Stalin's time.

It meant that under certain circumstances one might be 'subjectively' reactionary, anti-communist and anti-Soviet, but 'objectively' one's activities still served the Soviet Union. They might result in 'progress' and should therefore be welcomed. Soviet commentators used terms taken from their own history and the Russian revolution of 1917. Moscow radio referred to the existence of 'a dual power', of 'two apparatuses', of the opposition and of the government, 'which is already unable to carry out the duties incumbent upon it'.[32]

A week after the Shah's departure, the Soviets broke with him, denouncing him as a corrupt dictator who had brutally oppressed the people. This was the start of a flood of accusations directed at the Shah. Although the Shah died of cancer in a Cairo hospital on 27 July 1980, Soviet accusations of the Shah continued even after his death.

Notes

1. *Le Figaro*, 26 January 1979.
2. 'Iran in Ferment', *New Times*, no. 35 (August 1978), pp. 10-11.
3. *Pravda*, 12, 13 September 1978.
4. Interview with Tudeh Party First Secretary, Iraj Iskandari, and Second Secretary, N. Kianuri, *L'Humanité*, 27 November 1978.
5. *Pravda*, 31 October 1978.
6. *Za Rubezhom* (Moscow), no. 16, 12 April 1979, pp. 12-13.
7. A. Filipov, 'Iran: Days of Tension', *Pravda*, 3 November 1978.
8. Moscow radio in English to North America, 3 November 1978. In FBIS, USSR, 6 November 1978, pp. F8-F9.
9. 'Reply of L.J. Brezhnev to a question by *Pravda* Correspondent', *Pravda*, 19 November 1978.
10. Francis Fukuyama, 'Nuclear Shadow-boxing: Soviet Intervention Threats in the Middle East', *Orbis*, vol. 25, no. 3 (Fall 1981), pp. 579-605.
11. *Pravda* and *Krasnaya Zvezda*, 19 November 1978.
12. The Americans were 'trying to establish contact with opposition leaders who are considered to hold pro-Western views. The stakes thus appear to be played on two cards — support of the Shah and simultaneous wooing of the pro-Western wing of the opposition. This double game is as usual accompanied by an anti-Soviet and anti-communist propaganda campaign . . .' (A. Stepanov, 'Mysterious Mission', *New Times*, no. 50 (December 1978), pp. 9-10.)

13. *Pravda*, 7 December 1978.

14. TASS in English, 11 December 1978. In FBIS, USSR, 12 December 1978, p. F5.

15. Moscow radio in Persian to Iran, 12 December 1978. In ibid., p. F7.

16. The Shah said a month before his death: 'Somebody was interested in my leaving Iran because I was too independent in my way of thinking and decision'. (*La Revue du Liban*, 1 August 1980.) In his memoirs the Shah wrote that, although he had US Presidential Security Adviser Zbigniew Brzezinski's apparent support, he came to a realization in exile that 'the Americans wanted me out. Certainly this is what the human rights champions in the State Department wanted.' (Charles J. Hanley, 'A US-General-Aided Revolution, Shah's Book Says', *Philadelphia Inquirer*, 12 September 1980.)

17. 'Studio Nine' Programme, Moscow Domestic Television, 16 December 1978. In FBIS, USSR, 5 January 1979, pp. A11-A13.
For reviews of American policy see: Michael A. Ledeen and William H. Lewis, 'Carter and the Fall of the Shah: The Inside Story', *The Washington Quarterly* (Spring 1980), pp. 3-40; Walter Taylor, 'Sullivan Attacks Brzezinski Role in Iran. Ex-US Ambassador Charges Policy Errors', and William H. Sullivan, 'Envoy's Version of the Collapse. Brzezinski Blamed for Impeding Transition Period', *Washington Star*, 7 September 1980; *Foreign Policy* (New York), no. 40 (Fall 1980), pp. 175-86; Charles J. Hanley, *Philadelphia Inquirer*, 12 September 1980.

18. TASS in English, 11 December 1978 (in FBIS, USSR, 12 December 1978, p. F5) described 'mass anti-government demonstrations . . . held under slogans of liquidating the present monarchic regime'.

19. This, too, seemed to be exaggerated in Western press reports. The Tudeh Party claimed 'to be powerful' in the oil industry, but it was said that it had only 'old militants' at the Abadan refinery. (Bruno De Thomas, *Le Monde*, 8 May 1979.)

20. The December 1978 stoppage of gas supplies to the USSR (about one billion cubic feet per day during 1978) caused severe energy shortages in Soviet Transcaucasia.

21. V. Matvye'ev, 'Around the Events in Iran', *Izvestia*, 6 January 1979.

22. P. Demchenko, 'When the People Rise Up', *Pravda*, 24 January 1979.

23. S. Kondrashov, *Izvestia*, 24 January 1979.

24. Moscow radio in Persian to Iran, 27 January 1979. In FBIS, USSR, 29 January 1979, p. F1.

25. Moscow radio in Persian to Iran, 7 January 1979. In FBIS, USSR, 8 January 1979, p. A6.

26. *Sotsialisticheskaya Industriya*, 21 January 1979.

27. *Pravda*, 21 January 1979.

28. A. Petrov, 'Events in Iran', *Pravda*, 30 January 1979.

29. Ibid.

30. V. Ovchinnikov, 'International Review', ibid., 21 January 1979.

31. P. Demchenko, 'When the People Rise Up', ibid., 24 January 1979.

32. D. Volskiy, Moscow radio in Russian, 21 January 1979. In FBIS, USSR, 22 January 1979, p. A6.

5 THE SOVIETS AND THE FIRST STAGES OF THE ISLAMIC REVOLUTION (February-November 1979)

The Soviets Propose Co-operation

The return to Iran of Ayatollah Ruhollah Mosavi Khomeyni on 1 February 1979 was favourably reported in the Soviet media. So was Khomeyni's appointment, on 5 February, of Mehdi Bazargan to head a provisional government. The Soviet media had become increasingly critical of the Shahpur Bakhtiar government but preferred not to support any particular group. They were still uncertain what was going to happen: would there be a peaceful transfer of power from Bakhtiar to Bazargan, a civil war between their supporters, or a US-backed military take-over? Soviet commentators spoke a great deal about the latter possibility. They warned of an American intervention and talked about the need for co-operation between all anti-Shah forces to prevent such an eventuality. But they said all this indirectly, quoting others in a way that would enable the USSR to join the winners, whatever the outcome.

It was only after the army withdrew its support for Bakhtiar, forcing him to resign, that the USSR announced its official recognition of the Provisional Government headed by Bazargan.[1] After that, the Soviets made an effort to establish correct and stable working relations with the new regime. Their media praised the regime, stressing what they favoured and ignoring the regime's religious character.

An official Soviet position on the revolution in Iran was presented by Brezhnev in his 2 March 1979 election speech. He said:

We . . . welcome the victory of this revolution which put an end to the despotic oppressive regime . . . We wish new revolutionary Iran success and prosperity, and hope that relations of good neighbourliness between the peoples of the Soviet Union and Iran will be fruitfully developed on the firm basis of mutual respect, goodwill and non-interference in each other's internal affairs.[2]

A *Pravda* comment by P. Demchenko on 6 April 1979 appealed for greater co-operation between the Soviet Union and Iran. Now that Iran had been proclaimed a republic, 'the Pentagon's military bases have been abolished, the country has withdrawn from CENTO . . . this widens the aspect of coincidence in the USSR's and Iran's political positions on the international arena'. Iran's Deputy Prime Minister, A. Amir Entazam, was reported as stating that 'relations between Iran and the Soviet Union will be broadened and developed . . . bilateral relations should become much better than they were under the Shah's regime'.

As regards prospects for such co-operation, they are considerable in the sphere of industry, energy and agriculture. Soviet organizations have, for example, accumulated experience in conducting large-scale irrigation operations, which Iran needs and can thus help it to achieve self-sufficiency in foodstuffs. At present insufficient use is being made of the waters of the Tedzhen and Atrek rivers, where major hydro-power installations could be built to meet our mutual interests. The integration of the two countries' power systems would be of mutual benefit . . . the Soviet Union is prepared to make the greatest effort to strengthen and further expand Soviet-Iranian relations.[3]

Khomeyni completely ignored the appeal for co-operation.

The Tudeh Adapts Itself to the Situation

The Soviet media paid considerable attention to the Tudeh Party, its position and activities, but overestimated its strength and popularity. Tudeh influence appeared in three centres: the oil workers, the influential teachers' organization and in the universities, particularly Tehran University. After the revolution some 30 'cadres' who had been abroad returned. They were 'received favourably' in Tehran, especially among the students.[4] The Tudeh had many followers among workers of the Ahwaz oilfields and the Abadan refinery. In Tehran demonstrations took place adopting both Islamic and communist slogans. There were pro-Soviets and communists in the northern regions close to the USSR, although they were not necessarily Tudeh members or followers. (The Tudeh, as a party of Persian intellectuals, had less appeal in areas of minority ethnic groups.)

The Tudeh was headed for years by Iraj Iskandari. As a good communist, he was against the religious establishment and against Khomeyni, even when Khomeyni led the revolt against the Shah. This led to his removal on 4 January 1979, when he was replaced as First Secretary by

Nuraddin Kianuri, The latter is a grandson of Ayatollah Fazlollah Nouri, who was executed in 1907 by secular revolutionaries. Khomeyni and other clerics around him remembered it. Kianuri immediately published a communiqué in which he declared, in part: 'The Ayatollah [Khomeyni]'s programme coincides with that of the Tudeh Party . . . Any government which follows the policy outlined by the Ayatollah will have the Tudeh's support.'[5]

According to Tudeh (and the Soviets), the revolution in Iran had only just begun. Its first stage had come to an end but further stages were on the way in which opportunities for the Tudeh might appear. Meanwhile, the party had no chance to gain influence and could afford an open confrontation with Khomeyni. It preferred to do everything to enable it to carry on its activities legally and in the open, organizing and strengthening itself until its time came. Nuraddin Kianuri said:

> Ayatollah Khomeyni won our sympathy when he began to issue his resolute and radical slogans against the Shah. The Tudeh Party recognizes the objectively progressive elements in his movement. We are making every effort to find a common language with Khomeyni, because objectively he is playing a progressive role in Iran's development.[6]

However, this was a one-sided effort. There were no direct contacts between the Tudeh and Khomeyni. The Bazargan government was anxious to prevent the Tudeh and other Marxists from infiltrating the state machinery. Bazargan said of them:

> I distrust them . . . I have always come up against them . . . There is no way of co-operating with them. They always betray you. The Tudeh Party betrayed Mossadeq. When he was overthrown, its leaders admitted that and said they regretted it. It was too late.[7]

The Tudeh began legal activities, opening offices in Tehran and other cities. Its organ *Mardom* (The People) appeared twice a week. In the national referendum held at the end of March 1979, the party called for an Islamic Republic.[8] The Tudeh, however, was small and insignificant, with little influence. It was able to act more or less legally only because it was tolerated by Khomeyni and those around him.

The Nationalities and Ethnic Groups Issue

Traditionally the Soviets supported Iran's national minorities, and the prevailing Soviet slogan was to grant them national autonomy within the framework of the Iranian republic. However, the Soviets preferred not to go into details about the meaning and extent of such autonomy. A Tudeh Party document on the ethnic groups issue, published on 24 May 1973, reflected much of Soviet thinking on this matter. It stated that Iran was a multinational country in which various nationalities and other ethnic groups lived, namely Persians, Azerbaijanis, Kurds, Baluchis, Turkomans and Arabs. Other minorities are scattered throughout the country — Armenians, Assyrians and Jews. The term Persian was considered 'to denote all those living in Iran except the Azerbaijanis, Kurds, Baluchis and Arabs'. The Persians, along with the Azerbaijanis and Kurds, 'have achieved a higher level of national cohesion'.[9] Except for the Persians, 'national units are deprived of their right to manage their own social, economic, administrative and cultural affairs'. The document expressed support for:

> full equality of rights for all the peoples, ethnic groups and national minorities living in Iran, and their voluntary unity within a single homeland based on preserving the territorial integrity of the Iranian homeland . . . This can be achieved by securing autonomy for the deprived peoples and nationalities.

A middle course was advocated, opposing both 'deviationist nationalism and national isolationism' and 'the chauvinism of the greater nation'. Pan-Iranism was rejected, as it 'negates the existence of various national units in Iran . . . [and] tries to justify national oppression under the guise of national unity'.[10] This was in addition to pan-Iranist claims to parts of the Soviet Union inhabited by Persian-speaking peoples.

The Soviet position in 1979 did not differ greatly from that of the Tudeh Party. But both the Soviets and the Tudeh preferred to use generalized slogans and adapt themselves to current political situations. Soviet policy on this matter was a function of relations with Iran's leadership. When the Soviets saw a chance to co-operate with the Iranian authorities, they sided with them against autonomy for minority nationalities. This did not mean that the Soviets had abandoned all the ties they had fostered with these minorities — they simply gave them as low a profile as possible in order not to be seen to provide any open support for the Kurds, or other ethnic groups. This was the same attitude they had shown towards the Kurds in Iraq. Here, the Kurds had been supported by the Soviets in times of strained relations between the USSR and the Iraqi leadership, but when relations improved, the Kurds were abandoned and advised to accept whatever solution the Iraqi leadership offered them. For example, during Iraq's first Ba'thist regime, in 1963, the Soviets had provided aid to the Democratic Party of Kurdistan (DPK) in its revolt against the Iraqi authorities. After the Soviet-Iraqi friendship treaty was signed in 1972, the Soviets advised the Kurds (and also exerted pressure on them) to stop fighting and accept the administrative autonomy proposed by the Iraqi authorities.

The Soviets suspected that the Kurds in Iran were being used by 'outside forces' to destabilize the situation. They therefore decided to act against them (or at least to stop supporting them openly). The Kurds were advised by the Soviets to be cautious, not to allow themselves to be used by enemies of Iran's new regime, not to exaggerate their power and abilities, and not to demand too much.[11]

In April 1979 *Pravda* commented that the Iranian government had declared its readiness to deal with the question of ethnic groups on a basis 'of meeting their main demands'. However, a new conflict broke out in districts populated by Iranian Turkomans. There 'the forces of counter-revolution, teamed with local landowners and industrialists and with the Shah supporters who fled to this area, hand out armaments, form military units and organize actions directed against the authorities'. Any Soviet involvement was denied in both the Kurdish and Turkoman areas.[12] This was during the first weeks of the new regime, when the Soviets saw a chance that the Iranian revolution might develop in a direction they desired.

Careful Soviet Criticism

Soviet support for Iran's revolutionary regime had become less wholehearted and more reserved by mid-April 1979, and still more lukewarm by June 1979. Soviet commentators began talking about divisions among those who earlier had been united against the Shah and about 'a polarization of forces'. According to a senior Soviet commentator:

> A new, difficult and complicated period has begun in Iran . . . the forces that had been united by a common goal — the destruction of the Shah's regime and the fettering dependence on America — have begun to split into factions . . . differences are appearing not only

between political groups, but even within the religious groups which now play the main role in Iran. Its leaders sometimes take up differing, even opposing positions . . .

A considerable section of the bourgeoisie would prefer a bourgeois democratic structure. The left-wing forces demand to proceed still further . . . to extend the conquests of the revolution. The situation is complicated by the disorderly actions of various anarchist, Trotskyist, Maoist and leftist groups with their hangers-on . . . They organize bloody confrontations . . . provoke the authorities into repression.[13]

A Tbilisi daily spoke more openly about the 'reactionary priesthood' and the 'internal reaction' violent struggle:

Taking advantage of the social backwardness and profound and often blind and fanatical religiosity of significant strata of the population — the urban lower class and the peasantry — the reactionary segment of the priesthood, along with conservatively-minded circles of the haute and middle bourgeoisie, are doing their best to prevent substantial socio-economic transformations. Moreover, internal reaction is resorting to violent methods of struggle against detachments of the revolutionary movement.[14]

The writer was careful to distinguish between 'reactionaries' and Khomeyni — hinting that the Soviets wished to co-operate with him.

Soviet-Iranian bilateral relations worsened. The unstable situation brought about the cancellation of a number of joint economic projects. The most damaging of these, for the Soviets, was a reduction in the delivery of Iranian gas to the Soviet Union. This forced the Soviets to effect a costly redistribution of energy supplies for industries in the Transcaucasus region.[15] The construction work on a second gas pipeline was suspended and later cancelled. Iran also raised its prices to the USSR for natural gas.

The Soviet involvement in Afghanistan and reports of direct or indirect Soviet support and arms supplies for Iran's rebelling nationalities — Kurds, Turkomans, Arabs and Baluchis — increased Iranian suspicions and resulted in a considerable tension in relations. Soviet attempts to argue with leading Iranian personalities or to attack their pronouncements had been rare during the first months of the Islamic Republic. This changed in the second half of August 1979 and still more during September-October, when the Soviet media, although not official Soviet spokesmen, expressed growing reservations about developments in Iran.

Direct comments on Iran's 'official religious-theological doctrine' and 'religious fanaticism' were made by a senior Soviet commentator in early September 1979. In Iran, he said, 'hopes have been replaced by anxiety and alarm, uncertainty and disappointment'. The country's economy was being led by 'economist-theologians' who promised much but merely brought unemployment, inflation and chaos. He went on:

> All publications which have expressed views at variance with the official religious-theological doctrine have been closed down and banned. People advocating progressive social transformations . . . are being persecuted . . . the fratricidal war in Kordestan is continuing . . . Those demanding equality and autonomy are declared traitors, they are executed and the religious fanaticism of the Shi'ite masses is being aroused against them . . . Nobody can deny the Iranian clergy's positive role in the anti-Shah revolution . . . [and their] right to . . . participate in their country's political life. But there is obvious room for doubt that a theocratic concept of the state will help Iran to become a modern and flourishing country.
>
> It is obvious to me that the feeling of religious fanaticism, anti-communist hysteria and a desire to misrepresent the policy and intentions of a friendly country [the USSR] will not benefit the Iranian people . . . The coalition of political movements, forces and groups which secured victory for the revolution has already disintegrated . . . Repression of the extreme left of the political spectrum automatically strengthens the extreme right and creates favourable soil for outside pressure . . . All this is making the situation in the country unstable and fraught with conflicts and unexpected surprises.[16]

Moscow radio cited 'a listener' who said that Iran:

> represents something akin to a religious dictatorship. The revolution in Iran . . . was a religious one and it cannot solve the social and economic problems facing the country . . . it has turned the country into one big mosque . . . progressive movements are persecuted in the country and so is the People's Party of Iran [Tudeh].[17]

The Soviets, however, were not seeking to worsen relations but rather to improve them. An article by *Izvestia*'s Tehran correspondent spoke about co-operation between the two countries and Soviet support for Iran.

The Soviet Union has come out in support of the Iranian revolution. Our country is displaying its readiness to co-operate actively with the new Iran in the spirit of good neighbourliness, mutually advantageous co-operation, and non-intervention in each other's internal affairs . . .

A delegation of leaders of the Iranian metallurgical industry visited the Soviet Union recently and contracts were signed for the further expansion of the metallurgical plant in Isfahan. In Ahwaz Soviet specialists have commissioned the first turbine of the Rumin thermal power station, the largest in all southern Iran and of importance to the country's oil industry. Work has been completed on electrifying the railroad from the Soviet border to the city of Tabriz, and contracts have been signed for the construction of new grain elevators.

The article included a list of 'positive' steps in Iran's foreign relations:

Iran has ceased to be an appendage of the US military machine, withdrawn from the CENTO military-political alliance, and ceased to be the gendarme of the Persian Gulf and the outpost of the US . . . [and] has abolished the US surveillance bases on Iranian territory near the Soviet border . . . The Iranian government has stated its intention to adhere in its foreign policy to the principles of non-alignment and non-membership of military blocs.[18]

The Soviets feared a trend towards a *rapprochement* with the Western powers. TASS cited a *New York Times* report that the US administration was discussing with the Iranian government the question of resumption of deliveries of American arms and spares, and a new programme for training Iranian servicemen by American specialists.[19] The Soviets feared that this was the beginning of an American-Iranian reconciliation to which they were averse.

The Tudeh is Outlawed and then Legalized Again

On 20 August 1979 the Revolutionary Guards sealed off both the editorial office of the Tudeh newspaper *Mardom* and the secretariat of the Party Central Committee. It looked as if the Tudeh might be forced to go underground. Soviet reactions to this were cautious, trying to avoid a deterioration in relations between Tudeh and the Iranian authorities, and between the authorities and the USSR. The Soviet media reported

Tudeh protests against the act, but refrained from adding their own comments.

On 29 August 1979 *Pravda* published a letter from the Tudeh Party First Secretary to the Islamic Revolutionary Council and the government complaining against those measures. It said:

In most of the towns in Iran, the offices of the party and its youth organization are being subjected to attacks . . . Tudeh premises have been set on fire and the lives of many party members have been endangered . . . The latter demand an end to the persecution of the Tudeh Party and that the ban on the publication of the paper *Mardom* be lifted.[20]

A letter from the Tudeh Central Committee spoke about:

the closure of a number of newspapers and journals, including the newspaper *Mardom* . . . the pogroms against party representatives in other towns and provinces of the country, the attacks on party workers and their supporters, including the execution without trial in Kermanshah of two Tudeh members [and demanded] an end to the oppression of the Tudeh Party . . . to protect the party's activities by law from the raids and attacks.[21]

Both the Soviets and Tudeh preferred to avoid direct accusation either of the regime or of Khomeyni in person on this matter. The criticism was against 'reactionary' segments and tendencies of the Islamic revolution. Khomeyni was presented as acting against the 'reactionaries' and curbing their intentions. According to Kianuri:

It was Khomeyni who urged calm when the Islamic right started burning books and attacking the offices of left-wing organizations. It is he who has renewed the call for unity. Our entire policy is aimed at preventing Khomeyni from being relegated to the Islamic right.[22]

Restrictions on Tudeh activities were lifted, although not completely, and on 1 October 1979 the Tudeh newspaper *Mardom* resumed publication.[23] The Tudeh was satisfied with this. It knew its place well. Its aim was for the time being not to bring about a proletarian revolution, but rather to maintain the legality of the party's existence. The Khomeyni regime was not what the Tudeh wanted, but it feared a

Western-supported military coup or any other changes that would make the party illegal again.

The Revolt in Kordestan

The demands for autonomy by Iran's national and ethnic groups were represented by the Soviets during the first months of the Islamic regime as being justified in themselves, but in the existing circumstances they were being used by 'Shah supporters' to weaken the revolutionary regime and restore the old order. A Soviet comment in early May 1979 claimed that:

> The 3 million-plus local Kurds, the Arab tribes of Khuzestan and the nomads of Baluchistan are demanding that their regions be granted autonomy within the framework of a united Iranian state on federal principles . . . reactionary forces are endeavouring to channel into anti-government demonstrations the legitimate desire of the Kurds, Baluchis, Turkomans and Arabs for equality and national self-expression.[24]

During August-September 1979 the Soviet media gave detailed reports of the fighting in Iranian Kordestan. The reports were now more favourable to the Kurds than those of a few months earlier. *Pravda* quoted Tehran's *Iran Week* as saying that the main cause of the 'fratricidal conflict' was 'the central administration's stubborn reluctance to resolve the problem of granting national and cultural autonomy to the Kurdish population, which took an active part in the overthrow of the monarchy'. Representatives sent by Tehran, and Islamic Revolutionary Guards, disregarding the advice and feelings of local organs of self-government, 'committed lawless actions — which aroused the Kurds' indignation'.[25]

A Moscow broadcast to Iran announced that in Kordestan fighting was continuing:

> between the army and Kurdish revolutionaries who want national and cultural autonomy within the framework of a unified Iran. Most Iranians are of the opinion that the bloodshed and air raids are harsh measures which not only totally fail to rectify the situation, but actually make it worse.

The broadcast denied that the Soviets had anything to do with the events. It said that 'all true friends of Iran are witnessing today with great regret' the continuing bloodshed in Kordestan. 'The transfer of cultural autonomy to the Kurds within the framework of a unified Iranian nation has not yet appeared.'[26]

Iranian accusations of Soviet arms supplies to the Kurds were refuted by TASS on 4 September 1979. It said that 'some influential figures and the media in Tehran are making statements about some "involvement" of the Soviet Union' in Iranian Kordestan. *Keyhan International* reported that 'Soviet aircraft had made night flights over Kordestan and dropped weapons and equipment for the rebels'. TASS 'refuted categorically' such statements and reports.[27] It did not specify who 'the influential Iranian figures' were with whom it disagreed – but the reference was clearly to what Khomeyni had said a few days earlier.

The Secretary-General of the Democratic Party of Kordestan, Abd al-Rahman Qassemlou, denied that he had had direct contacts with Moscow. He admitted that the Soviet Union was an old friend of the Kurds. He noted that it had supported the Kurdish Mahabad Republic at the time, but so far the Kurds had not received any aid from the Soviet Union. 'But we shall not reject any aid should anybody offer us any ... political support by a superpower like the Soviet Union is already valuable to us.' The United States, apparently backing Khomeyni, was conducting negotiations with Tehran on renewed deliveries of US war materials and spare parts which the Iranian army urgently needed in its war against the Kurds. Moscow too had courted the Khomeyni regime. The Kurds had plenty of weapons – thousands of captured rifles, anti-tank missiles, ammunition and even tanks and artillery, all having come from the collapsed army of the Shah. Soldiers and officers of Kurdish origin had joined the guerrillas.[28]

The Soviets' position on the problem of the Kurds and other Iranian national and ethnic groups was primarily a function of their attitude to the Khomeyni regime. The way in which the subject was dealt with by the Soviet media during September-October 1979 indicated some Soviet criticism, although indirect, of the regime. It was a hint to Khomeyni that it was in his interest to maintain correct relations with the USSR, otherwise the Soviets might use the problem of ethnic groups, providing them with support in order to bring pressure on Khomeyni.

The Fall of the 'Bourgeois Liberal' Bazargan Government

On 1 November 1979 Prime Minister Mehdi Bazargan attended the Algiers celebrations marking the 25th anniversary of the Algerian revolution. This served as an occasion for talks between him and US President Carter's National Security Adviser, Zbigniew Brzezinski. Bazargan was accompanied by Foreign Minister Ibrahim Yazdi and Defence Minister Mostafa Chamran. The two had spent many years in the USA, studying at American universities, and were therefore viewed by the Soviets and some Iranians as pro-American.

Ibrahim Yazdi made an additional 'tactical mistake' of talking with US Secretary of State Cyrus Vance when he attended the UN General Assembly session in New York. Vance expressed the Carter administration's wish to improve relations with Iran. Agreements were arrived at on bilateral matters, such as the renewal of supplies of spare parts, ammunition and other much-needed equipment to the Iranian military forces. This coincided with an intensified Iranian campaign against the USA and thus the meetings and talks were frowned upon by Khomeyni and many of his followers, contributing to the already widespread criticism of the Bazargan government.

On 3 November 1979 the Iranian government decided to abrogate Articles V and VI of the friendship treaty of 26 February 1921 with the Soviet Union, and the co-operation agreement with the United States,[29] which permitted Soviet and American military intervention, respectively, in Iran, under certain conditions. Undoubtedly, the Soviets viewed this most unfavourably, but they refrained from reacting, avoiding any direct comment on the matter.

A few days later Khomeyni accepted the resignation of Prime Minister Mehdi Bazargan and on 6 November 1979 the provisional government was dissolved. An appraisal of the Bazargan government by the Tudeh leader Kianuri can, to a certain extent, be seen as a reflection of the Soviet position on the matter. Kianuri said:

A certain period following the revolution's victory was characterized by a dualism of power. There was, on the one hand, the revolutionary centre headed by Ayatollah Khomeyni, and on the other hand there was the government of the liberal opportunistic bourgeoisie . . . The revolutionary centre around Ayatollah Khomeyni resolutely declared itself against any compromise with US imperialism . . . Khomeyni also declared himself in favour of a change in the political and economic life of the country to the advantage of the working masses . . . The liberal bourgeoisie . . . by no means liked this situation and began to obstruct the revolutionary movement for the sake of its own economic interests.[30]

The fall of the Bazargan government was welcomed by the Soviets. A month before his death the former Shah said that Bazargan was 'an agent of Britain and the USA' and was being supported by them.[31] The Soviets too considered this to be so. The prevailing Soviet position *vis-à-vis* Iran was that the revolution had only just begun, that it must continue to expand, and that the more strained the relations between Iran and the Western world became, the better the chances for closer ties with the USSR.

Notes

1. *Pravda*, 13 February 1979.
2. Ibid., 3 March 1979.
3. P. Demchenko, 'The USSR and Iran: Horizons of Co-operation', ibid., 6 April 1979.
4. Interview with Tudeh First Secretary N. Kianuri, *Le Matin*, 27 November 1979.
5. Thierry Desjardins, *Le Figaro*, 26 January 1979.
6. *Horizont* (East Berlin), no. 16 (1979), pp. 14-15.
7. Paul Balta, *Le Monde*, 29 February 1979.
8. *Horizont*, no. 16 (1979), pp. 14-15; Asraf Akhmedzyanov, *Za Rubezhom* (Moscow), no. 16, 12 April 1979, pp. 12-13.
9. The Tudeh document used the standard Soviet definitions as given by Stalin. A nationality has to have a common territory, language, culture and economic relationship. (Josif V. Stalin, *Marxism and the National and Colonial Question*, International Publishers, New York, 1936.)
10. Radio Iran Courier (clandestine) in Persian to Iran, 14, 15 June 1973. In FBIS, Middle East, 20 June 1973, pp. K3-K6. See also: USSR Academy of Sciences, Institute of Ethnography, *Natsyonal'niye Protsesy V Stranakh Blizhnego i Srednego Vostoka* (National Processes in the Countries of the Near and Middle East) (Nauka, Moscow, 1970), edited by M.S. Ivanov, author of the chapter on Iran.
11. The existence of a Kurdish minority in the USSR might have helped the Soviets to develop relations with the Kurds in Iran, but it was not a major consideration in Soviet policy towards Iran. There are about 100,000 Kurds in the Soviet Union, concentrated in Transcaucasia and in parts of Central Asia and Kazakhstan. Because of their small numbers, and the fact that they do not form a majority in a particular area, there is no Soviet Kurdish national region. There are broadcasts in Kurdish, and a Kurdish newspaper *Riya Taza* (New Road) is published in the Armenian Soviet Socialist Republic. This newspaper is directed mainly at Soviet Kurds and their local affairs. Like any other local ethnic minority newspaper, its reporting of international affairs is mainly a repetition and popularization of what has been written in the (Moscow) central press.
12. A. Akmuradov, 'Slander — the Tool of Reaction', *Pravda*, 4 April 1979.

13. Yuri Zhukov, *Pravda* political observer on Moscow Domestic Television, 2 June 1979. In FBIS, USSR, 14 June 1979, pp. H6-H8.
14. V. Borisov, *Zarya Vostoka*, 1 June 1979.
15. Bruno De Thomas, *Le Monde*, 8 May 1979; *Washington Post*, 23 May 1979.
16. Aleksandr Bovin, 'With Koran and Saber!!!', *Nedelya* (weekly supplement to *Izvestia*), no. 36 (4 September 1979), p. 6.
17. Moscow radio 'Peace and Progress' to Asia, 16 September 1979. In FBIS, USSR, 17 September 1979, p. H3.
18. A. Akhmedzyanov, 'Iran: Processes of Renewal', *Izvestia*, 14 September 1979.
19. TASS in English, 22 September 1979. In FBIS, USSR, 24 September 1979, p. H2.
20. *Pravda*, 29 August 1979.
21. Ibid., 4 September 1979.
22. *L'Unità* (Milan), 30 September 1979.
23. *Pravda*, 4 October 1979.
24. *Novoye Vremya*, no. 19 (4 May 1979), pp. 12-13.
25. *Pravda*, 25 August 1979.
26. Moscow radio in Persian to Iran, 3 September 1979. In FBIS, USSR, 6 September 1979, pp. H7-H8.
27. *Pravda*, 5 September 1979.
28. D. Dummendey, *Die Welt*, 3 September 1979. Qassemlou summed up Kurdish aims in another interview:

> We do not want more than self-rule within the Iranian state ... We support the government and, of course, Khomeyni. But our support is conditional on self-rule and democratic freedoms ... We are about 20 million, and we must determine our future. But at present we do not want independence, not only for tactical reasons but also for economic and political reasons ... We do not wish to leave Iran ... We are working for the future, when conditions will have matured and become ready for some kind of federalism in the Middle East. Then the Kurds will have a right to be part of a federal state in the Middle East.
> (*Al-Hawadith*, London, 8 May 1979)

29. Tehran Domestic Service, 5 November 1979. In FBIS, Middle East, 6 November 1979, pp. R16-R17.
30. N. Kianuri to Bulgarian *Rabotnichesko Delo* (Sofia), 18 February 1980. A Tudeh Party Central Committee statement of 6 November 1979 appraising the Bazargan government was published in the East Berlin *Horizont*, no. 50 (1979), pp. 12-13.
31. *La Revue du Liban* (Beirut), 1 August 1980.

6

THE ISLAMIC REPUBLIC: THE SOVIETS SEE CHANCES AND OPPORTUNITIES
(November 1979–September 1980)

Divergences in Soviet and Iranian Outlooks

The seizure on 4 November 1979 of the American embassy in Tehran and the taking hostage of its personnel (see pages 77-8) were generally viewed favourably in the Soviet Union since they prevented an American-Iranian *rapprochement*. Questions were then asked in Iran as to how the Soviet Union would react in case of a probable attack on Iran by the United States in order to rescue the hostages. There were Iranian fears that if Soviet forces entered Iran to help it, in accordance with the 1921 Soviet-Iranian treaty, they might continue to stay there after that help was no longer needed. The end of December 1979 saw the Soviet intervention in Afghanistan, which was presented by the USSR as a response to a request for Soviet aid by the Kabul government, invoking the friendship treaty between the two countries. The Soviet-Iranian treaty might serve as a pretext for a similar Soviet intervention in Iran.

On 22 January 1980 the Iranian Revolutionary Council decided to abrogate Articles V and VI of the 1921 treaty with the Soviet Union, as these might allow Soviet troops to enter Iran. (A similar decision had been taken by the Bazargan government on 3 November 1979, three days before its resignation.) The Council deputy spokesman said that Iran had no intention of requesting assistance from 'any country whatsoever'. He added that Iran's government was keeping a close watch on Soviet troop movements on the Iranian-Afghan border.[1] The Iranian abrogation of the two articles was ignored in the Soviet Union and the Soviet media made no mention of it whatsoever. From time to time reference was made to the treaty. For example, in mid-March 1980 Igor Belyayev spoke about Soviet Russia's 1921 treaties with Turkey, Iran and Afghanistan, and used the argument that served to justify Soviet intervention in the latter at the end of 1979. He said:

> Now on the threshold of the eighties, the Soviet Union, as in the twenties, is interested in genuinely good-neighbourly relations with Turkey, Iran and Afghanistan. At the same time it is perfectly

obvious that, although it makes no territorial claims whatsoever on these countries, the Soviet Union cannot allow these countries to be used to undermine its security.[2]

While this Soviet interpretation was meant primarily to explain Soviet intervention in Afghanistan, it also referred to the possibility of a landing of American forces in Iran. The Iranian ambassador to the Soviet Union described his discussion with a Soviet Foreign Ministry official on this matter as follows:

I have informed the Soviet Union that in the likely event of an attack on Iran by America, we can defend ourselves alone, and we will not allow a single foreign soldier to enter the country on whatever pretext and by virtue of whatever friendship treaty.[3]

The divergences in Soviet and Iranian outlooks were evident in exchanges of official greetings. In Brezhnev's greetings of 3 February 1980 to Abolhassan Bani-Sadr upon his election as President of Iran, he said that relations would be based 'on the principles of good-neighbourliness, respect for sovereignty and territorial integrity, and non-interference in each other's internal affairs'.[4] The Bani-Sadr reply reiterated the same principles, but also mentioned 'the freedom of nations to choose their own destiny and to choose their social and political order'. He hoped that the USSR would 'act in such a way as not to give rise to any anxiety among its neighbours'.[5] This was a clear hint regarding the Soviet intervention in Afghanistan, and perhaps also a warning to refrain from intervention in Iran.

The following week Brezhnev sent greetings to Khomeyni and Bani-Sadr on the occasion of the first anniversary of the Iranian revolution, which was termed as the 'anti-monarchist and anti-imperialist revolution'.[6] Khomeyni's reply of 12 February stated that 'any aggression against Third World countries and Islamic countries, particularly in this region, is against the principles which should constitute the proper basis and foundation [of relations] between nations'.[7] Soviet press reports made no mention of Khomeyni's or Bani-Sadr's remarks. However, while Khomeyni was being praised and flattered by the Soviet media, criticism of Bani-Sadr began to appear, much of it intended as indirect criticism of what had been said by Khomeyni.[8]

As a reaction to the Soviet intervention in Afghanistan, Iran decided to join the boycott of the Summer 1980 Olympic Games in Moscow. No Soviet comments or reactions were forthcoming, since the Soviets had become very careful in their references to Iran. In their view, Iranian leaders had adopted an ungrateful attitude by attacking in equal measure both Moscow (which supported them) and Washington (which was against them).

The Soviet Union 'No Less Satanic than the United States'

The prevailing Iranian position after the Islamic revolution was that Iran need not worry about the superpowers, as the rivalry between the USSR and the USA neutralized both. Neither would allow the other to occupy Iran. However, experience of the history of previous Russian–British agreements made some leading Iranians think otherwise. The question was raised as to whether there was perhaps, in reality, an American–Soviet agreement regarding Iran, with both sides merely pretending to have differences.[9] Khomeyni said that the United States was 'playing games' with the USSR.[10] On 12 August 1980, in a speech to Majlis deputies, Khomeyni said that 'no matter how strong the powers are, when they are confronted with the entire [Iranian] nation, they will not be able to achieve anything'. There was nothing to be afraid of, said Khomeyni.

> Even if we imagine . . . that . . . they killed all the mullahs and destroyed all the believers, what are we frightened of? We will be taken from a place like this world to a place which is better . . . We have the same logic that existed in the early days of Islam, that if we kill them we will go to paradise, and that even if they kill us, again we will go to paradise . . . The person who believes in God, the Almighty, the All-Blessed, the person who believes in the Koran — his logic is that he cannot lose . . . If we are killed, we have changed our clothes and have put on a better suit . . . Therefore we have no fear concerning anything.[11]

The Soviets appeared as one of those powers that wished to subjugate Iran and impose its will on the country, taking away its faith. These were the powers against which the Islamic Republic had to defend itself. There was no fear that the Afghanistan episode would immediately be repeated; however, caution and vigilance were required. American diplomats had been taken hostage but Soviet diplomats were free, and it seemed that Khomeyni had ordered (or hinted at) restrictions on their number and activities.

Foreign Minister Sadeq Qotbzadeh announced on 3 July 1980 that the Revolutionary Council had decided that the number of Soviet diplomats in Iran should equal the number of Iranian diplomats in the USSR, and that the number of Soviet personnel in non-diplomatic institutions in Iran 'should not exceed two'. He also said that Iran had no need of a consulate in Leningrad, but would like to open one in Dushanbe, the Tadzhik capital. The USSR was told it must close one of its consulates, either in Rasht or Isfahan.[12] In early July 1980 Vladimir Golovanov, First Secretary at the Soviet embassy in Tehran, was declared *persona non grata* 'for having exchanged espionage documents' and was ordered to leave Iran.[13]

A statement published on 8 July 1980 by the USSR embassy in Tehran said that the Soviets had information that 'elements hostile to the Soviet Union' intended to seize the embassy. The embassy demanded that 'appropriate measures' be taken to prevent such an eventuality. Qotbzadeh replied that instructions had been given to take the security measures necessary to protect the Soviet embassy, like any other embassy in Iran. He stressed that foreign embassies in Iran 'should be protected as are Iranian embassies abroad'.[14]

The slogan 'neither East nor West' was the key motif in Iran's foreign relations. Tehran radio said that Khomeyni had 'always emphasized the dictum of following neither East nor West and only the heavenly path of Islam . . . Both the capitalist imperialism of the West and the social imperialism of the communist world are to be equally rejected.'[15] Khomeyni described the Soviet Union as an 'arch-Satan'. On 9 August 1980, addressing representatives of world liberation movements, he referred to 'this big satanic power the USSR, which is exerting all its power to suffocate Afghanistan'.[16] No Soviet reaction to this violent attack was forthcoming.

A message from Iranian Foreign Minister Qotbzadeh to USSR Foreign Minister Andrey Gromyko, sent on 11 August 1980, used a similar sharp tone in attacking the Soviets: 'Our Imam has described the United States as a great satan. Unfortunately, you too have proved in practice that you are no less satanic than the United States'.

Qotbzadeh referred to large quantities of Soviet-made weapons discovered in Kordestan, and Soviet money reaching the Kurds. Also, Soviet satellites were taking photographs of Iranian military positions in Kordestan, and the photographs were made available to 'counter-revolutionaries'. Qotbzadeh also accused the Soviets of sending agents to Iran to 'reorganize your fifth column, . . . publishing a paper [*Mardom*] propagating your views in their name, and sparing no financial or moral support for them . . . Members of your embassies and consulates, as well as other institutions, have not spared any efforts in establishing contacts with the enemies of our revolution and in gathering information.' The Soviet government had 'not yet paid any attention' to Iran's abrogation of Articles V and VI of the 1921 Iranian-Soviet treaty of friendship. The Soviet Union had sent troops to Afghanistan and interfered in its internal affairs. In Iran 'a great many of your officials, rather than attending to normal and current matters handled by a genuine embassy, are engaged in espionage operations'.[17]

Gromyko's reply stated that Qotbzadeh had tried 'to place the Soviet Union on the same level as the United States'. The 1921 treaty was 'mutually beneficial'. The USSR had not intervened in the internal affairs of Iran and wanted to have 'good and neighbourly relations' with it.[18] Thus the official published reply was mild; it attempted to ignore Qotbzadeh's sharp language and his attacks and accusations. It was already known that Qotbzadeh would soon be ousted as Foreign Minister, and the Soviets decided not to argue with him at the official level.

The proposed establishment of an Iranian consulate in Dushanbe was opposed by the Soviet Union. Iran closed its consulate in Leningrad and the Soviets announced the closure of their consulate in Isfahan, raising the consulate in Rasht to the status of consulate-general. Iran then asked the Soviets to close the Rasht consulate and maintain the one in Isfahan. On 20 September the consulate in Rasht was closed, thus ending the disputes and the exchange of numerous notes on the subject.[19] An Iranian Foreign Ministry official said that there were about 500 Soviet families in Isfahan, amounting to 2,000 people. Since the steel works built with Soviet aid was situated in Isfahan, the number of Soviet government personnel there was increasing. There were only 78 Soviet families in Rasht, numbering 250 people. Asked why the Soviet Union had insisted on keeping the consulate in Rasht, the reply was that 'this is an important strategic area for the Soviet Union' and the Soviet consulate in Rasht was 'in close proximity to the Guards Corps and the naval base'.[20]

The appointment, in August 1980, of Mohammad Ali Raja'i as Prime Minister served as an occasion for Kosygin to send greetings in which he spoke about good-neighbourly relations and co-operation. Raja'i's reply was cool and restrained.[21] Here and there, signs began to appear that the Soviets were starting to tire of flattering a regime of which they had a quite different opinion. Indirect hints slipped out — as to what, no one had yet dared to mention. Some among them began remembering 'the good old days' of the reign of the Shah, indirectly comparing him with the present-day rulers. There was a man with whom the Soviets could talk business, while the leaders of the Islamic Republic returned friendly greetings with an attack, and made quite unacceptable demands on the Soviet Union.

The Soviet media continued to emphasize the interests of both the Soviet Union and Iran in the maintenance of good relations between them. These words were meant not only for the Iranians but also for those in the Soviet Union who had begun to think otherwise. Broadcasts to Iran stressed that the USSR had supported Iran in times of danger in the past and would continue to do so in the future as well. The Soviets repeated this time and again, ignoring the fact that it was regarded in Iran as no small threat, a reminder of how the Soviet Union had 'helped' Afghanistan.

Economic Ties

Attempts were made by the Soviets to maintain the existing level of trade and aid, and to make economic relations relatively close, even if political ties were otherwise, but this was not easy. In the negotiations over the price of the Iranian gas delivered to the USSR, Iran was asking a price five times higher than that which the Soviet Union had previously paid.[22] In March 1980 talks broke down and Iran cut off its gas supplies completely.

The Soviets countered with a refusal to permit free transit of Iranian merchandise through their territory.[23] Iran had an interest in access to the Black Sea, from the Caspian Sea through the Volga river, and from there to the Mediterranean. The quantities of goods transported over the Volga route by Soviet ships in 1979 was only one third of that hauled in 1978.[24]

In April 1980 Reza Salimi, the Iranian Minister of Economy and Finance, conducted talks in Moscow on economic and industrial co-operation. While in Moscow he asked the Soviets to make transport facilities available to Iranian shipping — in particular the Volga river waterway, which joins the Black Sea and the Caspian.[25] Such proposals were also raised by Iran's ambassador to Moscow, Dr Mohammad Mokri, but he reported that the Soviets had refused them.[26] Negotiations were subsequently renewed and an agreement permitting the transit of Iranian commercial cargoes through the USSR, and of Soviet foreign-trade cargoes through the territory of Iran, was signed in Moscow on 16 September 1980.[27]

On 20 June 1980 a protocol was signed after a meeting of the Soviet-Iranian Permanent Commission on Economic and Technical Co-operation. TASS reported that it was 'the first official document sealing the basic principles for the development of business contacts' since the establishment of the Islamic Republic. TASS continued: 'The two sides agreed to co-operate on further development of such major sectors as ferrous metallurgy, coal mining, industrial engineering and the energy sector. The meeting also reached an agreement on co-operation in the training of Iranian cadres.'[28] Soviet experts stayed on in Iran and continued to work in the Isfahan steel complex, the coal mines, the Arak machine factory, the Ramin power plant, and in other production units.[29] 'We did not withdraw a single expert from Iran,' said Semyon Skachkov, Chairman of the Soviet State Committee for Foreign Economic Relations.[30]

The decline, almost to a standstill, of Iranian oil production indirectly influenced the Soviet economy. It was not a matter of direct oil sales to the Soviet Union, but rather of difficulties for East European countries which used to purchase oil from Iran, partly on a barter basis. Now they had to purchase their oil elsewhere for much higher prices, seriously aggravating their already difficult economic situation. This forced the Soviets to supply them with oil which they naturally preferred to sell to Western countries for hard currency. The Soviets, too, wanted to buy Iranian oil and the Soviet government asked to buy crude oil from Iran in order to balance the volume of commercial exchanges between the two countries. The Iranian response was that 'if the conditions for the deal were the same as that for exports to other purchasers from the viewpoints of price and procedures, there would be no objection to that'.[31] The Iranian side was ready to continue economic ties and co-operation with the Soviet Union, as long as this did not conflict with 'Islamic ideology and principles'.[32] The Soviets were aware of this and adjusted themselves to the situation.

'Khomeynism' and Soviet Muslims

The revival of Islam undoubtedly had an influence on the USSR and its policies, regarding both foreign and domestic matters. Leading Iranian personalities expressed their concern over the fate of Muslims in the Soviet Union. The Soviet media usually replied by describing the happy life of Soviet Muslims and their freedom to observe their religion. They tried to prove that no contradiction existed between communism and Islam and that Iran's existence as a Muslim state need not influence its relations with the Soviet Union. A similar position was expressed by Ambassador Mokri. When asked 'about the reflection of our Islamic Revolution in Muslim parts of the USSR', he replied:

> Although we try to maintain neighbourly relations with the USSR, we cannot cut our relations with Muslims in Russia. Just as we do not want anybody to interfere in our internal affairs, we in turn do not interfere in any other country's affairs. We maintain our spiritual connections and this enhances our friendly and neighbourly relations.[33]

This may have been the official position as it was presented to the Soviets, but it was not the real situation or what was said to the Iranian public. Iran's religious leaders constantly spoke about their intention of taking steps to improve the situation of Soviet Muslims; when the Iranians had asked to open an Iranian consulate at Dushanbe, in Tadzhikistan, it was with this in mind. This was why the Soviets had rejected the request.[34]

Is 'Khomeynism' a danger to the Soviet regime, or is Soviet Islam a relic of the past, limited in influence to a handful of elderly adherents? There are no clear-cut answers to this question. But the Islamic resurgence did indeed pose a problem for the USSR, which has some 40-50 million Muslims and is the fifth largest Muslim state in the world (after Indonesia, Pakistan, India and Bangladesh).

The term Muslim — in the USSR as elsewhere — refers to Muslim peoples, whether they are religiously inclined or not. The young and middle-aged Soviet Muslims have no doubt been influenced by the official anti-religious educational doctrine. Yet most of them maintain at least some customs which are decidedly Islamic — even if they are not orthodox 'religious'. Thus they observe holidays, visit the mosque occasionally, avoid eating pork and circumcize their children. Even Muslim communist officials bury their dead in Muslim cemeteries. Almost no Soviet Muslims intermarry or assimilate with non-Muslims.

The Soviet Muslim nationalities differ widely. Volga Tartars, for example, have little in common with Azerbaijanis or Tadzhiks. The Soviet leadership has consistently sought to emphasize these differences and fragment the Muslim population. Thus many of today's Soviet republics or autonomous national regions were formerly no more than ill-defined Turkic-speaking ethnic areas. In the past, the Soviets also struggled successfully to suppress pan-Turkish and pan-Iranian movements which laid claim to the allegiance of the Turkic- or Persian-speaking Soviet Muslim peoples. Leaders of such movements were either exiled or executed.

Islam, like other religions, has been assigned a well-defined — and limited — place in Soviet life. The October 1977 constitution gives all Soviet citizens the right to maintain either a religious or an anti-religious orientation. Religion is separated from the state, as are schools from churches and mosques. Religious observance is permitted in designated places, that is, only in mosques, not offices or schools. Religion may only be taught at home — not by teachers and not in groups. Anti-religious propaganda is permitted; religious propaganda is not. So far, the authorities have proved adept at confining Islam within the USSR, while simultaneously putting it on display for foreign eyes. Foreign guests from Islamic countries are shown well-kept mosques. They are given gifts of Korans printed in the USSR, in Arabic script which only few Soviet Muslims can read. A monthly publication, *Muslims of the Soviet East*, is issued in several languages.

Soviet Muslims are strictly controlled by the Soviet regime. If the regime finds it necessary, the control will be even more strict. What apparently concerns the Soviets at present is the demographic, rather than the strictly religious, aspect — in other words, the realization that the Muslim peoples have become a rapidly growing segment of Soviet society. In 1980 there were some 265 million Soviet citizens. Of these, 140 million were Russians, and 40 to 50 million were Muslims. Soviet census figures show that this Muslim population grew by approximately 50 per cent between 1959 and 1970 — while the Russians increased by only 13 per cent. Russians tend to marry late and have one or two children. The wife/mother usually works, and there is a very severe housing shortage. Among Muslim families, on the other hand, tradition reigns: couples marry young, the mother stays at home and has many children. If the present birth rate is maintained, there will be 80 million Soviet Muslims by the year 2000 and Muslims will constitute an absolute majority of the population within 80 years.

While the political consequences of this situation can still be postponed, the economic effects are already evident. Most of the Soviet Union suffers from a growing lack of manpower; but the Muslim regions have an excess. Most Muslim men do not have a sophisticated profession, and refuse to migrate to other parts of the Soviet Union. It is difficult to estimate the relative effect of this Soviet Islamic factor, in all its aspects, on the decision-making process which led to the invasion of Afghanistan at the end of 1979. Grave apprehension clearly exists that

Muslim-nationalist unrest and Khomeyni-style fundamentalism will spread into Soviet Central Asia.[35]

The Soviets and the American Hostages — the USA and Iran

On 4 November 1979 Iranian students seized the US embassy in Tehran and took its personnel hostage. As a condition for their release, the students demanded that the deposed Shah (who was at that time in the United States undergoing medical treatment) and all his wealth be turned over to them. They also insisted on a formal apology by the American administration for 'wrongs' done to Iran, and an undertaking to refrain from any interference in Iranian internal affairs. The USA was also required formally to recognize the new regime and lift all restrictions on Iranians and Iranian property in the USA.

During the first few days after the seizure of the hostages, Soviet Persian-language broadcasts were sharply anti-American. The USA protested to Iran at such broadcasts from the Soviet-run 'National Voice of Iran' (NVOI) radio station in Baku. A few days later these broadcasts became somewhat less inflammatory and even urged that the hostages be freed. The sharp anti-American tone continued, but more as quotations of what others were saying and less as direct Soviet positions. The Soviets quoted extensively the students who were holding the hostages, without adding their own comments. This, however, was often done in such a way that only a very careful reading enabled one to distinguish between the Soviets' own position and that of others who placed the blame for everything that was wrong in Iran on the Americans.

On 5 December 1979 A. Petrov, writing in *Pravda*, supported the Iranian position. He wrote that holding American hostages and seizing the embassy 'are themselves contrary to international conventions'. However, the USA itself had also flouted international law when, in 1953, it brought about the Shah's return to power; and again in 1980, by rejecting Iran's demands for the Shah's extradition and the return of the 'wealth he had plundered'. The USA was attempting to 'blackmail' Iran by concentrating forces nearby 'and dictating to it by force its line of conduct'. Petrov said that 'a just solution on a basis acceptable to both sides' had to be found. The Brezhnev statement of November 1978 came out 'against interference from outside in Iran's internal affairs by whoever, in whatever form and on whatever pretext'. The Soviet Union's stand on this, Petrov said, 'remains unaltered'.[36] Brezhnev had said, in 1978, that the USSR would consider such intervention as a threat to its security. The Petrov article omitted any reference to this, carefully avoiding any Soviet commitment one way or another in the event of an American intervention.

Throughout November and December 1979, Soviet editorial comments accusing the US remained relatively restrained, and were quite considerate of the American side. At the end of December 1979, after the Soviet intervention in Afghanistan, the Soviets abandoned this earlier restraint and spoke less, if at all, about respecting diplomatic immunity. They sharply attacked the USA as an enemy of Iran, as preparing a military intervention, and as trying to overthrow Iran's regime in order to restore the old one. On 13 January 1980 the USSR vetoed a UN Security Council resolution calling for economic sanctions against Iran. At that time the Soviets accused Washington of failing to take advantage of Iranian proposals to the United Nations to effect a release of the hostages.

The hostage issue led to a deterioration in Iranian-American relations, which the Soviets believed was to their advantage. They accused the United States of wanting to turn prevailing anti-Americanism into anti-Sovietism.[37] The Tudeh leader Kianuri stated: 'As long as we keep the hostages we will prevent a normalization of relations with the United States, a condition which some Iranian politicians are dreaming of.'[38]

Day after day the Soviet media tried to frighten Iran by describing details of American preparations for an invasion, due to start the following day. The Soviets said that the measures taken by the Americans, such as the break in diplomatic relations with Iran, were taken with an eye to the US elections. The Americans were using the issue to strengthen their position in the region, and not out of any concern for the hostages.[39]

The attempt to rescue the hostages on 24 April 1980 was the target of sharp Soviet propaganda attacks, but no official comments and no promises of Soviet support were made. On the propaganda level, the USA was accused of having been in a position to solve the problem, but preferring instead to use the situation for its own purposes. President Carter was accused of having exploited the situation for his election campaign.

The USSR Foreign Minister Gromyko said at a press conference in Paris on 25 April 1980: 'I can say that we are against all measures of a military, or generally forcible, nature on the part of the United States or anyone else against Iran. We decisively condemn such measures.' As to the possibility of Iran asking the Soviet Union for assistance if attacked by the USA, he refused to comment, saying, 'It is a hypothetical situation which does not exist today, and there is no need for me to consider such a hypothetical situation. At any rate I would prefer not to do so.'[40]

After a long silence on the part of the Soviet leaders as to the situation in Iran, a reference to it appeared in an address by Brezhnev in Alma Ata, Kazakhstan, on 29 August 1980. After reviewing the situation in Afghanistan, Brezhnev turned to American policy regarding Iran:

The USA is also using the situation in Iran. The economic blockade of that country continues unabated. The ships of the US navy, with aircraft and amphibian units on board, continue cruising around it.

We consider such actions inadmissible, and firmly adhere to the principle that only the people of Iran themselves can determine which way they should move ahead. The same approach, it seems, can rightfully be expected from the leaders of Iran by other states — and first of all by its neighbours.[41]

This last sentence referred to Afghanistan — a topic on which there was sharp disagreement between the USSR and Iran.

The Soviet Involvement in Afghanistan, and Soviet-Iranian Relations

The Soviet intervention in Afghanistan led to Soviet-Iranian differences, accusations and counter-accusations, with mutual suspicion and deteriorating relations. The Islamic Foreign Ministers Conference, convened in May 1980 in Islamabad, Pakistan, established a committee to deal with the Afghanistan crisis. Foreign Minister Sadeq Qotbzadeh, in his capacity as a member of this committee, made statements concerning Afghanistan to which the Soviets reacted immediately.

A TASS report condemned a Qotbzadeh statement alleging that bases for forces acting against Afghanistan's regime would be established on Iranian territory. It stated: 'This will have the most dangerous consequences. No matter from where the bloody hands of counter-revolution are stretched to Afghanistan, they will be cut off by the Afghan people.'[42] TASS was careful in its wording, specifying 'by the Afghan people' and not by the Soviets.

The Soviet media claimed that 'Afghan counter-revolutionaries in Iran', particularly from their centre in Mashad, also 'conducted subversive acts against Iran'. Such groups on Iranian soil were 'controlled by the United States and its agents' and used, 'on the one hand, to train gangs operating on the territory of Iran itself against the lawful Iranian government, and on the other, to infiltrate agents into Afghan territory'.[43]

Qotbzadeh's letter to Gromyko of 11 August 1980 included references to the Soviet role in Afghanistan, saying:

> Suddenly your government, on an imaginary pretext, sends troops to our neighbouring co-religionist country, Afghanistan, and crushes the brave resistance put up by the people of this land with fire and blood. Then we see America and its accomplices not moving a finger, rather confining themselves to verbal attacks. We are therefore justified in becoming sceptical, thinking that behind the scenes, the two superpowers have reached an agreement on dividing the spoils, and we become apprehensive of what is going on behind the scenes as far as our revolution is concerned.[44]

Qotbzadeh saw in this an American-Soviet agreement (on the pattern of the old British-Russian agreements) that divided the region between them, giving Afghanistan to the Soviets. He feared that such an agreement had been made or was going to be made concerning Iran, and that the Soviets might do in the Iranian areas 'that were given to them' what they had done in Afghanistan.

In his reply Gromyko avoided dealing with the main controversial issues. He said that 'those who can and will solve matters concerning Afghanistan are the Afghan people themselves and their government'.[45] Brezhnev's address at Alma Ata on 29 August 1980 also presented the problem in much the same way. He spoke out against foreign intervention in Iran's affairs and said that he expected the same approach from the leaders of Iran — in other words, no intervention in the internal affairs of Afghanistan.[46] The divergent approaches of the USSR and Iran to the Afghanistan problem and their support for opposing sides contributed greatly to the worsening in Soviet-Iranian relations.

The Soviets and the Iran-Iraq Conflict

Officially, the USSR had close ties with Iraq. It had an interest in friendly, or at least non-hostile, relations between Iran and Iraq, thus obviating the need to choose between them, or a situation in which closeness to one would influence relations with the other.

Iraq increased its power. It wanted to assume the role of 'policeman' in the Gulf region when this job fell vacant after the Shah was ousted. It had pan-Arab aspirations to be the leader of the Arab world. It was pursuing, or at least preaching, a socialist line in its economic development. Iraq demanded that Iran withdraw from the three islands guarding the Hormuz Strait: Greater Tunb, Lesser Tunb and Abu Musa, occupied by Iran in 1971. It called for an amendment of the 1975 Iraqi-Iranian agreement over the Shatt al-Arab river. Iran was not prepared either to give up the islands or to amend the agreement. Most of the Arab countries supported Iraq, as an Arab country against a non-Arab one. There were two reasons for this: first, because of the chaotic situation in Iran, Iraq was considered to be the stronger side; and secondly, because the Arab countries feared the spread of Khomeynism and its attempts to export the revolution.

The USSR was providing Iraq with political, military, economic and technical aid. However, Iraq's dependence on the Soviets diminished as it diversified its contacts and became less isolated. Its increased revenues from oil exports reduced its need for Soviet aid and enabled it to purchase Western equipment and technology. Differences were evident between the USSR and Iraq over a wide range of issues. A process of drifting away from the USSR began. The Soviets were interested in improving Iraqi-Iranian relations, but would not do much to bring this about. The Soviet media expressed concern at the situation, saying that it benefited only 'the imperialist forces, who are enemies of both countries'.[47]

As the Iran-Iraq conflict intensified, Ambassador Mokri, on Khomeyni's instructions, said on 11 April 1980 that Iran expected the Soviet Union, 'on the basis of neighbourly relations', to cease exporting weapons to Iraq.[48] He described his talks with an unnamed Soviet Foreign Ministry official on the subject. The Soviet official said that Iraq also purchased arms from France and West Germany, and if the supply of arms from the Soviet Union were to end, Iraq would increase its purchases of Western arms. The Soviets 'are not happy at events in Iraq', for example, the treatment of Iraqi communists, 'but these are Iraq's internal affairs'.[49] Appeals to the Soviets on this matter appeared in a number of messages and addresses by Qotbzadeh. In mid-August 1980 a Soviet broadcast to Iran finally replied, after a long silence:

Iranian Foreign Minister Qotbzadeh ... has proposed that the co-operation between the Soviet Union and Iraq — or putting it more precisely, this co-operation in one important field [arms supplies] — should almost totally end. In reality, efforts have been made to represent this support as the Soviet Union's support for Iraq in the actual dispute between Iran and Iraq . . . there are people to be found in Iran who have made the deterioration of relations between the Soviet Union and Iraq a condition for establishing good relations between the Soviet Union and Iran . . . the Soviet Union sincerely desires good relations with both Iran and Iraq. The dispute between Iran and Iraq is a source of regret for the people of the Soviet Union . . . The Soviet Union . . . wishes Iran and Iraq to be reconciled as soon as possible.[50]

The situation looked quite different in Iran. From there, Iraq seemed, aside from its own ambitions, to be a tool of both the USSR and the USA, which were using Iraq against Iran. According to Qotbzadeh (and this seemed to be Khomeyni's view too): 'Alone Iraq is nothing . . . the major powers want to use Iraq to isolate Iran — "the United States, so that it can regain its influence in our country, and the USSR, so that it can force us to enter the Eastern camp".'[51]

Clashes along the Iran-Iraq border intensified, but the Soviets preferred not to get involved or express opinions. They gave news from both sides. Nevertheless, they continued supplying arms to Iraq in accordance with the earlier agreements.

On 17 September 1980 the Iraqi Revolution Command Council decided to abrogate the 6 March 1975 agreement with Iran and 'to restore complete legal and effective sovereignty over the Shatt al-Arab'.[52] Iraq declared the Shatt al-Arab to be a national river, completely under its sovereignty. It was made mandatory for all ships using the river for navigational purposes to fly only the Iraqi flag and to follow Iraqi instructions and orders. Border fighting between Iran and Iraq intensified, developing into a full-scale war, with Iraqi forces invading Iran. The Soviets preferred to remain silent, saying nothing and not committing themselves.

The Soviets and Internal Iranian Politics

The Soviets had an interest in Iranian politics but their media scarcely referred to the subject, in order to forestall accusations of interfering in Iranian internal affairs. In Iran a number of competing power centres had developed, whose relative strength changed constantly. In Khomeyni's 'court' in the holy city of Qom, his quarrelsome assistants were engaged in a power struggle over the succession. They consisted of the

President, the Prime Minister, Ayatollah-politician Beheshti and other influential Ayatollahs. Each pulled in his own direction, acting against the others. Each had his own concept — if any — of the domestic political system, the economy and the international situation. The system somehow worked, or at least parts of it did.

In such a situation it was not easy for the Soviets to decide whom to back and whom to reject, or to predict future developments in order to guide their current policy. They sometimes attacked personalities whom they considered to be of little importance, only to find later that such people rose to high positions. They seemed to believe that in spite of the noisy anti-American and anti-Western proclamations, once the American hostage crisis had been solved, an Iranian-American *rapprochement* would be reached, since the Americans were 'the natural allies' of the Iranian 'reactionary clergy'. The Soviet media spoke of a 'progressive trend' in Islam, with Khomeyni being part of this trend. It is doubtful that they believed what they were preaching. For them, Khomeyni was a reactionary, an anachronism — someone belonging to medieval times. They saw him as no different from the Islamic groups fighting the regime in Afghanistan. However, they were wary of voicing this opinion, although they sometimes hinted at it indirectly so that intelligent Soviet readers would understand.

The Soviet view of the Majlis can be understood from the short remark, 'There are no representatives of workers and peasants.'[53] A description of Iran's socio-economic problems stated:

> The provisional organs of power did not succeed in adopting any important measures radically to restructure Iranian society or eliminate the socio-economic causes which gave rise to the mighty wave of the nationwide anti-Shah movement . . . There are about 3 million unemployed in the country . . . hidden unemployment . . . the monstrous rise in prices . . . the shortage of housing and transport, the enormous size of the lumpen proletariat and almost 4 million drug addicts.

As to political problems, there existed:

> a tremendous number of rival political organizations and parties with the most diverse doctrines . . . extreme right-wing reactionary elements and small but noisy groups of Maoists. They would like to return Iran once again to an alliance with Pakistan, . . . the monarchic regimes of the Arabian peninsula and, in the final analysis, the United States.[54]

Concern was expressed regarding the decision to close all the universities and send the students off to the countryside (a move aimed largely at weeding out leftist elements). The decision was said to have aggravated the internal political situation. It incurred the dissatisfaction of many students and certain leaders, specifically Bani-Sadr.[55] The Soviet media had criticized the latter as pro-Western and anti-Soviet. However, when Bani-Sadr began to be associated with the Soviet point of view, the attitude of the Soviet media towards him changed. He began to be viewed more favourably, as relatively more modern and less fanatic.

Foreign Minister Qotbzadeh was a target for sharp Soviet criticism — but not only for his anti-Soviet statements. Whenever Soviet commentators wished to criticize Khomeyni's statements, or those of influential persons near him, they did so by attacking Qotbzadeh. (Qotbzadeh was not included in the Raja'i cabinet appointed at the end of August 1980. He was later arrested and executed on 15 September 1982.) One of the ways of expressing Soviet positions on Iranian internal affairs was by quoting Tudeh Party statements and articles which were in accordance with Soviet positions.

Tudeh-Soviet Investment in an Option

The Tudeh Party flattered and praised Khomeyni, saying that he had done what he had to do and that it was for the good of Iran. According to the Tudeh leader, Kianuri: 'Our revolution, which is anti-imperialist, democratic and a people's revolution, [has] entered a new stage — the stage of intensified anti-imperialist people's orientation.'[56] No mention was made of the fact that it was an Islamic revolution, and that Khomeyni was a religious figure. Reading the above statement, one might reach the conclusion that Khomeyni was a communist and did what the communists would have done if they had come to power.

In the religious establishment Khomeyni was said to represent a 'progressive' trend. According to Kianuri:

Every time the situation seemed about to collapse, and the Islamic sectors with influence over Khomeyni seemed to be prevailing with their regressive thrusts, it was Khomeyni himself who stopped them and altered the course. This is what happened when the battle of the *chador* [women's all-enveloping gown] broke out. When the fanatics started burning left-wing books, when armed fighting broke out in Kordestan, every time it was Khomeyni who stopped them.[57]

It is not difficult to understand why the Tudeh, a communist party proclaiming 'scientific socialism' and Marxism-Leninism, supported an Islamic regime which could ban the party at any time. The Tudeh wanted to maintain its legal position, to express and disseminate its views freely and to publish its newspaper. It wished to continue to organize demonstrations and to keep party offices and officials. To appear to be against Khomeyni would mean an end to all this.

Why did Khomeyni, an anti-communist who had persecuted other Iranian leftist groups, tolerate the Tudeh? Several reasons might be given:

(1) Fear of the Soviets, who on the one hand generated considerable negative Iranian feelings towards the Tudeh, but on the other dictated caution. During the period when the party offices were closed, or the party newspaper was suspended, a strong anti-Khomeyni campaign appeared in the Soviet media. This ended when the Tudeh was allowed to continue its activities.

(2) Tudeh was not Iran's only left-wing organization, possibly not even the most 'dangerous'. By tolerating the 'official' communist party, the regime had a convenient lever for isolating it from other radical groups, preventing their unification. Thus, many Iranian leftists disparaged the Tudeh line of slavish submission to the Imam's line, with its sharp attacks on militant left-wing groups. Also, almost alone among the leftists, Tudeh did not actively support the Kurds and other ethnic groups in revolt.

(3) Lastly, unlike the other radical groups, the Tudeh maintained no armed military wing which could intimidate the regime.

The Tudeh called for 'co-operation among all Iranian revolutionaries' — Islamic and Marxist-Leninist. The other left-wing groups — the Mojahedin-e-Khalq and the Fedayeen-e-Khalq — were opposed to this. They were not ready to form a joint front with the Tudeh for the first round of parliamentary elections on 14 March 1980. Neither were they prepared to co-operate with each other. The Tudeh candidate then won some 100,000 votes in Tehran.[58] Tudeh failed in its efforts to persuade the other organizations 'that under the present conditions' of the revolution, 'the anti-imperialist struggle is the main issue and that all efforts must be joined in this struggle'.[59]

Does the Tudeh have a chance of increasing its power and influence? It is unlikely in the present circumstances. If Khomeyni's radical Islamic front were to become fragmented, or Soviet influence over Iran were to increase, then the Tudeh would try to exploit more actively its present, careful, quiet investment.

The Kurds and the Kurdish Problem

During the first months of Iran's Islamic take-over there was extensive Soviet press and radio coverage of the Kurdish problem. Soviet support of Kurdish demands was evident until the end of November 1979, when it suddenly stopped. Criticism then appeared of those 'who used the Kurds against Iran's regime', and this meant indirect criticism of the Kurds themselves as 'tools' of the enemies of Iran. The change seemed to come as the result of a Soviet reappraisal of the Iranian situation after the fall of the Bazargan government and the seizure of the American hostages.

Support for Kurdish demands was expressed by Aleksandr Bovin, senior commentator for *Izvestia*. He quoted Khomeyni on the Kurdish problem in such a way as to make the latter appear extreme, fanatic, unacceptable and unreasonable. Later he termed the Kurdish religious leader Hoseyni as moderate, acceptable and reasonable. Negotiations between the Iranian authorities and the Kurds were very difficult 'because there are influential forces in the government camp opposed to granting autonomy to the Kurds, and there are some extremist groups among the Kurds themselves'.[60]

Bovin said that 'extremist elements are operating on both poles, whose unrealistic position is aimed at destroying any agreement'. He quoted Hashemi Rafsanjani, who was then acting Minister of the Interior, as saying that 'in Iran there are no national minorities at all. This is why there is no one with whom to hold political talks.' That position was supported by the Islamic Revolutionary Guards, 'and not only by them'. Kurdish leaders 'were branded as traitors, counter-revolutionaries, agents of Zionism, agents of American imperialism, and so on. One can think of many such words.' The present events in Iranian Kordestan 'have not, of course, been inspired by the external enemies of the Iranian revolution', although they might be used by them. They were determined primarily by the Kurdish people's desire to survive as an entity, finally achieving 'national equality'.

Therefore, naturally, we Soviet people cannot but welcome the positive changes for the better in solving the Kurdish question which, it seems, are beginning to be seen there now. Satisfying the just demands of the Kurdish people is an important task of the Iranian revolution. The faster and the more thoroughly it is solved the better for all, both for the Kurds and for Iran as a whole.[61]

The Secretary-General of the Democratic Party of Kordestan (DPK), Qassemlou, was quoted by TASS as saying that 'the Kurds are not separatists. We are fighting for autonomy within the framework of democratic Iran, within the framework of its territorial integrity.'[62] This was a slogan long proclaimed by the Soviets on the Kurdish problem. Iranian representatives were told by the Soviets that the USSR had nothing to do with the events in Kordestan. Foreign Minister Gromyko said to Ambassador Mokri that the Soviet Union 'has never interfered nor will it ever interfere in Kordestan'.[63]

In April 1980 reports appeared about the DPK's having purchased arms from the Soviet Union. These allegations were denied by Qassemlou.[64] The Soviets tried to blame the CIA, saying that it had 'provoked, with the help of its agents and former SAVAK agents, new armed clashes in Iranian Kordestan, Baluchistan and Khuzestan in a bid to kindle national and religious strife'.[65] This was said for Iranian ears, but the Soviets also took into consideration the situation in Iranian Kordestan, where the main cities were occupied by government troops and Islamic Revolutionary Guards, but most villages and roads were controlled by the Kurds operating from their rear bases in the mountains. The government garrisons were isolated and supplied by air.

In early September 1980 a Moscow radio domestic broadcast spoke of the Kurds' struggle 'for autonomy within the framework of the Islamic Republic of Iran'. It stated that the Kurds wanted to decide 'all the domestic affairs of the province' by themselves and wished Kurdish to be recognized as the province's official language, having the same standing as Persian. They also asked that the authorities of the Islamic Republic should have 'responsibility only for foreign affairs, defence, finance and also other questions with the competence of the central authorities'. However, the government of Bazargan, and later that of Bani-Sadr, 'did everything possible to crush the demands of the Kurds for any sorts of reforms'. As a result, Kurdish fighting units 'took shelter in the mountains and turned to the tactic of waging guerrilla warfare'.

The unwillingness of the Iranian leaders to grant autonomy to the Kurds was blamed on the Kurds' striving to break away from Iran and create their own independent state. The Soviet commentator quoted 'the religious and political leader of the Kurds, Hoseyni,' as saying that 'the separation of Kordestan from Iran is not in the interests of the

Kurdish people'. Their only desire was 'to participate more actively in the decisions made on domestic affairs' and to solve the problem peacefully.[66] Soviet support for the Kurdish demands now appeared more openly than a few months previously, but, as in the past, the Soviets left their options open. This was even more apparent in the second half of September 1980, with the outbreak of the Iran-Iraq war. The Soviets then preferred not to take clear positions, delaying their decisions on this and other matters concerning Iran until the outcome of the war and its results were clearer.

Notes

1. AFP in English, 22 January 1980. In FBIS, Middle East, 22 January 1980, Iran Supp., p. 13.
2. *Literaturnaya Gazeta*, 12 March 1980, p. 14.
3. *Ettela'at*, 12 May 1980.
4. TASS in English, 3 February 1980. In FBIS, USSR, 4 February 1980, p. H1.
5. Tehran Domestic Service, 9 February 1980. In FBIS, Middle East, 11 February 1980, Iran Supp., pp. 22-3.
6. *Pravda*, 11 February 1980.
7. Tehran Domestic Service, 12 February 1980. In FBIS, Middle East, 22 February 1980, Iran Supp., p. 16.
8. TASS in English, 25 March, 2 April 1980. In FBIS, USSR, 26 March 1980, p. H3; 13 April 1980, pp. H1-H2.
9. Ayatollah Montazeri said that any military attack by America on Iran would certainly be carried out in agreement with the Soviet Union (*Keyhan*, 30 August 1980).
10. Tehran Domestic Service, 14 August 1980. In FBIS, South Asia, 15 August 1980, pp. I6-I7.
11. Tehran Domestic Service, 12 August 1980. In FBIS, South Asia, 13 August 1980, pp. I3-I6.
12. Tehran Domestic Service, 2 July 1980. In FBIS, South Asia, 3 July 1980, p. I3.
13. Tehran Domestic Service, 3 July 1980. In FBIS, South Asia, 7 July 1980, p. I3.
14. *Pravda*, 8, 9 July 1980.
15. Tehran radio in English to Europe, 9 July 1980. In FBIS, South Asia, 10 July 1980, pp. I2-I3.
16. Tehran Domestic Service, 9 August 1980. In FBIS, South Asia, 11 August 1980, pp. I12-I14.
17. Tehran Domestic Service, 14 August 1980. In FBIS, South Asia, 15 August 1980, pp. I2-I6 and ibid. (correction), 18 August 1980, p. I22.
18. Moscow radio in Persian to Iran, 28 August 1980. In FBIS, USSR, 29 August 1980, pp. H1-H2.
19. *Keyhan*, 25 August 1980; *Ettela'at*, 6 September 1980; BBC World Service, 20 September 1980.
20. *Keyhan*, 21 August 1980.

21. Moscow radio in Persian to Iran, 22 August 1980. In FBIS, USSR, 25 August 1980, p. H2; Tehran Domestic Service, 25 August 1980. In FBIS, South Asia, 25 August 1980, p. I3.
22. Iran charged $3.80 for each 1,000 cubic feet of gas, whereas formerly that figure was 76 cents. (Tehran radio in English to Europe, 13 February 1980. In FBIS, Middle East, 15 February 1980, Iran Supp., pp. 25-36.)
23. AFP in English, 8 August 1980. In FBIS, USSR, 11 August 1980, pp. H1-H2.
24. Moscow radio in Persian to Iran, 27 June 1980. In FBIS, USSR, 1 July 1980, pp. H2-H3.
25. *Bamdad* (Tehran), 15 June 1980.
26. *Keyhan*, 26 June 1980.
27. *Pravda*, 17 September 1980.
28. TASS in English, 20 June 1980. In FBIS, USSR, 23 June 1980, pp. H2-H3.
29. Moscow radio in Persian to Iran, 25 August 1980. In FBIS, 27 August 1980, pp. H2-H3.
30. *Keyhan*, 21 June 1980.
31. PARS (Tehran) in English, 7 September 1980. In FBIS, South Asia, 9 September 1980, pp. I13-I14.
32. *Al-Safir* (Beirut), 21 August 1980.
33. Tehran Domestic Service, 2 August 1980. In FBIS, South Asia, 4 August 1980, p. I17.
34. 'Dushanbe is a city inhabited by Muslims, we can publicize Islam there and allow the people there to avail themselves of embassy publications if they wish,' said an Iranian Foreign Ministry official. (*Keyhan*, 21 August 1980.)
35. 'Muslims of the Soviet Union. Why the Kremlin is worried', *Arab Report* (London), 20 June 1979, pp. 5-7; Alexandre Bennigsen and Chantal Lemercier-Quelquejay, 'Muslim Religious Conservatism and Dissent in the USSR', *Religion in Communist Lands*, vol. 6, no. 3 (Autumn 1978), pp. 153-61; *idem*, ' "Official" Islam in the Soviet Union', ibid., vol. 7, no. 3 (Autumn 1979), pp. 148-59; A. Philips, *Monday Morning* (Beirut), 22-28 October 1979; *The Economist*, 30 December 1978, p. 30; A. Manakov, M. Mullodzhanov interview with Soviet Mufti Babakhan, *Literaturnaya Gazeta*, 26 September 1979; Leonid Medvedko, 'Islam and Liberation Revolutions', *New Times*, no. 47 (October 1979), pp. 18-21; *idem*, 'Islam – Religion or Political Banner?', *Moscow News*, no. 38, 21 September 1980, p. 7.
36. A. Petrov, 'Display Prudence and Restraint', *Pravda*, 5 December 1979.
37. *Literaturnaya Gazeta*, 12 March 1980, p. 14.
38. Kianuri to Eric Rouleau, *Le Monde*, 18 April 1980.
39. A. Bovin, *Izvestia*, 12 April 1980.
40. Moscow radio 'Peace and Progress' in Arabic, 13 May 1980. In FBIS, USSR, 19 May 1980, p. H2. See: A.K. Kislov, 'The Middle East and American Strategy', *SShA – Ekonomika, Politika, Ideologiya* (USA: Economics, Politics, Ideology), no. 6 (126), (June 1980), pp. 15-26. The author is head of the Middle East Department in the Institute of USA and Canada of the Soviet Academy of Sciences.
41. *Pravda*, 30 August 1980; *Moscow News*, no. 36 (2920), 7 September 1980, Supp., p. 3.
42. TASS in English, 2 June 1980. In FBIS, USSR, 2 June 1980, p. H1.
43. *Kommunist Tadzhikistana* (Dushanbe), 22 July 1980.
44. Tehran Domestic Service, 14 August 1980. In FBIS, South Asia, 15 August 1980, p. I5.
45. Moscow radio in Persian to Iran, 28 August 1980. In FBIS, USSR, 29 August 1980, pp. H1-H2.

46. *Pravda*, 30 August 1980.
47. Moscow radio in Persian to Iran, 8 April 1980. In FBIS, USSR, 9 April 1980, p. H4.
48. Tehran Domestic Service, 14 April 1980. In FBIS, South Asia, 15 April 1980, pp. I19-I21.
49. *Ettela'at*, 12 May 1980.
50. Moscow radio in Persian to Iran, 16 August 1980. In FBIS, USSR, 19 August 1980, p. H1.
51. AFP in English, 6 September 1980. In FBIS, South Asia, 8 September 1980, p. I14.
52. Baghdad radio, 17 September 1980. In FBIS, Middle East, 18 September 1980, p. E8.
53. *Izvestia*, 15 May 1980.
54. M. Krutikhin, *Zarya Vostoka* (Tbilisi), 5 June 1980.
55. *Pravda*, 17 June 1980.
56. *Rabotnichesko Delo* (Sofia), 18 February 1980.
57. *L'Unità* (Milan), 26 November 1979.
58. At the autumn 1979 elections for a constituent assembly, some 50,000 people voted in Tehran for the Tudeh. (Kianuri interview in *Le Matin*, 27 November 1979.)
59. Interviews with Kianuri in *Rabotnichesko Delo*, 18 February 1980, and *Daily Telegraph*, 11 March 1980; Eric Rouleau, *Le Monde*, 18 April 1980.
60. Moscow Domestic Television, 18 November 1979. In FBIS, USSR, 11 December 1979, pp. H2-H3.
61. Aleksandr Bovin commentary, Moscow Domestic Service, 20 November 1979. In FBIS, USSR, 21 November 1979, pp. H3-H6.
62. TASS in English, 22 November 1979. In FBIS, USSR, 23 November 1979, p. H7.
63. *Ettela'at*, 27 November 1979.
64. Tehran Domestic Service, 13 April 1980. In FBIS, South Asia, 16 April 1980, p. I20.
65. TASS in English, 16 May 1980. In FBIS, USSR, 19 May 1980, p. H1.
66. Moscow Domestic Service, 5 September 1980. In FBIS, USSR, 9 September 1980, pp. CC4-CC5.

IRAN AT WAR: CLOSER TO THE SOVIETS BUT STILL DISTANT AND UNAPPROACHABLE
(September 1980 – end 1982)

The Iran-Iraq War: The Soviets are Neutral and Wait for Opportunities

On 22 September 1980 Iraqi forces began a full-scale war against Iran. The Soviets attempted to utilize the occasion to improve their relations with Iran. They were even reported as having indirectly passed to Iran Iraq's secret plans for an offensive. When the extent of the increasing Iraqi military build-up became clear and President Bani-Sadr called for measures against it, he was accused by his opponents of exaggerating the threat for internal political reasons. The army then underwent a series of purges and an extensive reorganization. It was kept busy trying to pacify Kordestan and preparing itself against a possible Soviet invasion. On the very day that Iraqi tanks entered Khuzestan, a thousand Iranian tanks were guarding the border with the USSR.[1]

Iraq made itself more independent of the Soviets, often acting against their advice and interests. It did not consult them or even inform them in advance about the war, as it should have done in accordance with the friendship treaty between the two countries. Soviet statements in the media, which had earlier made frequent references to the Soviet-Iraqi treaty, now ceased all mention of it, as if it had never existed.

President Saddam Husayn addressed the Iraqi National Assembly on 17 September 1980 and abrogated the Iraqi–Iranian agreement of 6 March 1975. His address included indirect criticism of the USSR, claiming that Iraq had been forced to sign the March agreement because it was weak and lacked arms and ammunition. Even after it had signed the friendship treaty with the USSR in 1972, and the latter had then committed itself to help Iraq, the Soviets did not do so. Although he did not say this directly, the hints were clear enough.[2]

On 22 September 1980 the Iraqi Deputy Prime Minister Tariq 'Aziz visited Moscow and held talks with CPSU Secretary Boris Ponomarev and First Deputy Foreign Minister Viktor Maltsev.[3] The aim of the Moscow visit, he said, was to inform the Soviets that it was in their interest to watch the situation on the Iraqi–Iranian border and understand what was happening, without their intervention being required, as long as the conflict was confined to Iraq and Iran.[4]

In Tehran Dr 'Aziz's visit to Moscow was regarded as a sign of Soviet support for Iraq. On 23 September 1980 President Bani-Sadr said that he had told the Soviet ambassador that 'your assistance to aggressive Iraq is proof of your enmity toward us'.[5] In Moscow that same day, the Vice-President of the USSR Supreme Soviet, Inamadzhan Usmankhod-zhayev, received Ambassador Mokri, at the latter's request. The meeting was attended by Viktor Maltsev, who had participated a day earlier in the Ponomarev-Tariq 'Aziz talks.[6] Mokri reported on the talks, saying that he had protested at the presence in Moscow of Tariq 'Aziz and said that the Soviets 'should condemn the Iraqi action'. According to Mokri:

> They replied: 'We are taking a neutral stand which we shall endeavour to maintain.' I told them: 'We are neither satisfied nor content with your neutrality, which is like giving a dagger to one of two men in a fight, then standing back and saying "I am neutral." If you do not cease arms shipments to Iraq, our future generations will never forget whose rockets and MiGs bombed their cities and destroyed them . . .'
>
> They replied: 'We shall raise this matter with Mr Brezhnev and others, and we shall try to play a role which will put an end to this war . . .'
>
> Elsewhere in the discussion, I told them: 'If you do not stop send-ing arms to Iraq, the Iranian government will doubtless recall me, and our relations will be reduced in scope.'[7]

Mokri reported that the Soviet government had 'formally assured' him that Moscow 'intended to remain neutral' in the Iran–Iraq conflict. The Soviets had refused further military aid to Iraq and maintained that the Tariq 'Aziz visit to Moscow was 'a failure'. Mokri reported that the Tehran government was 'very grateful to the USSR for this neutrality'.[8]

At a Kremlin dinner in honour of Sanjiva Reddy, President of India, on 30 September 1980, Brezhnev spoke of Iran and Iraq as equally friendly to the USSR — ignoring the Soviet–Iraqi treaty and Soviet arms supplies to Iraq. He called for negotiations to reach a partial settlement on what was possible, delaying the remainder for an unspecified time in the future, when it would be easier to reach an agreement.[9]

References to the Iran–Iraq war were made by Brezhnev at a dinner in the Kremlin for the Syrian President Hafiz al-Asad on 8 October 1980. Brezhnev said: 'We are not going to intervene in the conflict be-tween Iran and Iraq. We stand for its earliest political settlement by the efforts of the two sides. And we resolutely say to others: Hands off these events.'[10] These words were uttered on the day that he and Asad had signed a USSR–Syrian friendship treaty. This was interpreted in Baghdad as an anti-Iraqi action, coming as it did at a time of strained Syrian–Iraqi relations, after Iraq had broken off diplomatic relations with Syria in August 1980.

Soviet reports on the fighting tried to be even-handed, but the more difficulties the Iraqi forces met, the more it appeared that the USSR was criticizing Iraq as the guilty party and was desirous of getting closer to Iran.

Soviet Attempts to Attract Iran

The Soviets used two approaches — often simultaneously — in dealing with the Khomeyni regime. The first viewed the Islamic Republic as a temporary phenomenon and Soviet actions were adjusted accordingly; the USSR moved carefully and tactfully and always kept future events in mind. The second, based on short-term considerations, adapted Soviet behaviour and policy to the existing situation. The Soviets avoided arguing with the Iranians over matters that did not particularly affect the USSR, even when concern for their own prestige might require them to act otherwise. They kept trying to improve relations, no matter what they thought of the regime, and whatever its character. They were unceasing in their attempts to obtain the greatest possible immediate advantages.

Neither approach was always successful. The Soviet media portrayed, for temporary tactical reasons, a certain image that was more wishful thinking than a true picture of the real situation, and Soviet officials often acted as if that image were actually true. The result was 'a dialogue of the deaf'. In their discussions with Iranian officials, the Soviets were unable to find a common language, and so concluded that 'you can't talk with them'. Contacts remained mainly at the lower official levels (compared to the frequent top-level contacts during the Shah's regime). But they did exist and were sufficient to make the position of each side known to the other.

Top-level ceremonial greetings or condolences and expressions of sympathy were sent by the Soviets on all possible occasions. These messages were often signed by Brezhnev and addressed to Ayatollah Khomeyni. The Soviets' aim was to show that they were good friends and neighbours who cared about what was going on in neighbouring Iran, participating in its joys and sorrows. Iranian replies were often cool and restrained but this did not discourage the Soviets.

Iran found itself isolated and with few friends. It was suspicious of the Soviets, seeing them as standing behind Iraq and supporting it, in spite of declared Soviet neutrality. An Iranian Foreign Ministry announcement on 9 October 1980 said:

> There are clues which clearly show that both the United States government and the Soviet Union were informed of the Iraqi attack against Iran, for the attack had been planned long ago, but that neither of the two countries really wished to prevent this war, because each of them somehow supposed itself able to benefit from it.[11]

An adviser to President Bani-Sadr mentioned an American–Soviet agreement to divide the region, 'to control the area and secure their interests'.[12] The Soviets tried to counter such Iranian positions, to persuade Iran that its suspicions were unfounded, and that the Soviets were its friends.

The USSR ambassador Vladimir Vinogradov met the Iranian Prime Minister Mohammad Ali Raja'i on the pretext of inviting him to the Soviet pavilion at the Tehran international fair. The ambassador was reported as saying: 'We can co-operate in various fields and are prepared to help you with military equipment.' Raja'i rejected the proposal, saying:

> Our people have not forgotten your stand at the time of Dr Mossadeq and during that of the former regime; then suddenly they were faced with your invasion of Afghanistan . . .
>
> I am expressing my deep anxiety over your delivery of 100 T-72 tanks to Iraq, your receiving Tariq 'Aziz on the eve of the war, your reconnaissance flights over Iranian territory and the sending of Soviet experts to Jordan [which helped Iraq in the war]. This is at a time when you cannot deny that our revolutionary people have expelled your highest rival from their country.

Vinogradov reiterated the USSR's desire to befriend Iran. He claimed that the Tariq 'Aziz visit to Moscow had not been initiated by Moscow and that 'Aziz had come on his own initiative, meeting only the Deputy Foreign Minister. The Soviets 'condemn the conflict between Iran and Iraq . . . We are against this war. Obviously, we shall condemn whoever started it.'[13]

When the text of the conversation was published the next day by the Tehran press, the Soviets protested. TASS denied American reports (omitting to mention that they had been leaked by Raja'i):

> alleging that the Soviet Union had recently offered to supply Iran with Soviet arms and that the Iranian Premier had rejected the proposal . . . there have been no proposals from the Soviet side to Iran concerning arms deliveries and, consequently, the Iranian Premier had nothing to reject.[14]

On 6 October Vinogradov conferred with Hashemi Rafsanjani, Speaker of the Islamic Consultative Assembly, the conversation dealing mainly with the Soviet intervention in Afghanistan. Then came an air raid. 'What is that noise?', asked the ambassador. 'That is the sound of your MiGs,' replied the Speaker, and both had to run for shelter.[15]

A few days later, on 11 October, President Bani-Sadr met Vinogradov and strongly condemned Soviet aid to Iraq. He referred to Iraq's use of Soviet long-range Tupolev-22 bombers in raids on Iranian targets, saying that they had been supplied to Iraq on condition that they be used only against Israel. The President pointed out that Moscow had informed the Iranian government of this condition prior to delivering the bombers to Baghdad. Bani-Sadr also asked for clarification of the USSR's position regarding the supply of arms to Iraq via the Jordanian port of Aqaba. In addition, he raised the question of the 'regular supply of essential strategic information' to Iraq by Soviet spy planes. Bani-Sadr wanted to know whether the Soviet Union would supply Iran with weapons and what stance they would adopt at the UN.

Vinogradov replied that his government had been committed to a policy of neutrality since the war began, and added that his country was seeking to establish good and friendly relations with Iran. He denied that the Soviet Union was sending arms to Iraq through Aqaba, and protested at Iran's announcement that the USSR had offered to supply it with arms, saying that this was untrue and had caused great embarrassment to the USSR. At the mention of the Tupolev bombers, he lost patience, saying, 'Obviously we cannot ask for the Tupolevs back, so stop irritating the only country prepared to lend you a hand.' Vinogradov continued:

> In this war . . . we are neutral . . . Our greatest worry is an extension of the conflict, with possible US interference. But we are also keen to achieve the political result that is most important to you — Saddam Husayn's downfall . . . he shows all the symptoms of the evil

syndrome which seized the Egyptian President Sadat in 1975. But we
are also sure that one sector of the Ba'th Party . . . is still healthy and
plans to return to a policy of friendship with Syria and therefore
with us. We are counting on this sector and on certain sectors of the
army with which we still maintain excellent relations.[16]

The Soviets, however, were unwilling to 'lose' Iraq completely. They
also hoped that the Iran-Iraq conflict would not turn into an Arab-
Iranian one, a situation that would limit Soviet possibilities of manoeuvre. They therefore viewed Syrian and Libyan aid to Iran with
favour. The visit to Syria and other Arab countries by Hashemi Rafsanjani, the Speaker of the Iranian Majlis, at the end of November 1980
was given wide publicity in the Soviet media, with particular emphasis
on Syrian-Iranian statements against Egypt and Israel. Rafsanjani was
reported to have expressed willingness to buy Soviet arms. 'If we needed
arms and the Soviet Union were prepared to supply them we would buy
them,' he said.[17]

On 14 February 1981 Prime Minister Raja'i met the USSR ambassador. Raja'i said he could not ignore the Afghan issue and the continued
Soviet silence regarding Iraq's attack on Iran. It made Iran 'see no difference between the actions of the two superpowers'. The ambassador
said that Soviet leaders had stated that they would like to see an end
to the Iran-Iraq war as soon as possible: 'The USSR has suspended
arms deliveries to Iraq. Even Iraq has stated that the Soviet stand is
not neutral, but favours Iran . . . This war is in neither Iraq's nor Iran's
interest.'[18]

On the whole, Khomeyni did not attack the Soviets directly. However, he very frequently spoke against 'the superpowers', and for 'independence of the East and the West' and 'against the Eastern and Western
world-devourers'.[19] While the Soviet media often reacted sharply to
such statements by Iranian officials, they ignored them when they came
from Khomeyni. They quoted him only when he said the things they
favoured, for instance, when he attacked the United States or Israel.

Brezhnev's report to the 26th CPSU Congress (Moscow, 23 February
1981) included a reference to Iran. As with his earlier remarks on the
subject, it was repeated again and again by the Soviet media, finally becoming the official Soviet line on developments in Iran. Brezhnev said:

The revolution in Iran has a special character. It is one of the major
international events of recent years. With all its complications and
contradictions, it is fundamentally an anti-imperialist revolution,

even though internal and foreign reaction is striving to change its nature. The Iranian people are seeking their own path to freedom and prosperity. We sincerely wish them success in this and we are ready to develop relations with Iran on the basis of equality and, of course, reciprocity.[20]

The Brezhnev speech reflected Soviet attempts to be friendly and attract Iran's leadership. However, it was couched in Soviet language which did not say much to Iran's ruling clergy, who reacted to it with coolness and suspicion.

Growing Co-operation with the USSR; Indirect Soviet Military Supplies

By late 1981 and early 1982 a less hostile Iranian attitude towards the USSR became evident. It showed itself in the form of fewer attacks on the USSR, first in the speeches of leading Iranians and the government-controlled media. Then there was greater readiness to talk with the Soviet Union, renew economic co-operation and accept Soviet technical aid and arms. The arms did not come directly from the USSR but from the Soviet Union's friends in the region, such as Syria and Libya, and from more distant Soviet allies: the East European countries, Cuba and North Korea, of whose intentions the Iranians were less suspicious.

In Iran and around Khomeyni, the position strengthened of those who advocated adopting a line similar to that of Libya — in other words, accepting a functional alliance with the Soviet Union to enable them to concentrate more efforts against the United States; stressing anti-Americanism and less opposition to the East; equipping the military forces with Soviet arms; and strengthening relations with the radical Arab states, Syria, Libya and the PDRY. The Libyan-style trend was not a dominant one, but yet strong enough to be influential on certain occasions. It seemed, too, to be increasing. The Soviets hoped that they would become stronger and perhaps gain the upper hand. Thus they were prepared to contribute to this tendency. However, they were uncertain as to how to go about it. The Soviet media often spoke as if such a situation already existed, believing that the pretence would help make it a reality. In particular, they increased their efforts in the fields in which the Iranian side was ready to co-operate — economic relations, military supplies through third parties, and limited technical aid. The Soviets hoped that a possible deterioration in relations with the USA would bring about an extension of this co-operation. They also assumed that Iran, having become used to the Soviet arms it had received through third parties, might ask for them directly if an urgent need arose.

In September 1981 a Paris-based Iranian opposition paper reported the arrival of Soviet military equipment in Iran. It said that every week two jumbo jet planes from North Korea and one from East Germany were arriving in Tehran, and that other shipments were coming from Libya and Syria.[21] In late 1981 Iranian opposition sources claimed that the USSR had supplied replacements for armaments destroyed in the war. During the Shah's regime Iran had received conventional weapons and vehicles, including artillery, as part of the gas supply agreement with the USSR. The Soviets were interested in keeping their part of the agreement, hoping that this would persuade the Iranians to renew gas supplies to the USSR. There were also reports of an arms deal between the Soviet Union and Iran, worked out through Syria, by which the Soviets were said to be providing Iran with arms worth $860 million. The deal reportedly included Soviet ground-to-air missiles, artillery, mortars, light arms and mines. Other reports said the deal had been made directly between the USSR and Iran, and that the equipment came to Iran directly over the border.

At the end of 1981 TASS quoted the Iranian Premier Mir Hoseyn Musavi Khamene'i as denying any Iranian arms purchases from the USSR. Iran, he said, was buying arms on the open market.[22] In February 1982 President Ali Khamene'i was asked how far Iran would go in accepting Soviet military and technical aid. He replied:

> Purchasing arms and equipment is not considered aid. Military aid means the use of foreign advisers or the intervention of foreign advisers. We will never accept such a thing. But whenever we deem it useful, we buy military equipment. We cannot close these doors.[23]

This was not far from an admission that arms deals were being made with the Soviet Union. Reports at the end of 1981 also mentioned Soviet training of Revolutionary Guards, with the object of making them a counter-weight to the military forces, whom they suspected were not completely loyal to the regime. Soviet advisers had reportedly helped to establish a large training camp at Mashad which was able to turn out 3,000 trained Revolutionary Guard recruits per course.

There were also reports in late 1981 about the arrival in Iran of Soviet intelligence advisers. The Soviet embassy in Tehran offered to provide the Islamic regime with security and training assistance after the explosion in the IRP headquarters on 28 June 1981. The proposal was rejected at that time. After a second explosion on 30 August 1981 which killed the President and the Prime Minister, the Islamic leaders reviewed the Soviet offer with greater interest. Negotiations were conducted for Soviet aid in this matter.[24] From mid-October 1981 KGB and other Soviet advisers have reportedly been arriving in Iran to help organize its intelligence and security forces.[25] A report to this effect in New York's *Time* magazine was immediately and sharply denied in the Soviet media.[26]

The relative improvement in Soviet–Iranian relations was, in part, the result of efforts by the Soviet ambassador Vinogradov, who had been in Iran from January 1977 and was quite familiar with Iran's leading personalities. Vinogradov contributed much to a shift in the Iranian viewpoint: from seeing both the USA and the USSR as equally 'Satanic powers', to considering the Soviet Union less dangerous, and able to help Iran during the time of its isolation and need for foreign support. Nevertheless, Iran continued to suspect Soviet intentions. Vinogradov had frequent meetings with Iran's leaders, trying to persuade them that the Soviet Union was a friendly country, ready to help Iran. It is doubtful, however, whether his achievements were fully understood in Moscow. The Kremlin leaders wanted much more than this, but they did not understand the situation in Iran.

In June 1982 the appointment was announced of Vil Konstantinovich Boldyrev as USSR ambassador to Iran. Boldyrev had served in the USSR embassy in Iran from 1956 to 1960, and later in Algeria and India. From 1978 he had been head of the USSR Foreign Ministry Department of Middle East countries. This office handles affairs pertaining to Soviet relations with Iran, Afghanistan and Turkey, so Boldyrev was quite familiar with developments in Iran.[27] He presented his credentials to the Iranian Foreign Minister Velayati on 7 August 1982 and to President Khamene'i three days later. Boldyrev spoke about 'friendly relations and good-neighbourliness' and said that there were great possibilities for the expansion of co-operation between the two countries.[28]

Iran's ambassador to Moscow, Dr Mohammad Mokri, could well be considered 'Moscow's man'. He was sent to Moscow as soon as Khomeyni came to power and has remained in his post ever since. Foreign Ministers Ibrahim Yazdi and Sadeq Qotbzadeh both tried to dismiss him. Qotbzadeh even recalled him to Tehran once, but he was returned to his position — reportedly after intervention by the Tudeh through the IRP,[29] but more probably after the Soviets expressed a wish that he remain at his post. Both ambassadors contributed much to the improvement in relations between the USSR and Iran, an improvement which expressed itself particularly in economic co-operation.

Economic and Technical Co-operation

The closure of Iranian ports in the Persian Gulf as a result of the war with Iraq has increased Iran's use of overland routes through the Soviet Union, for trade with European countries, with Japan and with the Soviet Union itself. According to an official in the USSR State Committee for Foreign Economic Relations, transportation between the Soviet Union and Iran was by sea, rail and road. By the end of 1980 more than 250 wagons a day, carrying various products, reached the rail station on the Julfa border from the Soviet Union. Soviet river-sea vessels carried goods from Western Europe and from the Soviet Union to the Caspian Sea ports Nawshahr and Enzeli. Since the Caspian Sea is shallow in the area of these two ports, special Soviet vessels dredged these areas. 'Goods are transported day and night by trucks via the bridge on the border river Astara-Chay. Every day hundreds of tons of cargo are delivered to the Iranian authorities in Astara.'[30] Goods from Shanghai were reportedly shipped via China and the Trans-Siberian railway to Tehran.[31] However, no agreement was reached regarding the export of Iranian gas to the Soviet Union.[32] With diminishing Iranian oil exports, negotiations on the subject were delayed.

The freeing of the American hostages in January 1981 led to an increase in Iranian–West European trade, especially with West Germany. Part of the goods traded passed through the Soviet Union. Iranian cargoes were transported through the Volga-Don by Soviet sea-going vessels from Iranian ports to Western Europe via the Caspian Sea, the Azov Sea and the Black Sea.[33]

By the end of 1981 the increase in trade had led to congestion at the Soviet–Iranian border because of difficulties in handling the cargoes on the Iranian side. In late November 1981 it was reported that the Soviet All-Union Cargo Transit Corporation, which is in charge of the Siberian overland trade route by way of the Trans-Siberian railway, had asked the Japanese transport companies temporarily to suspend shipping of cargo bound for Iran. Soviet aid was provided for the purpose of improving the Iranian transportation network in the border areas and further southward. It included both Soviet equipment and technicians. This in turn contributed to the further expansion of trade.

Among the steps taken to deal with this situation was the leasing by

Iran at the end of 1981 of ten Soviet locomotives to run on the Tabriz–Tehran line. These were driven and serviced by nineteen Soviet engine-drivers, instructors and maintenance staff.[34] The railway linking the cities of Tabriz and Julfa had been electrified, with the aid of Soviet specialists. 'Several tens' of Iranian railway specialists were sent for training in the Soviet Union.[35]

Signs of improving relations included talks in Moscow from 7-12 October 1981 between delegations from TASS and the Iranian news agency PARS regarding co-operation between them.[36] On 19 October there was a meeting between the Chairman of the Soviet State Construction Agency and the Iranian Minister for Housing and Urban Planning at which co-operation was discussed.[37] Seven new grain storage silos were reportedly to be constructed in Iran with the help of the Soviet Union.[38] By itself, none of these developments was of particular significance, but taken together they indicated a definite, if slight, improvement in relations.

Iran's Energy Minister Hasan Ghafuri-Fard visited the USSR and on 15 February 1982 signed a protocol in Moscow on economic and technical co-operation between the two countries.[39] The protocol included a speeding up of the construction of two power stations, in Isfahan and Ahwaz (Ramin station).[40] The Minister said that relations between the two countries were good and that Moscow had expressed support for the Islamic revolution. The co-existence as neighbours of 'a communist Soviet Union and an Islamic Iran does not pose any problem, as neither country interferes in the domestic affairs of the other', he said.[41]

Izvestia, summing up Soviet–Iranian economic relations after this visit, said that the transit of commodities into Iran and back via the territory of the Soviet Union had risen from 1 million tons in 1978 to 3.4 million tons in 1981. The volume of trade between the two countries had reached 800 million roubles (more than US $1,000 million) in 1981, compared to 671 million roubles in 1978. The USSR had increased its supplies of timber, fertilizers and steel-building equipment. Iran chiefly supplied dried fruit and concentrates of lead-zinc and copper ores. In 1981, for the first time, Iran supplied the USSR with over 2.2 million tons of oil. This meant that, by buying oil from Iran on a barter or rouble basis, the USSR could increase by the same amount the oil which it could sell for badly needed foreign currency.

The Soviet Union has been co-operating with Iran on the construction of 153 projects, 104 of which have already been commissioned. Chief among them is the Isfahan metallurgical combine. An agreement has been signed to expand the combine's production to 1.9 million tons a year. The expansion work has largely been completed, according to *Izvestia*.[42]

With regard to co-operation in job training, the Soviet Union is helping Iran to establish training schools for specialized workers and technicians for the construction and operation of production units built in Iran with Soviet technical help. Approximately 23,000 technicians and skilled workers have been trained directly on the job in 13 training and technical schools built and equipped with the aid of Soviet experts. Over 1,000 workers, technicians and engineers have been trained in the Soviet Union and 120 skilled experts have graduated from Soviet training schools.[43] If we consider the number of years over which this occurred, and the number of projects for which this training was undertaken, we see that they were not many. In Iran in early 1982 there were about 2,000 technicians and military advisers from communist and pro-communist countries, including the Soviet Union.[44]

Iran's trading partners were mostly Eastern bloc countries. Iran was making deliveries of oil to Romania, Yugoslavia, Bulgaria, Hungary and the USSR, and was also making purchases in those countries.[45] This was during a period of acute foreign exchange shortages in Iran and a drastic fall in Iranian government reserves. West European trading partners had no wish to enter into barter deals with Iran at a time when crude oil was in over-supply. The USSR and East European countries were ready to exchange Iranian crude oil for supplies of food, medicines, machinery and raw materials, many of them of low quality, which the Soviets and East Europeans had difficulty selling to Western countries.

Economic relations were generally subordinated by the Soviets to political considerations. They were ready to make economic investments in order to support their political aims, and were prepared to compromise and agree to Iranian terms. They wished to create a situation where Iran would get used to close economic co-operation with the USSR, while loosening ties with the Western world. The Soviets believed that this would sooner or later lead to a certain measure of Iranian dependence on them, thus influencing political relations.

Soviet Grievances and Disappointments

In meetings between Soviet and Iranian representatives, each side had its own viewpoint and each said something different, often irrelevant to what was being communicated by the other side. Even when the

Soviets and the Iranians used the same terms, each side interpreted them differently.

On 28 December 1980, a year after the Soviet intervention in Afghanistan, demonstrators marched on the Soviet and Afghan embassies in Tehran. Some 100 Afghan refugees managed to enter the Soviet embassy and about 3,000 others staged a sit-down on the street outside. The invaders broke windows and furniture and burned a Soviet flag. Revolutionary Guards in the street fired shots in the air and drove the rioters away.[46] The Soviets had praised and justified events of this sort when they concerned the American embassy and American diplomats. This time, when it affected the Soviets, TASS described the demonstrators as 'hooligan-type elements whose actions have obviously been inspired by reactionary forces'.[47]

The USSR Foreign Ministry delivered a note of protest to the Iranian ambassador in Moscow. It accused the Iranian authorities of having been informed in advance that the attack was being prepared, and not taking 'urgent and effective enough measures' to prevent it. The Soviet government 'reserves the right to make claims' for the restoration of the damage 'and to consider the question of appropriate measures to protect the lawful interests of the Soviet Union'.[48] The note made no mention of the attack having been staged by Afghans.

On 12 January 1981 the Iranian ambassador was summoned to the USSR Ministry of Foreign Affairs. He was told that the attack on the embassy was:

> a violation of both the norms in relations between states . . . and elementary notions of decency characteristic of civilized countries . . . The Soviet side naturally expected that the government of Iran would unequivocally and resolutely condemn the crimes committed and strictly punish their organizers and direct participants.

But no official condemnation by Iran was forthcoming.

> The Soviet Union, as before, is ready to build its relations with Iran on the basis of good neighbourliness and mutual respect. At the same time no one should have any doubt that it will have to protect the legitimate rights and interests of the Soviet state and its citizens if the Iranian government does not wish, or finds itself unable, to perform its duty regarding the ensurance of the safety of the Soviet institutions and their personnel in Iran. The Soviet government also expects full compensation for the material damage caused to the

property of the USSR embassy in Tehran.[49]

The Soviet statement was sharply worded, but put in such a way as to
restrict it only to the incident itself, making it clear that the USSR had
no intention of exacerbating relations with Iran because of the incident
— but rather wanted to improve them. The language used in the statement, however, offended Iran's leadership and public opinion.

The general Soviet tendency was to pretend that friendly relations
existed. *Pravda* cited the Speaker of the Majlis, Hashemi Rafsanjani, as
saying that Soviet-Iranian relations 'are developing perfectly normally,
without any trend towards the aggravation of tension between the two
states'.[50] *Izvestia* commentator Aleksandr Bovin was more frank about
Soviet-Iranian relations and the situation in Iran. Commenting on the
removal of President Bani-Sadr from office on 22 June 1981, Bovin
referred to an address by Khomeyni, saying:

> This is what Khomeyni said: All the attempts by this faction — that
> is, Bani-Sadr's faction — amount to attempts to turn Iran towards
> America. His logic goes further than this: if they draw us closer to
> America, then the Soviet Union will be an accomplice. America can-
> not do this alone, they must be in it together. This is how the Imam
> viewed the situation.

Bovin referred to Foreign Minister Hoseyn Musavi's reply to the question, 'Whom must Iran fight in the first place — the Soviet Union or
America?' According to Bovin, the Minister said:

> In Iran, the slogan 'Death to America' and the slogan 'Death to com-
> munism' are one and the same thing. We must destroy any stronghold
> of the Eastern superpower — meaning the Soviet Union — as well as
> of other oppressor powers ... In our country, opposition to com-
> munism and Marxism is generally a universal conviction.

Bovin added another description:

> A detachment of painters and artists was sent to our [USSR] embassy
> [in Tehran] and on the fence around the embassy they painted, in
> enormous letters more than a metre high, sayings by Khomeyni —
> such as, 'World communism is more dangerous to us than the Amer-
> ican threat,' and 'America is worse than England, England is worse
> than America, but the Soviet Union is worse than both of them.'

Bovin wrote: 'I will not comment on these rather colourful statements
. . . I am telling you this so that you may know the real atmosphere that
now prevails there.'[51]

A *Pravda* article of 9 March 1982 spoke of both 'positive changes
in Iranian policies' and grievances and disappointments. Commercial
and economic relations between the USSR and Iran were 'not bad' and
even steadily expanding. But there were still many limitations: the number of Soviet diplomats and journalists permitted to work in Iran; the
closure of the Soviet consulate in Rasht; a reduction in Soviet cultural
and propaganda activities; restrictions on the Iran–Soviet Bank, and
branches of Soviet insurance and transport services and organizations.
The Soviets were also unhappy at being lumped together with the
United States when the Iranians spoke equally negatively of the two
powers, viewing them both as threats to their country. Iran was opposed
to the Soviet military intervention in Afghanistan; in February 1982 a
Soviet Muslim delegation, which had arrived in Iran to help mark the
third anniversary of the Islamic revolution, left the official celebrations
because 'hostile slogans' were chanted there against the Soviet Union.
Pravda blamed 'a few among the Iranian leadership who are opposed to
good-neighbourly relations and co-operation' between the Soviet Union
and Iran and 'conservative factions' around Khomeyni 'which include
groups with extreme right-wing views'.[52]

Pravda expressed a Soviet wish to extend aid but also asked for some
positive Iranian gestures in return, especially redress for at least some
of the Soviet grievances which they then listed. *Pravda* also expressed
Soviet frustration and disappointment at achieving so few results from
the investment of such great efforts.

The 'neither East nor West' slogan was repeated in Iran again and
again. Khomeyni said on 25 July 1982 that Iran had been isolated:

> Nearly the entire East and West are either our direct or indirect op-
> ponents . . . Today we are facing the East and West; the Eastern bloc
> and the Western bloc . . . Today nearly all the propaganda of the
> media in both East and West is aimed at the Islamic Republic . . .
> The Iranian nation has managed to stop all powers from interfering
> in its country.[53]

But while Khomeyni opposed interference by others in Iran's affairs,
he was nevertheless trying to extend his brand of Islamic revolution to
neighbouring and even more distant countries. Whereas the Soviets might
welcome Iranian activities that led to the destabilization of Western-

oriented countries in the Persian Gulf, they took a quite different view of Iranian support for the Muslim revolt in Afghanistan. They also considered Iranian appeals to Soviet Muslims for an Islamic revival as being directed against them. Continuous Iranian broadcasts to Soviet Transcaucasia and Central Asia were aimed at subverting the loyalty of Soviet Muslims to the Soviet regime. An Azerbaijani official complained that 'various "radio voices" broadcasting to our country in the ethnic languages of the East, including Azeri, are appealing to all Muslims to unite under the green banner of Islam'.[54] This clearly meant broadcasts coming from Iran and being heard in Soviet Azerbaijan. There were reports that a powerful broadcasting station was being built in northern Iran, close to the Soviet border, to transmit programmes to Muslims in the Soviet Union.[55] The Soviets undoubtedly considered such a step as hostile to them, since even now broadcasts intended for local audiences in Iran are heard clearly in the Soviet Union and are listened to in regions populated by Soviet Muslims.

After Khomeyni came to power, the Iranians tried to use visits to the Soviet Union as occasions on which to propagate Islam and Iran's Islamic revolution. This was also done by Iranians going on the *hajj* (pilgrimage) in Saudi Arabia, and often brought about clashes and incidents there. In September 1982 an Iranian wrestling team scheduled to take part in a competition in Makhachkala, the capital of Muslim-populated Soviet Dagestan, planned to act in a similar manner. To avoid incidents there, the Soviet embassy in Tehran refused to grant the team entry visas. Iran's Minister of Labour and Social Affairs was cited by *Keyhan* as saying that the refusal was because the Soviets were 'afraid of Islam'. He told the members of the team: 'If you had gone there, you would certainly have chanted "Allah-o-Akbar" (God is Great), and they were afraid of this.'[56] For the Soviets the subject is very sensitive and Iranian attempts to try to operate among Muslims in the Soviet Union will undoubtedly encounter a sharp Soviet reaction and influence Soviet-Iranian relations.

War with Iraq: the Soviets Help Iran but do not Want it to Win or to be Strengthened

The first weeks of the Iran-Iraq war (September-October 1980) were marked by Iraqi advances into Iran and by some Iraqi military successes. Iraq, however, failed to gain any political aims — in other words, to bring about the downfall of the Khomeyni regime and a popular revolt in the Khuzestan area. Iraqi military forces reached a number of Iranian cities, but in order to conquer them they would have had to suffer heavy losses and this they tried to avoid. Even if the Iraqis had succeeded in conquering these cities and advancing still further into Iranian territory, they would still not have achieved the political ends for which they had gone to war. The Iranians were determined to fight, and reorganized their forces to strengthen their resistance.

The second stage of the war (from the end of 1980 until the end of 1981) was marked by a stalemate. The Iraqi forces stopped their advance and waited for Khomeyni's regime to fall and for the opposition to grow stronger. This did not happen; in fact the opposite came about. Even those who had opposed the regime now consolidated around it.

The third stage (from the end of 1981) saw an Iranian offensive. Reaching the conclusion that they were unable to achieve their political aims, the Iraqis retreated. The roles of both sides were now reversed, with Iran assuming the role that Iraq had had at the beginning of the war. Iran was intent on overthrowing the Saddam Husayn regime and establishing a Shi'ite Islamic Republic in all of Iraq, or at least in the Shi'a-populated areas. The Iranians hoped that the Iraqi Shi'ites would revolt and join them.

The fourth stage ran from July 1982. On 13 July 1982 Iranian forces crossed the Iraqi border and moved towards the solidly Shi'ite city of Basrah, the second largest city in Iraq and site of Iraq's major oil installations. But now the Iraqis were fighting on their own territory and so were motivated to fight, and the Iraqi Shi'ites did not revolt but militarily backed Saddam Husayn. Even Syria (which supported Iran) did not wish to witness the downfall of Iraq's Ba'th Party regime (although they would have been happy to see Saddam Husayn deposed) and thus to have a neighbour dependent on Iran. Neither the USA nor the USSR wanted to see any kind of close co-operation between Iran and Iraq under an Islamic banner. In early August 1982 the Iranian offensive towards Basrah stopped. Minefields, barbed wire and machine-guns were waiting for those who were ready to be martyred. Opinions were divided in Tehran. The professional soldiers and some of the less militant mullahs were unenthusiastic about a war on foreign soil.

The Soviets continued to demonstrate a position of even-handedness, not supporting either side. The Soviet media repeatedly called for an end to the war, saying that it was against the interests of both Iran and Iraq and that they should reach a political settlement through negotiation. The Soviets were careful not to say what kind of settlement they would prefer.

A broadcast from the USSR-based National Voice of Iran (NVOI) sided with Iran and supported its conditions for ending the war. These included an unconditional withdrawal of Iraqi forces from Iranian territory, the payment of reparations to Iran, and an admission by Iraq that it was the aggressor. The broadcast, as all Soviet comments at the time, called for an end to the conflict through negotiations.[57]

Moscow radio in Arabic welcomed the Iraqi leadership's decision to withdraw its forces from the Iranian territory they had occupied, calling it 'a positive step'.[58] The Soviets were worried at the possibility of the war extending deep into Iraq, so their media continued to call for an end to the fighting. Since this became Iraq's position too, it meant that in practical terms the Soviet and Iraqi viewpoints were coming closer together than those of the USSR and Iran. A senior Soviet commentator said of this war:

> This is a senseless war which has caused, and is still causing, great damage both to Iran and to Iraq . . . some circles in Tehran call today for the continuation of the war in order to punish the Iraqi leaders and spread the Iranian type of Islam. Are those countries not paying too high a price in trying to clarify, with the aid of military operations, the point as to who is better, the Sunnis or the Shi'ites?[59]

Time and again the Soviet media stressed that a continuation of the war was in America's interests, benefiting only the USA and enabling it to strengthen its positions in the region. Iranian advances into Iraq made Arab countries in the Persian Gulf turn closer to the USA, facilitating the presence of the American Rapid Deployment Force on their territory and causing much Soviet anxiety.[60]

The Soviets were interested in helping Iran as long as it remained weak, but an Iranian victory in the war would not be to their advantage, since it would weaken Soviet positions in the region. Arab countries in the Gulf area would turn still closer to the USA, thus damaging Soviet efforts to win acceptance in the Arab world. A stronger Islamic Iran meant increased support for the Islamic anti-Soviet revolt in Afghanistan, increased appeals to Soviet Muslims to turn to Islam, and less need for Soviet aid. But although this would diminish the Soviets' chances, it prevented them from acting openly against Iran and forced them to try harder to attract Iran.

The Soviet Union and Iraq: Attempts to Keep Positions and Options

Soviet–Iraqi relations have followed an uneven course. At the outbreak of the Iran–Iraq war in September 1980 relations cooled. Both sides, however, were interested in preventing any further deterioration. They even tried to improve matters as far as the existing situation allowed, without substantially altering their fundamental positions. By 1982 relations had improved slightly, although they did not reach the peak of the early 1970s. Moscow wanted to stop Iraq from getting closer to the West European countries and to prevent the establishment of official US-Iraqi relations. They also wanted to keep alive the possibility of closer relations with Iraq.

When the war broke out, a few Soviet ships carrying cargoes for Iraq unloaded in Aqaba for trans-shipment overland to Iraq. Other ships, *en route* to ports through which the arms could be delivered to Baghdad, never arrived at their destination. They had been diverted to other destinations.[61] Some Soviet military equipment, mainly spare parts and ammunition, continued to arrive in Iraq indirectly, through Middle Eastern (Jordan, North Yemen, and so on), East European and other countries.

Tariq 'Aziz, Iraq's Deputy Prime Minister and Vice-Chairman of the Revolution Command Council, visited Moscow on 11 November 1980 for the second time during the war.[62] He described Soviet policy as one of 'wait and see'.[63] By the end of 1980 he was said to have commented that the USSR had stopped arms deliveries to Iraq at the start of the war.[64] A Soviet broadcast to Iran in mid-February 1981 reported that, from the beginning of the Iran-Iraq war, the Soviet Union 'has not delivered and will not deliver arms to either side in the conflict'.[65] Tariq 'Aziz visited Moscow again on 4 June 1982, where he met CPSU Politburo member Ponomarev.[66] The Soviets gave scant publicity to the visit, even though it took place while Soviet–Iraqi relations were improving somewhat.

Official Soviet-Iraqi relations are specified in the treaty of friendship and co-operation signed on 9 April 1972. The Soviet intervention in Afghanistan was explained by the USSR as a consequence of the USSR–Afghan friendship treaty, which obliged the Soviet Union to help its friends. In Iraq this line of reasoning caused the Iraqis to consider abrogating the treaty lest it serve as a pretext for similar Soviet intervention in Iraq. Reports that Iraq was intending to abrogate the treaty have appeared from time to time.[67] Both sides, however, have decided to keep up the appearance of the treaty, even if neither of them actually observes its provisions. Differences over a great number of issues continue between the two countries:

(1) *Iraqi communists.* The persecution of Iraqi communists has been deeply embarrassing to Moscow, which has had no choice but to abandon them. For the Iraqis the persecution of communists, in addition to its significance in internal policy, has been aimed at 'punishing the Soviet Union' and demonstrating Iraq's independence from Moscow.

(2) *The Kurds.* The Iraqis suspect the USSR of inciting the Kurds to revolt.

(3) *Gulf security.* The Iraqis have called for the Gulf to be outside the sphere of influence of non-Gulf powers, making it clear that these include the USSR.

(4) *Afghanistan.* The Soviet intervention in Afghanistan increased Iraqi suspicions that the Soviet Union might do the same in Iraq, supporting 'its people' and helping them to come to power. This suspicion led to even greater persecution of the communists.

(5) *Eritrea.* The Soviet Union supports the present Ethiopian regime, while the Iraqis support Eritrean organizations fighting Ethiopia and trying to establish an independent state.

(6) *The Iraqi–Syrian conflict.* Soviet efforts not to become involved in this conflict have met with failure. Their support of Syria was seen by Iraq as acting against its interests, particularly because of Syria's support of Iran in the war against Iraq.

By the beginning of 1982 Soviet–Iraqi relations had improved slightly. The USSR was again prepared to provide some arms indirectly, through third parties. On 17 July 1982, on the fourteenth anniversary of the Iraqi Ba'th Party's rise to power, the Iraqi ambassador to the Soviet Union spoke on Moscow television. He described Iraq as a progressive revolutionary country, whose friendship with the Soviet Union was based on the USSR–Iraqi friendship treaty. 'Our relations in all areas of life are developing successfully,' he said.[68] A Moscow radio broadcast in Arabic that same day listed Soviet irrigation co-operation projects with Iraq, the construction of the al-Tharthar–Tigris Canal and the Fallujah and al-Hadithah dams on the Euphrates river, all with Soviet aid.[69] In an exchange of greetings between Soviet and Iraqi leaders in August 1982, both sides expressed confidence that relations between the two countries would continue to develop on the basis of the friendship treaty.[70] Both sides were eager to avoid any further deterioration of relations, even though they each moved in different directions.

Soviet Reactions to Iran's Attempts to Export its Revolution to the Gulf Region

The Iranian advances in the war with Iraq increased the fears of the Arab Gulf states' rulers that Iran would attempt to export its Islamic revolution to adjacent Muslim countries, especially those with a considerable Shi'ite population. These fears increased after the discovery, at the end of 1981, of an attempt to overthrow the ruling family in Bahrain in order to establish an Islamic regime like the Iranian one. Investigations uncovered large caches of smuggled arms and revealed the fact that support for the plot was coming from Iran, where an Islamic Front for the Liberation of Bahrain has offices and is given training facilities and other support.

The Soviet media generally treated the situation as a purely internal affair of the Gulf countries. They stressed the social character of such occurrences, while attempting to ignore or play down their religious nature. The Soviets were in favour of attempts to destabilize and overthrow conservative and Western-oriented regimes. Therefore they were critical of such regimes' defensive measures: more co-operation within the framework of the Gulf Co-operation Council; and bilateral defence and economic arrangements confronting Iran and making Shi'ite uprisings within their territories more difficult. The Soviets also decried these states' dependence on the USA and Britain for aid and protection. The USA also gave aid to Gulf countries supporting Iraq. This in turn led to Iranian reactions and threats. The Soviet media denied the existence of such a situation, or that Iran had any aggressive intentions toward the Gulf countries. They claimed that reports were being spread by the Western powers in order to frighten the Gulf rulers, thus making them more receptive to an American military presence and to security defence agreements with the USA.

Afghanistan: Iran Supports the Muslim Revolt against the Soviet-installed Regime

The USSR's military intervention in Afghanistan greatly influenced Soviet-Iranian relations. Iran refused to recognize the regime installed in Kabul as representing the people of that country. Instead, it supported Muslim groups fighting the new Afghan regime, providing them with aid, shelter and protection. There were more than one million Afghan refugees in Iran, providing a constant reminder of the problem. Talks on the subject between Soviet and Iranian representatives often turned, on the Iranians' initiative, to the situation in Afghanistan. The Soviets frequently reacted quite sharply to any introduction of the subject by the Iranians. For example, the Soviet ambassador once went to meet Prime Minister Raja'i 'to warn . . . against the new plots and conspiracies of the Reagan administration', but the Prime Minister turned the talks to the Afghanistan problem. According to a NVOI broadcast, the head of an Iranian delegation to the Soviet Union, 'instead of reviewing problems of interest to both countries, again raised the problem of Afghanistan'.[71]

The Soviet media repeatedly attacked 'the Afghan counter-revolutionary groups who have found backing and hiding places in Iran'. They were described by the Soviets as former 'big feudal landlords', no different from the 'counter-revolutionaries' in Iran who served the Shah, and as murderers and bandits, trading in narcotics and disobeying Iran's laws. They were branded as speculators, trying to create conditions under which American agents could penetrate into Iran. The Soviet media criticized 'anti-Afghan remarks' by 'some very influential' and 'powerful' figures in Iran.[72]

An Iranian Foreign Ministry proposal of 10 November 1981 demanded that Soviet troops in Afghanistan be replaced by Islamic forces, and the current regime by a clergy-dominated government.[73] These proposals were not directly rejected by the Soviets, but they pointed to Afghanistan's official rejection of them. Moscow radio, quoting an Afghan Foreign Ministry spokesman, said the Iranian proposal was 'trying to impose a government of reactionary clergymen on the Afghan people . . . to subjugate the Afghan people to foreign occupation by using the so-called Islamic peace-keeping force, which is to consist of Iranian and Pakistani military units'. The spokesman reported that the offer had been strongly rejected by the Afghan government, and called for a normalization of relations between Iran and Afghanistan according to proposals presented by the Afghan government.[74] Moves to normalize Iran's relations with Afghanistan were frequently made by the Soviet media,[75] but met with no Iranian response.

The Soviets Desire the Continuation of Tension between Iran and the USA

The Soviet media blamed the United States for the outbreak of the Iran-Iraq war,[76] accusing the US of using the war as a pretext to build up its military forces in the region, and increase its presence and influence there, in preparation for an armed intervention in Iran, designed to overthrow the regime.

According to *Izvestia*, American fear of a possible Soviet reaction had prevented a US military intervention. The paper maintained that the USA had wanted to intervene but had not dared, first because of a possible violent Iranian reaction. Then, 'Washington cannot fail to take into account the Soviet Union's possible reaction ... The factor of Soviet foreign policy itself undoubtedly limits the possibilities for "gunboat diplomacy" and this is affecting the US line in the Iran-Iraq conflict.'[77]

Reports appeared in the Soviet media which attempted to increase Iranian suspicions of the USA and prevent an Iranian-American *rapprochement*. Indirect criticism was levelled at those in Iran who called for an agreement with the USA to solve the problem of the hostages seized in the Tehran embassy. Soviet commentators constantly said that the USA was not interested in solving the issue, but only in using it as 'a pretext' to increase its military presence in the region.[78] Over and over again, they repeated stories about American plans to attack Iran and release the hostages by force. Such Soviet propaganda became more intense during the last days of the Carter administration, when it appeared that the problem was about to be solved. The Soviet goal was to undermine the talks, weakening those in Iran who wanted a settlement and strengthening its opponents.

The American hostages were released on 20 January 1981, the day that President Reagan took office. The Soviet media repeated their warning that the new administration was not going to honour the terms of the US-Iranian agreement, i.e., not to interfere in internal Iranian affairs and to transfer to Iran the Iranian assets frozen in the United States. They claimed that the United States could have solved the problem much earlier but had not wished to.

The Soviet media, and their broadcasts to Iran in particular, sharply attacked the USA, accusing it of bombings, plots, terrorism, attempts to overthrow the Islamic regime, supporting Iranian refugees and terrorist groups, using 'Afghan counter-revolutionary robbers' to create unrest and difficulties in Iran, and 'destroying essential commodities ... burning and storming buildings and killing prominent figures'. The USA had not officially declared war on Iran, they said, 'yet the war against the Islamic Republic of Iran continues with widespread dimensions'.[79] The USA had concentrated a huge naval armada in the Persian Gulf near the Iranian coast and might 'start any adventure to regain its positions in the region'.[80]

Day after day the Soviet media accused the USA of acting to destabilize the situation in Iran and restore the old regime. To divert the
attention of the Iranian public from their machinations, the Americans
— it was claimed — had 'raised the bogey of a Soviet threat'.[81] Such
Soviet propaganda was an attempt to create a rift between Iran and
the Western world, placing Iran in political, economic and social isolation and segregating those in Iran who wished to return it to a Western
orientation.

Iran's Islamic Regime: Soviet Tactical Approval and Basic Opposition

Generally, the Soviets were interested in internal Iranian affairs only
in so far as they were relevant to the Soviets themselves. According to
Iran's ambassador to the USSR, Dr Mokri:

> The Soviet government . . . only pays attention to us and accepts our
> revolution to the extent that it is in its interests to do so. The Soviet
> government always defends our anti-imperialistic stand strongly,
> but never has much to say about the Islamic side. The Soviet Union
> states, through its media, that our revolution is anti-imperialist and
> [its media] reflect only the anti-American aspect of our struggle.[82]

This, however, was only outwardly true; the Soviets carefully
watched ongoing power struggles in Iran, like that between President
Bani-Sadr and the Islamic Republican Party (IRP). The former favoured
a more non-aligned approach and the maintenance of contacts with the
Western world, while the latter opposed any *rapprochement* with the
USA.

'We are exerting all efforts to sever all relations . . . between the
United States and the Western bloc on one side and Iran on the other.
We must eliminate these inherited relations and then decide if there is
any need for relations,' said IRP leader Ayatollah Beheshti. If ties could
be established on Iranian terms, 'some relations between us and those
states will be created. Otherwise, none shall exist.'[83] For the time being,
this was the position preferred by the Soviets.[84] A strange situation now
developed, in which the Soviets supported those whom they generally
termed 'reactionary' (those who rejected Western culture and concepts
of which communism too was a part), while opposing those who had
called for modernization and relative secularization.

Universities in Iran were closed because they were centres of modernization, leftist activity and opposition to rule by the clergy. According to Khomeyni, universities were 'a trench for the communists, a war office for the communists . . . in the grip of communists, the guerrillas and other hypocritical groups'. He said:

Whether we want it or not, it is the university which is dragging us towards America or the Soviet Union . . . Bazaar tradesmen cannot lead us towards America or the Soviet Union; peasants cannot do this either; factory workers cannot do this; nor can the clergy . . . Such a university must not reopen.[85]

This led to discussions in the Soviet Union as to whether, against all the Soviets' principles, they could accept such viewpoints solely because of Iran's anti-Americanism, or whether there was a limit to the lengths to which the Soviets could go in adapting themselves to the situation. A discussion of this kind appeared on Moscow television between Aleksandr Bovin, *Izvestia* senior political observer, and Yevgenyi Primakov, Director of the Institute of Oriental Studies at the USSR Academy of Sciences:

Bovin: Iran is now living through a period of what I would call a slump and a retreat from the revolution . . . The universities are closed there now and a cultural revolution is in progress . . . Ayatollah Khomeyni . . . said: 'It is the universities which submitted Iran to the authority of the superpowers. Do you want to reopen the universities now so that they can again become a bastion of communists who would not let the faithful work and learn?' This is Ayatollah Khomeyni's reasoning. I consider it difficult to call it a development of the revolutionary process . . .
Primakov: There is an objective side to this. One cannot talk only of the subjective features connected to any words said by the leader . . . Yes, when the universities were closed, it happened in a definite situation when the Western agencies operated in these universities . . . an objective situation exists. This objective situation has not lost its very strong anti-imperialist charge . . .
Bovin: . . . it is naturally an anti-American course when you call it anti-imperialist. You know very well that the thunder and lightning raging against the United States are immediately accompanied by thunder and lightning against the Soviet Union.[86]

Soviet views of the situation in Iran also reflected internal Soviet interest groups. Their military commentators found it difficult to accept Iran's downgrading of the regular army, giving preference to revolutionary militias and allowing the clergy to intervene in military operational matters of which they had very little understanding. The Soviet military saw this as one of the reasons for Iran's difficulties in the war, while for most of the Soviet public it served as a reminder of the supremacy of the party over the military, as exists in the Soviet Union.

The Soviet press reported the curtailment of President Bani-Sadr's powers without comment.[87] However, Soviet commentators tended to favour the IRP. *New Times* cited the Tehran paper *Keyhan*, which listed among Bani-Sadr's supporters:

the liberal-bourgeois National Front (the pro-Western sentiments of some of its leaders are well known), the Maoist group that calls itself the Party of the Iranian Working People . . . For tactical reasons, the Leftist People's Combatants [Mojahedin-e-Khalq] sided with Bani-Sadr. In short, the former President drew his main support from the bourgeoisie, both small and big.[88]

Khomeyni dismissed President Bani-Sadr on 22 June 1981. Initially, the Soviet media withheld comment and refrained from taking sides, but later they increasingly identified Bani-Sadr with the pro-American camp or said indirectly that he himself was pro-American.

On 28 June 1981 a bomb exploded in the IRP headquarters killing 64 people, among them IRP leader and Chief Justice Ayatollah Beheshti, and several ministers, deputy ministers and members of parliament. Soviet reports claimed that this had been engineered by the USA, acting 'to destabilize the situation by using the most outrageous methods, including terrorism'. They also claimed that the USA had tried to stage a coup in Iran similar to that in Chile against President Salvador Allende.[89] The Soviet media refrained from accusing the Mojahedin-e-Khalq organization of perpetrating bombings and assassinations, and this could be construed as a positive appraisal of their organization. Later Soviet comments also avoided publicly associating the Mojahedin with the bombings, or mentioning them in the numerous accounts of street clashes involving 'counter-revolutionaries' and supporters of Bani-Sadr.

Pravda published a report which could be interpreted as a favourable appraisal of the Mojahedin-e-Khalq. It cited the French communist *L'Humanité* writing about the execution of one of the Mojahedin leaders who had 'spent much time in the Shah's prisons'. The execution, along with others, caused 'legitimate concern on the part of all democrats who supported the Iranian revolution'.[90]

A Soviet report in March 1982 gave a more directly favourable appraisal of the Mojahedin. It described the group as a left-wing organization which had played a considerable part in the overthrow of the Shah's regime. The report added that at least 2,000 of its members had been executed by the Islamic authorities, but it still continued to have a large number of supporters, particularly among young people.[91] The Soviets were undoubtedly impressed by the ability of the Mojahedin, its effective organization and the support it received from a wide cross-section of the public, ranging from technocrats and bazaaris to intellectuals. They therefore seem to have concluded that they should not appear to be openly against it, since the Mojahedin might one day come to power or become part of a victorious coalition.

Generally the Soviet media were careful not to say anything that could be interpreted as being against Islam, but they also wished to make their position clear to the Soviet public. A Moscow radio panel described the clash between the IRP, 'which embodies the Shi'ite clergy', and forces representing 'the interests of various levels of the Iranian bourgeoisie'. *Pravda* commentator Demchenko said that 'the bourgeoisie blamed the clergy for destroying the economy, the culture, and Iran's traditional foreign links', and for 'subjugating' Iran to 'the canons of Islam, which have become obsolete in the twentieth century'.[92]

A discussion was again shown on Moscow television as to what should be stressed most: Iran's anti-Americanism and anti-Westernism in general (which should be favoured) or its Islamic fundamentalism (which had to be rejected). The first view was presented by Primakov, the second by Bovin. Primakov said that Bani-Sadr and those supporting him 'were oriented towards the United States . . . towards the West, towards Europe', whereas Islamic fundamentalists adopted 'patriotic' (i.e. anti-American) positions on a wide range of issues. Bovin admitted that this was generally so, but the struggle 'against the Western devil' appeared together with 'a struggle against the Eastern devil' (i.e. the Soviet Union). As to the future:

It appears that it is impossible to reorganize the country and rebuild its social life in accordance with the principles being proposed by the fundamentalists — in other words, to return to a way of life set down in the Koran nearly 1,500 years ago. I do not think this experiment will be successful.[93]

Soviet criticism of Iran's steps towards Islamization also appeared without comment in news reports, as, for example, the announcement, in early 1982, of an Iranian ban on skiing for women. The reason for the ban was said to be 'the "non-Islamic" nature of women's sports clothing'. There was also a report saying that separate sea-bathing for men and women had already been introduced in Iran.[94] For Soviet readers, communications of this nature described 'the reactionary nature' of Khomeynism more accurately than any direct criticism.

A NVOI broadcast in February 1982 said that the revolution in Iran was progressing very slowly, due in no small measure to those who 'raise obstacles' in its path and 'stamp every positive and revolutionary measure of the Islamic government with a communist label'. The broadcast praised the expulsion of the 'government of liberals' and the dismissal of Bani-Sadr and his associates. 'However, one cannot and should not overlook the fact that what has been accomplished is negligible compared to what could have been accomplished.' This was one of the most negative appraisals of the situation in Iran. The cause of such conditions was said to be not only plots and subversion by the enemies of the revolution, 'but also incompetence and, in many cases, the creation of difficulties by some superficial and monopolist officials'.[95]

Iran's instability during this period made the Soviets avoid comment on its internal situation. A brief summary of events between July and November 1981 reveals this instability all too clearly:

24 July 1981 — Mohammad Ali Raja'i elected President of Iran.
5 August 1981 — Hojjat al-Islam Mohammad Javad Bahonar, IRP Secretary-General, appointed by the Majlis as Prime Minister.
30 August 1981 — Raja'i and Bahonar killed by an explosion in the office of the Prime Minister.
31 August 1981 — Hojjat al-Islam Hoseyn Ali Khamene'i elected IRP Secretary-General.
2 September 1981 — Hojjat al-Islam Mohammad Reza Mahadvi-Kani nominated Prime Minister.
2 October 1981 — Hojjat al-Islam Hoseyn Ali Khamene'i elected President of Iran.
2 November 1981 — the Majlis approves a cabinet headed by the President's brother, Prime Minister Mir Hoseyn Musavi Khamene'i.

Unrest was rife in Iran: bombings, shootings, the killing of government officials and executions of opposition members. The Soviet media usually reported all these without comment, merely giving the numbers of those executed and saying that it was because of 'anti-government activities'. Sometimes they even branded the victims as 'terrorists'. The picture presented was one of the regime's inability to control the country in the face of widespread opposition. This line enabled the Soviets to refrain from committing themselves to particular positions concerning Iran's internal affairs, thus avoiding direct Soviet support of particular groups or personalities.

The opposition was strong enough to conduct a campaign of terror, but not to overthrow the regime. The Mojahedin-e-Khalq was weakened after sustaining heavy losses. Opposition groups were unable to unite and devoted much of their efforts to fighting each other. Those in exile abroad could not do much against the regime, and their importance was more in their potential as a possible alternative after the fall of the existing regime than as a direct and immediate threat to it.

In the ruling IRP groups, factions and personalities all struggled and fought one another. They could be variously described, depending on the observer's point of view, as progressive or conservative, pro-Soviet or anti-Soviet, moderate or extreme, radical, fundamentalist, revolutionary, and so on. But the struggle among them was more personal — for power and influence in the current situation, and even more for the times that would follow Khomeyni's death. All claimed to be true followers of the Khomeyni line, and that their opponents were the ones who had deviated. They all cited relevant quotations from the Holy Koran and statements by Imam Ali to prove they were right.

Those who continued to seek the true revolution called for radical reforms, such as land reform and the nationalization of the import trade. Conservatives, and those looking for a return to 'normality', spoke about respecting the right of ownership as recognized by Islamic law. Khomeyni used his personal influence and pressed for reforms, but those who opposed them succeeded in postponing their implementation.

The radicals advocated a certain degree of approach to the Soviet Union. They feared the return of American influence, considering that those who had opposed them were now anxious to seek a *rapprochement* with the USA. The radicals wanted to diminish the role of the oil sector in the economy, thus leading to fewer ties with the industrial world. The moderates wanted to increase oil exports, create a modern sector and strengthen industry. This situation posed a dilemma for the Soviets. Their aid strengthened the state, but in doing so, automatically led to industrialization, modernization and stronger ties with the industrialized world. Thus, the greater the Soviet economic investments, the

the more they strengthened those forces in Iran which were politically closer to the Western world.

Ethnic Uprisings: to what Extent were they Supported by the Soviets?

The unstable situation in Iran made it easier for the Kurds to control about half of the Kurdish territory south of Tabriz. They ruled a few towns, almost all the countryside and the most important highways, while government forces controlled only the major Kurdish cities, such as Sanandaj and Kermanshah. Battles raged for a long time in the city of Mahabad, with the Iranian air force bombarding it countless times, killing or wounding hundreds of its Kurdish inhabitants. The number of Kurdish dead had risen to 10,000 between March 1979 and March 1981. Kurdish forces had accumulated sufficient arms to last them for several years, but they were short of ammunition, fuel, food and medical supplies.

There was extensive co-operation between the Democratic Party of Kordestan (DPK) and the Mojahedin and other forces opposing the Khomeyni regime. As for the Tudeh Party and the Fedayeen movement, the DPK leader Abd al-Rahman Qassemlou said:

> we will not co-operate with them . . . because the Tudeh Party supports the present regime. This party is constantly attacking us and supporting the authorities. As for the Fedayeen organization, it had sent groups to fight alongside us but then these groups later withdrew and rejoined the regime.

In reply to a question 'about your relationship with the Soviet Union', Qassemlou said his party sympathized with the Soviet Kurds 'but, in the final analysis, we are an Iranian party'.

> As far as we are concerned, the Soviets are our friends and we need their political support. I stress the word 'political'. I would like to point out that no government is helping us.
>   The Soviets take into consideration the actual forces present in the arena. Our party represents 80 per cent of the Iranian Kurds . . . As for the Tudeh Party, its influence is weak and limited.[96]

The Soviet media refrained from commenting on the Kurdish problem. Occasional news reports that the Kurds were fighting for autonomy showed that Soviet sympathies lay with them. For example, a July 1981 *Pravda* item said that in Kordestan, 'the armed struggle for autonomy in this region has not ended'. There were cases in which soldiers refused 'to carry out orders of the command regarding punitive operations'. Soldiers and officers who attempted 'to go over to the side of the Kurdish rebels' were executed.[97] A NVOI broadcast supported Kurdish demands and called for an end to the fight against them. It said:

> The problem of Kordestan . . . should be resolved by peaceful means and through recognition of the Kurds' ethnic rights . . . These people want to enjoy their indisputable national rights within the system of the Islamic Republic of Iran . . . Unfortunately . . . no practical, decisive and democratic measures have been taken to resolve the ethnic problem, including the settlement of the Kurdish problem.[98]

In the existing situation, the Soviets preferred to avoid committing themselves publicly on the Kurdish problem. They wished to leave all their options open on this matter. In dealing with the problem, the Soviets could not consider it entirely in the Iranian context since it existed also in Iraq in particular, and also in Turkey and other places.
In 1974 the Ba'th authorities in Iraq had established an autonomous Kurdish government which in fact did very little and had little power. The Iraqi Kurds continued to fight the Ba'thist regime, and succeeded in establishing control in areas in the mountains and in forcing the Iraqi authorities to keep large military forces in these areas. The two main Kurdish groups in Iraq were the left-wing Patriotic Union of Kurdistan (PUK) under Jellal Talibani, and the more conservative Democratic Party of Kurdistan (DPK) under two of Mustafa Barzani's sons, Idris and Mas'ud. Although there was no co-operation between them, they no longer fought one another. The PUK, working closely with the Kurds in revolt in Iran, operated in southern Kurdistan, centred on Sulaimaniyah. The DPK worked in the north near Rawanduz, co-operating with Syria. Here too the Soviets preferred not to have any public ties with the Kurds. However, such ties did exist between the Iraqi Communist Party and the PUK.[99]
The Soviets viewed uprisings of the Iranian Qashqa'i tribes less favourably, probably because they had no influence or ties with the Qashqa'i as they had with the Kurds. At the end of April 1982 *Izvestia* reported clashes between government forces and Qashqa'i near Firuzbad, in Fars province. The paper said that the Qashqa'i nomads were cultivating opium poppies in secret plantations and maintaining links

with organizations preparing an uprising against the regime in Iran.[100] A
Moscow radio broadcast to Iran spoke about Qashqa'i links with 'the
imperialist forces and the forces of reaction'. It said that 'the feudalist
hierarchy of the half-million strong Qashqa'i tribe have been imperialist
puppets for many years'. They had links with the German Nazis during
the Second World War, and with the British during Dr Mossadeq's rule
at the time of the Iranian-British oil company crisis, and were now
reportedly being used by the Americans.[101]

The Soviets took a constant interest in the problems of Iran's ethnic
groups, trying to maintain contact with their leaders and influence them.
The Soviets also made it known to Tehran that they might exploit the
ethnic problem and support the various groups opposing the central
authorities unless relations between the two countries improved. They
made it clear that they were able to influence the situation, whether
Iran continued to be a united state or was divided into separate ethnic
units.

Tudeh's Continued Support for Khomeyni; the Soviets Keep a Lower Profile in Support of the Party

The Tudeh Party was officially recognized but its activities were semi-
clandestine. It no longer had official offices. The Tehran headquarters
had been shut and since July 1980 were occupied by religious extrem-
ists. The party's daily newspaper *Mardom* had been closed in mid-1981.
Mardom, at the time when it was still tolerated by the regime, had had
a 60,000 print-run and figured among the four large dailies distributed
in the newspaper kiosks. The Tudeh press also included a monthly
periodical called *Donya* (World) and 20 other publications aimed at
women, secondary school students, university students, peasants,
workers, and so on. They were more widely accepted and read by the
intellectuals than by the masses. However, they did wield a certain influence even in religious circles, and some of the Tudeh concepts came
to be used even by the mullahs. For instance, the latter learned from
the Tudeh that the label 'liberal' meant 'reactionary'. Radio Tehran
broadcast courses in Marxist economics based on extracts from a work
published by Abolhossein Agahi, a member of the Tudeh Party. On
television, Soviet and Yugoslav films replaced the American westerns
shown during the Shah's regime. Tudeh members held top posts in Iran's
press, radio and television, the central bank, the national oil company
and in important ministries.

Relative to other groups, there had been few arrests and executions of Tudeh members, who tended to avoid protests and armed clashes. Its relatively small number of 'militants' kept a low profile and avoided provocations, and limited their protests at the closure of *Mardom*. When Tudeh's leader, Kianouri, was questioned about this, he said that even if the party were banned and its members persecuted, it would continue to defend the Khomeyni line, 'which consists of fighting imperialism and its local agents'.[102]

Three different attitudes to the Tudeh prevailed among the ruling classes:

(a) Those who refused to consider any party other than the IRP.
(b) Those who opposed the Tudeh but conceded that it had a role to play.
(c) Those who saw it as 'a major element'.[103]

The second view had prevailed during the first years of the Islamic Republic, but since late 1981 the first attitude had assumed the upper hand. Some people in the religious establishment were in favour of permitting the Tudeh legal activities, because they did not regard it as dangerous; it conducted no violent activities and could not compete with the leftist groups who were advocating terror.

Deputy Foreign Minister Ahmad 'Azizi, when asked about the regime's attitude to the Tudeh, said: 'We do not need the Tudeh, and Islam has nothing to do with Marxist ideology'. In an attack on the Mojahedin, he commented on the Tudeh: 'The Tudeh is different; it has never taken up arms against us, so why persecute it? It has no influence, and moreover the population hates it and the government distrusts it.'[104]

The Mojahedin-e-Khalq leader, Mas'ud Rajavi, explaining his organization's attitude to the Tudeh, said:

We exclude the communist party from the forces with which we co-operate since it is one of Khomeyni's agents and would not hesitate to divulge the names of our members to Khomeyni's repressive organs so that they might arrest and execute them.[105]

The existing Tudeh policy was not unanimously accepted by its cadres and members. The party in fact consisted of three main groups, each of which held a different position. Outwardly they maintained an appearance of unity, but those who did not accept the official line continued to call for changes in internal debates. The various trends were as follows:

(1) Those who supported the party line by backing Khomeyni. These included former exiles trained in the GDR and headed by the party leader Kianouri.

(2) Local underground cadres, unwilling to accept the leadership of former exiles who support Khomeyni. They called for underground work against the regime.

(3) Cadres who had lived a long time in Western countries and had turned 'Euro-communist'. These were against a close reliance on Moscow.[106]

Former exiles led the party and decided its official line, but the party apparatus consisted mainly of underground cadres who preferred to join the Mojahedin rather than Khomeyni, particularly since support for Khomeyni did not halt persecutions of party members. Party supporters consisted mainly of students (the closure of universities was therefore a blow to the party), oil industry workers, the lower ranks in the military, and ethnic minorities. The latter were strongly represented in the party. Tudeh strength was concentrated mainly in the cities and less in the rural areas which championed Khomeyni. The party had the support of intellectuals and the well-educated, but not of the common people.

The Tudeh, as a communist party, used Western concepts, proclaiming Western ideas of secularism and the separation between religion and state. They used terms like progress, socialism, nationalism, industrialization and modernization. Khomeynism, on the other hand, was a revolt against the acceptance of Western ideas and against intellectuals who tried to adapt themselves to Western culture. It called for a return to roots, and faith, and a rejection of all that came from the West, including communism. In this there was a basic difference between the Tudeh and Khomeynism. The Tudeh therefore appealed more to Westernized intellectuals and less to the masses who followed traditional life and concepts.

The party's problem was how to find a middle road between accepting the internal socio-economic policy of the Khomeyni regime, and upholding Soviet positions on international affairs. It even tried to adjust itself to accept the 'neither East nor West' slogan, which it interpreted as aiming towards self-sufficiency and independence while not excluding co-operation with the socialist countries. The prevailing party concern was simply to ensure its legal existence. It tried to find allies wherever possible, particularly among the religious establishment, intending to influence them to adopt an 'anti-imperialist' policy while co-operating with the Soviet Union.

The party had no illusions. It knew that sooner or later it would be suppressed and would have to go underground, and it prepared itself for this. In July 1982 the Tudeh weekly *Ittihad-e-Mardom* (People's Unity) was banned.[107] An appeal by the Tudeh Party to the Iranian authorities, published in July 1982, said that 'the party has been practically deprived of all possibilities for political work'. Tudeh members were intimidated and thrown into prison, 'only on the charge of being committed to the programme and policy of the party'. The petition called for an end to this situation.[108]

This appeal was published in East Germany but not in the Soviet Union, where the Soviets now played down their support of the Tudeh. Indeed, from 1981 the Soviet media, which had often referred to the party during the first two years of the Islamic Republic, scarcely mentioned it. The Soviets wanted to give the impression that they were not interfering in Iran's internal affairs, and they did not want to be too closely identified with the Tudeh. On the other hand, they relied a great deal on the Tudeh in case a situation should arise which was similar to that in Afghanistan — a civil war or an opportunity of some other kind in which the Tudeh might be helpful.

Notes

1. Eric Rouleau, *Le Monde*, 6 January 1981; Giancesare Flesca, *L'Espresso* (Rome), 26 October 1980.

2. Baghdad Domestic Service, 17 September 1980. In FBIS, Middle East, 18 September 1980, pp. E1-E7. For Iraqi positions and aims, see: Claudia Wright, 'Behind Iraq's Bold Bid', *New York Times Magazine*, 26 October 1980, pp. 43ff.

3. TASS, 22 September 1980. In FBIS, USSR, 23 September 1980, p. H1.

4. *Ash-Sharq al-Awsat* (London), 30 September 1980.

5. Tehran Domestic Service, 24 September 1980.

6. TASS in English, 23 September 1980. In FBIS, USSR, 24 September 1980, p. H3.

7. Interview with Ambassador Mokri, *Ettela'at*, 2 December 1980.

8. AFP in English, 23 September 1980. In FBIS, USSR, 24 September 1980, p. H3.

9. *Pravda*, 1 October 1980.

10. Ibid., 9 October 1980.

11. PARS (Tehran) in English, 11 October 1980. In FBIS, South Asia, 14 October 1980, pp. I23-I24.

12. Interview given by Mohammed Hasan Pir-Hoseyni, adviser to President Bani-Sadr, to *An-Nahar al-Arabi wa ad-Duwali* (Paris), 13-19 October 1980.

13. Tehran Domestic Service, 5 October 1980. In FBIS, South Asia, 6 October 1980, pp. I8-I9.

14. TASS in English, 8 October 1980. In FBIS, USSR, 9 October 1980, p. H10.

15. Tehran Domestic Service, 7 October 1980. In FBIS, South Asia, 7 October 1980, pp. I7-I8.

16. Giancesare Flesca, 'Ayatollah Brezhnev', *L'Espresso*, 26 October 1980, pp. 54-6; KUNA (Kuwait), 27 October 1980. In FBIS, South Asia, 27 October 1980, pp. I17-I18; Tehran radio in Arabic, 12 October 1980. In ibid., 14 October 1980, p. I11.

17. Tehran Domestic Service, 2 December 1980. In FBIS, South Asia, 3 December 1980, p. I1.

18. Tehran Domestic Service, 15 February 1981. In FBIS, South Asia, 17 February 1981, pp. I7-I9.

19. Tehran Domestic Service, 19, 21 January 1981. In FBIS, South Asia, 21 January 1981, pp. I35-I40.

20. *Pravda*, 24 February 1981.

21. *Iran Libre* (Paris), 28 September 1981.

22. TASS in Russian, 28 December 1981. In FBIS, USSR, 31 December 1981, p. H7.

23. *Yanki* (Ankara), 22-28 February 1982, p. 19. See also *Newsweek*, 22 February 1982, p. 15.

24. *Iran Libre*, 28 September 1981.

25. *Time*, 23 November 1981, p. 19.

26. TASS in English, 20 November 1981. In BBC, SU/6888/A4/2, 24 November 1981; Moscow radio in Persian, 24 November 1981. In BBC, SU/6893/A4/6, 30 November 1981.

27. *Pravda*, 2 June 1982; *Izvestia*, 3 June 1982; Moscow radio in Persian to Iran, 2 June 1982. In BBC, SU/7044/A4/1, 5 June 1982.

28. Tehran Domestic Service, 7, 10 August 1982. In FBIS, South Asia, 9 August 1982, pp. I12-I13, and 11 August 1982, p. I2.

29. Voice of Iran in Persian (clandestine), 2 April 1982. In FBIS, South Asia, 6 April 1982, p. I13.

30. Moscow radio in Persian, 13 December 1980. In FBIS, USSR, 15 December 1980, pp. H2-H3.

31. Shanghai City Service in Mandarin, 6 January 1981. In FBIS, PRC, 8 January 1981, p. I1.

32. Tehran Domestic Service, 12 December 1980, citing the head of the Iranian delegation to the OPEC meeting. In FBIS, South Asia, 15 December 1980, p. I20.

33. Moscow radio in Persian to Iran, 15 February 1982. In FBIS, USSR, 17 February 1982, p. H2.

34. *Izvestia*, 15 December 1981.

35. TASS in English, 6 January 1982. In FBIS, USSR, 7 January 1982, p. H5.

36. *Izvestia*, 13 October 1981.

37. *Pravda*, 20 October, 1981.

38. Moscow radio in Persian to Iran, 8 December 1981. In FBIS, USSR, 9 December 1981, pp. H4-H5.

39. *Izvestia*, 17 February 1982.

40. Tehran Domestic Service, 16 February 1982. In BBC, ME/6957/A/3, 18 February 1982; AFP (Paris), 15 February 1982. In FBIS, USSR, 16 February 1982, pp. H5-H6.

41. AFP, 15 February 1982. In FBIS, USSR, 16 February 1982, pp. H5-H6.

42. A. Akhmedzyanov, 'Strengthening Independence', *Izvestia*, 11 February 1982.

43. Moscow radio in Persian to Iran, 15 March 1982. In FBIS, USSR, 22 March 1982, p. H9.

44. *The Economist*, 20 March 1982, pp. 56, 58.

45. Interview with the Director of Iran's Central Bank, Mohsen Nurbakhsh, in *Der Spiegel*, 5 April 1982, pp. 185-9.

46. AFP in English, 27 December 1980. In FBIS, South Asia, 29 December 1980, pp. I20-I21.

47. TASS in English, 27 December 1980. In FBIS, USSR, 29 December 1980, p. H1.

48. TASS in English, 28 December 1980. In FBIS, USSR, 29 December 1980, p. H1.

49. 'At the USSR Ministry of Foreign Affairs', *Pravda*, 13 January 1981.

50. *Pravda*, 25 March 1981.

51. Moscow Domestic Television in Russian, 25 July 1981. In FBIS, USSR, 30 July 1981, p. CC10.

52. P. Demchenko, 'USSR-Iran: In the Interests of Good Neighbourliness', *Pravda*, 9 March 1982.

53. Tehran Domestic Service, 25 July 1982. In FBIS, South Asia, 26 July 1982, p. I1.

54. *Komsomol'skaya Pravda*, 30 June 1982.

55. *Ettela'at*, 24 July 1982.

56. IRNA (Tehran), 2 September 1982. In FBIS, South Asia, 3 September 1982, pp. I1-I2, citing *Keyhan*, 2 September 1982.

57. National Voice of Iran (NVOI) radio (clandestine) to Iran, 20 April 1982.

58. Moscow radio in Arabic, 21 June 1982. In FBIS, USSR, 22 June 1982, p. H7.

59. Valentin Zorin, Moscow Domestic Television, 5 August 1982. In FBIS, USSR, 6 August 1982, p. H12.

60. Yevgeniy Primakov, Director of the Institute of Oriental Studies at the USSR Academy of Sciences, *Literaturnaya Gazeta*, 7 July 1982, p. 14; Moscow radio 'Peace and Progress' in Arabic, 29 July 1982. In BBC, SU/7095/A4/A, 4 August 1982.

61. *Financial Times*, 11 November 1980.

62. TASS in English, 11 November 1980. In FBIS, USSR, 12 November 1980, p. H3.

63. *Al-Mustaqbal* (Paris), 15 November 1980.

64. Eric Rouleau, *Le Monde*, 24 December 1980.

65. Moscow radio in Persian to Iran, 16 February 1981. In FBIS, USSR, 19 February 1981, p. H1.

66. *Pravda*, 5 June 1982.

67. *An-Nahar* (Beirut), 17 July 1982, cited diplomats in Beirut, saying that Iraq might annul its friendship treaty with the Soviet Union unless Moscow maintained its commitments in the light of Iran's invasion of Iraq.

68. Moscow Domestic Television, 17 July 1982. In FBIS, USSR, 19 July 1982, pp. H4-H5.

69. Moscow radio in Arabic, 17 July 1982. In FBIS, USSR, 19 July 1982, pp. H6-H7.

70. TASS in Russian and Moscow radio in Arabic, 6 August 1982. In BBC, SU/7100/A4/4, 10 August 1982.

71. NVOI in Persian to Iran, 20 February 1981. In FBIS, South Asia, 25 February 1981, pp. I17-I19.

72. *Pravda*, 8, 13 April, 28 July 1981; *Izvestia*, 13 April 1981; Moscow radio in Persian to Iran, 15 February, 27 April, 9, 16 May, 1981, 31 August 1982. In FBIS, USSR, 17 February 1981, p. H8; 27 April 1981, pp. D1-D2; 11 May 1981, p. H6; 18 May 1981, pp. H5-H6; 2 September 1982, pp. H9-H10.

73. Tehran Domestic Service, 10 November 1981. In FBIS, South Asia, 12 November 1981, pp. I1-I2.

74. Moscow radio in Persian to Iran, 17 November 1981. In FBIS, USSR, 19 November 1981, p. D1.

75. Moscow radio in Persian to Iran, 1 January 1982. In FBIS, USSR, 5 January 1982, p. D1.

76. P. Demchenko, 'Who Is Kindling Conflicts?', *Pravda*, 18 October 1980; *Krasnaya Zvezda*, 14 October 1980.

77. S. Kondrashov, *Izvestia*, 3 October 1980.

78. Moscow radio in Persian to Iran, 4 November 1980. In FBIS, USSR, 5 November 1980, pp. H1-H2; Moscow radio in Persian to Iran, 19 November 1980. In FBIS, USSR, 20 November 1980, pp. H1-H2.

79. Moscow radio in Persian to Iran, 1 July 1981. In FBIS, USSR, 10 July 1981, p. H1; Baku International Service in Azeri, 12 July 1981. In FBIS, USSR, 14 July 1981, p. H4.

80. Moscow World Service in English, 2 July 1981. In FBIS, USSR, 2 July 1981, p. H3.

81. V. Sisnev, 'Who Paid the Killers?', *Trud*, 2 September 1981; Moscow radio in Persian to Iran, 1, 10 September 1981. In BBC, SU/6819/A4/1 and FBIS, USSR, 14 September 1981, pp. H3-H4.

82. *Keyhan*, 11 November 1980.

83. Tehran radio in Arabic, 5 February 1981. In FBIS, South Asia, 6 February 1981, pp. I5-I6.

84. Hasan Nazih, opposition leader and former National Iranian Oil Company Chairman, was cited as having said that Ayatollah Beheshti was 'a Russian agent'. (*Le Figaro*, 4 October 1980.) Hasan Nazih denied having made such a statement: 'What I in fact said was that Ayatollah Beheshti is a very ambiguous person who cannot suppress his lust for power. He is prepared to co-operate with the Russians or the Americans or any other international power that will guarantee his assumption of power.' (*Al-Hawadith*, London, 24 October 1980, pp. 36-7.)

85. Tehran Domestic Service, 18 December 1980. In FBIS, South Asia, 19 December 1980, pp. I1-I3.

86. Moscow Domestic Television in Russian, 'Studio Nine' Programme, 27 December 1980. In FBIS, USSR, 5 January 1981, pp. CC7-CC9.

87. 'Khomeyni Decree', *Pravda*, 12 June 1981.

88. Y. Bochkaryov, 'The Ousting of the President', *New Times*, no. 27 (July 1981), p. 13.

89. Moscow radio in Persian to Iran, 29, 30 June 1981. In FBIS, USSR, 1 July 1981, pp. H2-H3.

90. *Pravda*, 30 July 1981.

91. Moscow Domestic Service, 18 March 1982. In FBIS, USSR, 23 March 1982, p. H1.

92. Moscow Domestic Service, 5 July 1981. In FBIS, USSR, 6 July 1981, pp. CC5-CC6.

93. Moscow Domestic Television, 25 July 1981. In FBIS, USSR, 30 July 1981, pp. CC10-CC11.

94. *Sovyetskaya Rossiya*, 21 January 1982.

95. NVOI, 27 February 1982. In FBIS, South Asia, 3 March 1982, pp. I16-I17.

96. Interview given by the Kurdish leader Qassemlou to *al-Hawadith*, 3 April 1981, pp. 26-9.

97. A. Filipov, *Pravda*, 15 July 1981.

98. NVOI, 4 February 1981. In FBIS, South Asia, 5 February 1981, pp. I15-I16.

99. A joint statement of the Iraqi Communist Party and the Patriotic Union of Kurdistan was broadcast by the clandestine Voice of the Iraqi Revolution on 7 July 1982. Cited in FBIS, Middle East, 9 July 1982, pp. E5-E7.

100. *Izvestia*, 27 April 1982.

101. Moscow radio in Persian to Iran, 29 April 1982. In FBIS, USSR, 30 April 1982, pp. H3-H4.

102. *Le Monde*, 24 July 1981.

103. *Le Matin*, 27 August 1981.

104. Ibid., 11 September 1981.

105. *Al-Majallah* (London), 5 September 1981.

106. Robert Rand, Radio Liberty Research (Munich), RL 361/81, 1 September 1981.

107. Tehran Domestic Service, 18 July 1982. In FBIS, South Asia, 20 July 1982, p. I9.

108. *Horizont* (East Berlin), no. 28 (1982), p. 19.

8 RIFTS WITH MOSCOW GROWING AGAIN: THE SOVIETS WAITING FOR OPTIONS

Changes in the Soviet Leadership: the Rise of Andropov

Leonid Ilich Brezhnev, General Secretary of the Central Committee of the Communist Party of the Soviet Union (CPSU) and Chairman of the Presidium of the USSR Supreme Soviet, died on 10 November 1982. He was succeeded by Yuriy Vladimirovich Andropov as CPSU Secretary-General. Born in 1914, Andropov served as Chairman of the Committee for State Security (KGB) from May 1967 to early 1982, when he became Secretary of the Central Committee of the CPSU. He has been a full member of the CPSU Politburo since 1973.

Andropov will undoubtedly try to replace Brezhnev's protégés with 'his own people'. On 22 November 1982 Geydar Ali Aliyev, First Secretary of the Communist Party of Azerbaijan, was elevated from candidate membership in the CPSU Politburo to full membership and was also made First Deputy Prime Minister of the USSR. Aliyev, of Shi'a Muslim origin, was, until 1969, head of the KGB in Soviet Azerbaijan, and since that time has been the 'boss' of that Soviet republic. He is a specialist on Iran, and probably the man in the Politburo responsible for USSR-Iranian relations.

Aliyev has expressed the wish that the Azerbaijanis, both in the USSR and in Iran, may be reunited. He is undoubtedly conscious of the dangers inherent in the spread of the Khomeyni brand of militant Islam to Soviet and Soviet-controlled areas, but he is probably also aware of the possibilities that might open up for the Soviets if it spreads to Western-oriented Muslim countries.

Bilateral Relations: Growing Suspicion and a Growing Rift

Although the Soviets are pleased by the downturn in Iran's relations with the USA, the 'Great Satan', Iran considers the USSR to be satanic too — a smaller devil but a devil none the less. It views both superpowers as enemies to be rejected. The slogans 'Death to America, Death to the USSR, Death to Israel' often go together and are repeated again and again.[1] Iran's leaders continue to proclaim 'neither East nor West', for which they are repeatedly attacked by the Soviet information media. The latter reiterate that Iran's leaders must distinguish between its friends (i.e. the Soviets) and its enemies (the Americans).

Iran's improving economic situation and the rise in its oil production have permitted it once again to welcome the foreign experts it shunned and expelled in the early days of the Islamic revolution. Foreign investments have revived and with them have come foreign specialists: West Germans and Italians from the West, as well as Yugoslavs, East Germans and Soviets from the East. More and more opportunities have arisen for the engagement of Soviet personnel. They continue to work in projects that were started earlier with their assistance.

'At present there are 1,600 [Soviet] experts in Iran,' said I.A. Kulev, First Deputy Chairman of the USSR State Committee for Foreign Economic Relations, in January 1983. 'The Soviet Union has repeatedly expressed its readiness to continue to expand its economic and technical co-operation with Iran' and specific proposals have been made. 'However . . . regretfully there are elements in Iran,' he continued, which 'obstinately insist on obstructing co-operation.'[2]

Transit trade passing through Soviet territory and linking Iran with European countries continues to operate. About one third of all Iran's imports are carried through Soviet territory.[3] In early 1983 the Julfa–Tabriz electric railroad, built with Soviet assistance, became operational. The railroad depot in Tabriz has been modernized and renovated with the aid of Soviet experts and with Soviet machinery and equipment. After the visit of an Iranian geological delegation to the USSR, Soviet mining equipment has been delivered to Iran.[4] The Soviets have asked for the renewal of operations of the Soviet–Iranian gas pipeline and of Iranian gas supplies to the Soviet Union, but Iran has ignored these requests. The Soviets are also interested in intensifying educational and cultural exchanges, but the Iranian authorities have held back. Each year the Soviet Union offers education subsidies and other benefits for 30 Iranian students to study in Soviet schools of higher education, but there have been almost no takers.[5] The mullahs are afraid to expose Iranian students to communist-atheist indoctrination.

Direct military co-operation is limited and Soviet offers to increase it have been ignored. The Soviets were ready to supply military equipment directly to Iran, but Iran has preferred to purchase it indirectly, through Syria, Libya and North Korea. The purchases include hundreds of tanks, heavy field guns and anti-aircraft guns, missiles and automatic rifles.

North Korea supplied about 40 per cent of the approximately $2 billion worth of weapons, ammunition and military equipment that Iran acquired in 1982. Most of this was Soviet-made, but some came from the PRC or from North Korea's own arms factories. The supplies included 150 Soviet-made T-62 tanks, 400 guns, 1,000 mortars, 600 anti-aircraft guns, machine-guns, smaller weapons and ammunition. Iran paid for them partly in cash and partly in oil. In order to pay for these procurements, Iran increased its oil production beyond the limits set by the Organization of Petroleum Exporting Countries (OPEC). It also cut its prices to below those set by OPEC, and established a guns-for-oil barter arrangement with North Korea and other countries.[6]

Reports have been published about limited military training co-operation between the USSR and Iran. They indicated that Soviet military experts had arrived in Iran, and that Iranian military personnel were being trained in Soviet military academies and schools. An agreement over such co-operation was reportedly signed on 20 May 1982,[7] but even if it was signed (or agreed in principle), it is very doubtful whether it was implemented.

Visits of Soviet officials to Iran have been rare and mostly at a low level. In April 1983 Vasiliy Safranchuk, head of the Middle East Department of the USSR Foreign Ministry, visited Tehran. Talks were held regarding mutual ties, the expansion of economic relations, and regional and international problems.[8]

In summer 1982 a Soviet vice-consul in Tehran and a senior KGB official, Vladimir Andreyevich Kuzichkin, defected to Britain. Kuzichkin disclosed that 'Soviet people', members of the Tudeh and others had infiltrated revolutionary organizations and the regime's bureaucracy. He indicated that the infiltrators were much more numerous than expected, which made the regime more alert in this respect. Soon afterwards Tudeh centres were raided and some Tudeh underground leaders were arrested.

On 28 April 1983 the new Iranian ambassador to the Soviet Union, Kia Tabataba'i presented his credentials in Moscow.[9] On 4 May, the day the Tudeh Party was banned (see pp. 142-4), 18 Soviet diplomats (of a total of about 70 stationed in Iran) were ordered to leave. The statement announcing the expulsion did not directly link the diplomats with the Tudeh, saying only that the diplomats had been 'accused of interfering with the internal affairs of the Islamic Republic through establishing contacts and taking advantage of treacherous and mercenary agents'.[10]

The Soviets tried to avoid arguing with Iranian officials about these steps (which were directed against them) and the Soviet media have generally avoided criticism of Iran's regime and policy. Such criticism has, however, frequently been voiced in broadcasts by the USSR-based

National Voice of Iran (NVOI) and indirectly by Moscow radio broadcasts in Persian to Iran. One such commentary dwelt on the war with Iraq, with the Soviets urging an end to the hostilities.

The Iran-Iraq War: the Soviets Call for an End to the Fighting

In September 1982 Iranian forces, having succeeded in ousting the Iraqis from Iranian territory, proceeded to invade Iraq, where they met strong resistance. In Iran itself, opinions were divided as to whether to continue to advance further into Iraq or to be satisfied with present achievements. The military and some of the conservative clergy advised a waiting policy, in order to reorganize the troops and let them rest. Khomeyni rejected this approach.[11] He saw in his mind's eye the vision of Islamic forces advancing as they had during the first glorious years of Islam, crushing the infidels, smashing enemies, and bringing the true faith everywhere. He also expected an uprising by Iraq's Shi'ites, but it never took place.

The Soviets now oppose the war even more strongly than they did earlier. An Iranian victory is not in their interest. Inside Iran, it would strengthen the clerical regime and make Soviet aid less essential. Such a victory could lead to the establishment of a pro-Iranian Islamic regime in Iraq which, from a Soviet point of view, would be worse than the present Ba'thist regime. The new regime would be more anti-communist, and anti-left, with a strong religious character; it would attempt to spread the Islamic revolution and thus cause instability. This would lead the Arabian peninsula–Persian Gulf states to seek American protection, thus damaging Soviet efforts to win wider acceptance in the Arab world. It might also inhibit the ongoing improvement in relations between the Soviet Union and Iraq, and hinder chances for improving them further.

On 1 October 1982 the USSR Foreign Minister Andrey Gromyko said in his address to the UN General Assembly:

> For almost two years now bloody hostilities have been going on between Iran and Iraq. This is a senseless war . . . The fire should be put out before it spreads further. The more reasonable thing to do would probably be for Iran and Iraq to put aside arms . . . to settle their differences at the negotiating table. The Soviet Union has invariably come out in favour of putting an end to the war between the two states with which our country has maintained traditional ties and is doing all in its power to bring that about.[12]

Gromyko was trying to be even-handed and spoke about the Soviets' 'traditional ties' with both Iran and Iraq. The Soviet position, however, was closer to that of Iraq, which wanted to end the war, while Iran had decided to continue. According to a Soviet commentator:

> As the conflict dragged on, Baghdad reached a growing understanding of the senselessness of continuing attempts to resolve its dispute with Tehran by military means . . . Iraq came out in favour of seeking ways to a settlement by peaceful means using mediation missions . . . the Iranian leadership rejects the peace proposals put forward by mediation missions. Iran does not agree to a cease-fire and continues offensive operations . . . Thus the senseless bloodshed goes on . . .
>
> As for the Soviet Union, from the very beginning of the conflict it has advocated the speediest end to the bloodshed, warning that it only benefits the forces of imperialism.[13]

On 23 April 1983 another Soviet comment, by Leonid M. Zamyatin, Chief of the International Information Department of the CPSU Central Committee, said, *inter alia*:

> Our position — like the position of many states in this region — is to force Iran and Iraq to sit down at the conference table and have them set aside their antagonistic sentiments and attempt to solve this issue through peaceful means . . . So far such talks have yielded no results.[14]

Iraq: a Soviet Renewal of Direct Arms Supplies and a Relative Improvement in Relations

USSR-Iraqi relations have now begun to improve somewhat. Soviet arms supplies have been resumed in accordance with earlier agreements. In the spring and summer of 1982 a new arms deal appears to have been signed. Considerations influencing the Soviets in their decision were:

(1) Iran had not moved closer to the Soviet Union.
(2) Iraq might turn to the West.
(3) The Iraqis had succeeded in defending themselves against an Iranian invasion. Saddam Husayn had remained in power and would continue to do so in the near future.
(4) Soviet weapons had performed poorly in Lebanon and the Soviets

wished to show that it was not the weapons which had caused the
failures there. They wanted another chance to demonstrate that
Soviet equipment is of high quality and that the Soviets do not abandon their friends.

In December 1982 Saddam Husayn announced that the Soviet Union
had resumed arms sales to Iraq, noting that prepaid contracts had been
signed with the Soviet Union before the war so that it was only natural
for the Soviets to honour them. Soviet military supplies appeared to
include MiG-25 planes, T-72 tanks and SAM-8 missiles. There were
also reportedly about 1,000 to 1,200 Soviet advisers and technicians in
Iraq.[15]

An Arab League delegation headed by Jordan's King Husayn visited
Moscow from 2 to 4 December 1982 to explain the Arab summit's
September 1982 proposal for solving the Arab–Israeli conflict.[16] In his
meetings with Andropov and other Soviet leaders, the King utilized the
opportunity to discuss the Iran–Iraq war and to urge the Soviets to take
a clear stand.

King Husayn's talks paved the way for a high-level Iraqi delegation
to visit the USSR at the beginning of 1983. It was headed by Deputy
Prime Minister Taha Yasin Ramadan and included Deputy Prime Minister
Tariq 'Aziz and Chief of Staff Abd al-Jabbar Shanshal. The delegation
concluded an agreement on supplies of Soviet military equipment that
soon began to arrive in Iraq. With it came more Soviet experts, increasing the number of those already there.[17]

This is a reversal of previous Soviet policy regarding the Iran–Iraq
war. Under Brezhnev, Soviet policy was even-handed, supplying arms
already under contract. All this has changed under Andropov, who has
decided to pursue a more active policy in the region, including turning
closer to Iraq.

The Soviet *rapprochement* with Iraq's Ba'thist regime has been influenced by the ineffectiveness of the Iraqi opposition to the Ba'th. The
Iraqi Communist Party (ICP) tried to co-operate with local Shi'ite organizations but failed. The Iranian invasion prevented the opposition groups
in Iraq — Kurds, communists, lay-Shi'ites, dissatisfied military — from
doing anything that could be construed as stabbing their country in the
back. Saddam Husayn gained confidence from the ICP's weakness and
in July 1982 he ordered the release of about 280 communist prisoners.
This contributed considerably to an improvement in the atmosphere
between the Soviet Union and Iraq. Most of the released communists
were said to have been reinstated in their government positions.[18]

Interestingly enough, this relative improvement in Iraq's relations with the Soviet Union has been accompanied by a parallel upswing — in both the economic and the political spheres — in Iraq's relations with the USA. There has been no official re-establishment of diplomatic relations, but the American interests section in the Belgian embassy in Baghdad performs almost all the functions of a fully operating embassy. Trade between the two countries has increased and American business-men visit Iraq. The USA has done nothing to prevent American arms from reaching Iraq — it has not, for instance, made any attempt to dis-courage Jordan or Egypt from providing Iraq with weapons, or Saudi Arabia and the Gulf states from giving it an estimated $30 billion in aid since the start of the war.

Saddam Husayn has been in favour of moving closer to the USA, but not too close, thus playing the Americans and the Soviets off against each other. In this way, he hopes to demonstrate to the Soviets that he has other policy options and that their future actions will determine whether he uses them or not.

The war has also brought Iraq closer to the conservative pro-Western Arab states, and away from the radical Steadfastness and Confrontation Front of Syria, Libya, Algeria, the PDRY and the PLO. This is due in no small measure to the support shown for Iran by countries of the Front, while Iraq has received arms, money and political support from Saudi Arabia, the Gulf states, Jordan, Egypt, Sudan and North Yemen. Iraq's international posture has gradually shifted from political and eco-nomic alignment with the Soviet Union to a more even-handed approach to the superpowers, both in international and regional affairs.[19]

Iranian Attempts to Destabilize the Gulf Region — in Line with Soviet Interests

Iranian attempts to export the Islamic revolution and destabilize the Gulf region are contrary to the interests of the Western powers, which would like to preserve the *status quo* there. The Soviets would be glad to see this oil-rich region, so vital to the Western economy, plunged into chaos, through no action of their own. Any direct move by them, on the other hand, could lead to American intervention, or at least to US reactions in other places. The Soviets would prefer a local power to bring about the unrest, with the USA seemingly powerless to combat it.

Iranian advances in the war with Iraq have greatly influenced the policy of the Gulf states. American offers of joint military manoeuvres have gone unanswered by all but Oman. They are trying to avoid overt ties with the USA or even with local US-oriented states such as Egypt. Some Gulf rulers believe that they can successfully co-exist with revolutionary Iran, and have tried to adapt themselves to living with it. So long as they refrain from open co-operation with the USA, Soviet interests are well served. Although American military planners hope to be able to use bases in Saudi Arabia and Oman in the event of a Soviet invasion of Iran, it is by no means certain that they would be able to do so since there is considerable local hesitation in allowing the bases to be handed over to them in time of crisis.

Kuwait has refused any consultations on security policy with the USA, and has helped Iraq in the war by acting as a supply line through which military supplies are delivered. Iran has threatened to regard Kuwait, or any other Gulf country which helps Iraq, as a hostile party against which it might take retaliatory action. Saudi Arabia, struck by Iran's Islamic revolution and Iraq's relative inter-Arab moderation, has developed a measure of tactical alliance with Iraq while still trying to maintain a working relationship with Iran. But this is not so easy — Iran's revolutionary radicals reject Saudi overtures, preferring to destabilize the situation in Saudi Arabia, which they consider a reactionary state. They also believe that its regime will be short-lived.

Similarly, the Soviets do not believe that the present Gulf regimes will last long, and hope for revolutionary upheavals and changes. They are therefore unhappy at the establishment of the Gulf Co-operation Council (GCC), which might serve as a framework for the Gulf countries to help those of their members who might be endangered by internal unrest or attempts at insurrection. Another reason for Soviet opposition to the GCC is their suspicion that it serves as the nucleus for a Western-sponsored military alliance, a sort of mini-version of NATO. Kuwait's policy within the Council serves Soviet interests, since it has urged neutrality in international affairs, avoiding close relations with the USA. The Council has turned into a loose grouping, more on the pattern of the European Economic Community (EEC) than of NATO. But while Kuwait tries to retain Soviet goodwill and appreciation, the Soviets see its stance as weak, and they encourage those that wish to supplant its existing regime.[20]

The course of the third GCC summit held in Bahrain from 9 to 11 November 1982 led the Soviets to believe that the Council was in fact weak and ineffective, a far cry from their earlier opinion. The GCC has been unable to forge a common stand regarding the Iranian challenge. Some member states view it as a severe threat, while others maintain that a negative attitude towards Iran would undermine their security.

Among the issues facing the GCC and splitting it are the members' differing perceptions of the following events:

(1) The Iran–Iraq war.
(2) The attempted coup in Bahrain in December 1981, which Iran supported and perhaps even staged.
(3) The implications of the November 1979 revolt at the Grand Mosque in Mecca.
(4) The clashes between Iranian pilgrims and Saudi security forces in Medina.
(5) The ferment in OPEC concerning prices and production quotas.

The six GCC members have failed to reach any agreement on shoring up their own defence, security and economic future, and a defence pact has been delayed because of differences over relations with the super-powers. Kuwait has urged neutrality, while Oman has refused to break its agreement on bases with the USA. The swing in Iran's favour in the war prompted certain states to initiate a *rapprochement* with it, so the GCC summit communiqué did not even condemn the Iranian invasion of Iraq.[21]

The weakness of the GCC is well suited to Soviet policy in the area. Even since the GCC's establishment, the Soviets had sought ways to weaken it and prevent closer integration of its members. Now the members have achieved this all on their own, with no need for Soviet intervention for which the USSR could later be blamed.

Afghanistan: Will the Soviets Remain and Encircle Iran?

The Soviet intervention in Afghanistan continues to affect adversely Soviet relations with Iran, which supports the Muslim revolt against the Soviets and the Soviet-installed regime. An Iranian Foreign Ministry statement of 26 December 1982 on the situation in Afghanistan sharply attacked the Soviet Union. It spoke of 'the savage behaviour of the occupying forces and their internal mercenaries', and named the Soviets an 'oppressive power'. It called for an immediate and un-conditional withdrawal of Soviet forces, the return of Afghan refugees and 'the right of the Muslim people of Afghanistan to determine their destiny'.[22]

The next day, 27 December, crowds of protesters gathered at the

Soviet embassy in Tehran. TASS described the demonstration as organized 'with the obvious connivance of the Iranian authorities', and a Soviet protest was lodged.[23] A few days later the Iranian Ministry of Islamic Guidance withdrew the accreditation of the TASS correspondent in Tehran and refused to accept a successor. This has led, for the time being, to the closure of the Tehran TASS office.

In Afghanistan, meanwhile, facts were being established on the ground, reflecting the Soviet intention to remain. Insurgents reported that by November 1982 the Soviet Union had nearly completed six airfields in southern Afghanistan, putting the Gulf within range of Soviet planes. The reports also disclosed that in summer 1982 the Soviets had begun building an airbase in Shindand, western Afghanistan, whereas the other bases had been built mostly between Shindand and Kandahar in the south. This latter location is the site of a Soviet base where they were said to have enlarged the storage facilities.

The Soviet military intervention in Afghanistan in 1979 and its aftermath were purported to have been undertaken in order to ensure the survival of the existing Afghan regime. The Soviets have constantly claimed that their forces will withdraw as soon as the threat ends. The construction of airfields, however, indicates that they intend to maintain a long-term military presence, turning Afghanistan into a Soviet forward military base aimed at the Persian Gulf and the Indian Ocean, thus encircling Iran even further.[24]

Internal Struggles in Iran: a Turn to the Right; Fewer Chances for the Soviets

Soviet policy regarding revolutionary Iran is greatly influenced by the waxing and waning of the power of the mullahs. When the regime appears strong, with good prospects of remaining in power, the Soviets increase their efforts to co-operate with it. When it shows signs of weakness and dissension at the top, the Soviets change their tune, according to what they feel will be the scenario after Khomeyni has gone.

Iran's gains in the Gulf war have made its regime more popular. The opposition has become much weaker and its calls for upheaval have been much less heeded. The bazaar — which first tended to support Khomeyni, but later turned to Bani-Sadr and the Mojahedin-e-Khalq — has now gone back to supporting the regime, or at least to accepting it and co-operating with it. The people have concluded that they have no choice since the present regime gives every indication that it will be around for a long time. However, the main support for the regime comes from the lower classes, such as the south Tehran lumpen proletariat. One of the main problems faced by those in power is how to bridge the gap between the expectations of the poor and underprivileged, on whose support they depend so much, and their actual miserable situation, which has not improved much since the fall of the Shah. Khomeyni consoles them by pointing out that the once rich and powerful are now oppressed and suffering, rather than by fulfilling their needs and expectations.

Many of the rich have managed to adapt themselves to the situation; they have been joined by a new class of privileged people who have discovered the advantages of this world and wish to enjoy them. The common people find it easier to adapt to the mullahs' rule than to fight it, and so opposition to the regime has weakened. The dissenters can disseminate propaganda and make trouble by assassinating officials and mullahs, but they have not been able to overthrow the regime. This would be possible only if they had allies inside the regime or if a split developed among its supporters.

At one time the opposition had great hopes of the military, believing that at least some of the commanding officers would join them if an opportunity arose. The radicals around Khomeyni advocated purging the military command and absorbing the army into the Revolutionary Guards. This could perhaps have been achieved in peace-time, but during the war the officers have emerged with an enhanced reputation for having saved Iran from foreign invasion; and the more protracted the fighting, the stronger their position may become. When the war ends, however, the radicals will probably try to break the power of the military, who may take pre-emptive action.

Could an Iranian Bonaparte arise? The mullahs have long feared such a possibility and have done their utmost to prevent it. A new generation of commanders has replaced the old generals and colonels and, for the time being, they are obedient to the regime and co-operate with the Revolutionary Guards. They are now less of a threat to the regime than they might have been during the earlier stages of the revolution.

While in Khomeyni's lifetime unity among the leaders of the regime seems to prevail, at least outwardly, this situation could change after his departure. A split may develop between the more radical clergy, and those who are considered moderate traditionalist-conservative. This might lead to a civil war, with the Soviets deciding to intervene. They are in fact ready for such an eventuality and have reportedly concentrated military forces close to the Iranian border. A USA-USSR proxy war could then develop, assuming much larger proportions than the situation that has developed in Afghanistan.

A power struggle has now developed, both for the present and over the succession to Khomeyni. There is a radical group, led by President Khamene'i and his brother Prime Minister Musavi, which includes the students and mullahs who seized the American hostages. They initially maintained ties with the Tudeh and the Soviets but later lost influence and power. Their loss strengthened the position of the Majlis speaker Rafsanjani, a radical who favours nationalization and land reform. Rafsanjani, however, has begun to prepare himself for leadership after Khomeyni, and for this he needs the support of the right and the conservatives. He already has the backing of a group led by Sadiq Khalkhali, the regime's executioner. Another group led by Hojjat al-Islam Musavi Ardabili, President of the High Judicial Council, claims to unite the different streams and sees itself as a centrist wing.[25]

The Islamic revolutionaries who enjoy the support of Khomeyni are opposed by the strictly fundamentalist-conservative Hojjatis (Hojjatiha). In the Majlis some 50 deputies are considered to belong to them. They are not a majority, but as a well co-ordinated group they have great influence. They are opposed to the tendency of the more radical clergy to link the Islamic revolution with a social one. In the Majlis they had opposed both the nationalization of foreign trade and land reform; and after these laws had been accepted by the Majlis, the Hojjatis acted to minimize their implementation. They are not enthusiastic about continuing the war against Iraq, as Khomeyni urges so strongly. They lay less stress on spreading the Islamic revolution in the Muslim world and more on strengthening the Islamic regime in Iran itself. They do not see Khomeyni as 'the Imam', reserving this term for the long-awaited Mahdi, the Twelfth Imam, who, according to Shi'ite tradition, disappeared in AD 879, is in hiding, and will return some day. When these conservative fundamentalists shout 'The Imam will come,' they mean 'the true Twelfth Imam' and not Khomeyni. The Hojjatis call for a holy war against both communist atheists in the Soviet Union and Afghanistan, and the Tudeh Party in Iran.

The Soviet media have generally refrained from attacking or praising particular entities. In the early stages of the Islamic revolution they would criticize particular groups or personalities, but later they found that some of those censured became leading personalities or were relatively more friendly to the Soviets than others. This does not apply to the Hojjatiha, who are sharply attacked by the Soviet media and accused of serving American interests.

A comment in the *New Times* of January 1983 attacked the Hoj-jatiha, 'the conservative wing of the clergy and its secular supporters'. It said that 'the clerical right' was in favour of continuing the war with Iraq, wanted to outlaw the Tudeh Party, and spread 'anti-Soviet insinua-tions'. In the view of the commentator:

> It is obvious that the policy of the conservative clergy is bound to disenchant, to put it mildly, those who once believed that the over-throw of the Shah would open practical opportunities for solving the problems facing the country . . . it is bound to disappoint . . . The Iranian revolution finds itself at a crucial and dangerous cross-roads.[26]

The strengthening of the right is seen by the Soviets as part of a tendency to lean more towards the West. 'The mullahs like to curse the West in public but to have ties with them in private,' said a former Iranian diplomat.[27] Meanwhile, the Soviets prefer to wait quietly and see who will emerge victorious.

The Tudeh: Banned and Persecuted

The Tudeh Party initially supported Khomeyni and went along with the steps he had taken since coming to power, even in cases which con-flicted with Tudeh principles. For a long time the regime saw no reason to fight the Tudeh, which had remained loyal, even providing the regime with information about its opponents. Khomeyni's policy was, how-ever, to rid himself of all the forces that had supported him during the initial stages of the Islamic revolution, eliminating all allies and sup-porters once they had played the roles expected of them. At first, the Tudeh Party was left alone and allowed freedom of activity. Not long afterwards, however, its turn came too. The party's property, offices and publications were confiscated and party cadres were arrested. The Tudeh went underground, but still did not join the opponents of the regime.[28]

The Tudeh leader Nuraddin Kianuri was arrested by Islamic Revolu-tionary Guards on 6 February 1983, together with 30 other Tudeh members (including 7 prominent party leaders). They were accused of spying for the Soviet KGB and forging passports and birth certificates to cover their real identity.[29] Soviet reactions were restrained. *Pravda* reported the arrests from Paris, quoting 'foreign information agencies' and refraining from further comment.[30] The Soviet Azerbaijan-based NVOI, however, gave the event wide coverage, criticizing the 'reactionary clergy' but not Khomeyni.[31] Two weeks elapsed before *Pravda* published an editorial comment on the arrests.

The accusations against Tudeh leaders, *Pravda* said, were of a 'groundless and slanderous nature'. The Tudeh Party 'supported the democratic and anti-imperialist principles of the Iranian revolution.' But today:

Reactionary conservative circles have become active in Iran . . . These groupings appear to be gaining strength . . . the social reforms . . . have come to a standstill . . . Now a blow is being struck at the Tudeh . . . The reactionary circles are undermining Soviet–Iranian relations . . .

. . . the Soviet Union does not seek any special rights or advantages for itself in Iran, has no territorial claims on Iran, is not interfering in its internal affairs . . . As for the anti-Soviet campaign that has been launched in Tehran, it only darkens relations between our countries and peoples, harming, above all, the interests of Iran itself.[32]

The *Pravda* article was broadcast to Iran during the following few days, but after that Soviet media avoided further reference to it. Tudeh Party statements were reported in NVOI broadcasts and in international communist publications but not in the Soviet media.[33]

In an interview on Tehran television on 30 April 1983 Kianuri confessed to espionage, treachery and deceit. He admitted that the Tudeh had been guilty of six errors: dependence on the Soviet Union and engaging in espionage on its behalf; illegally retaining secret arms caches; maintaining a secret political organization; establishing a secret group of officers who became an agency for collecting information for dispatch to the USSR; infiltrating the administration; and arranging illegal departures from the country. Perhaps the confessions of Kianuri and other Tudeh leaders were made because they had been shown evidence which they could not deny. But they might no less be the result of 'hellish means of torture', as was charged in a NVOI broadcast.[34]

On 4 May 1983 Chief Prosecutor Hojjat al-Islam Musavi-Tabrizi announced that the Tudeh Party was to be dissolved and banned. During the next few days more Tudeh members were arrested and others were required to register. Clandestine weapons stores were seized. A commentary over Tehran radio on 5 May said, *inter alia*:

The mercenary leaders of that party pretended that they were independent of the Soviet Union . . . they tried . . . to infiltrate society
. . . portrayed themselves as much as possible as supporters of the
revolution and the Islamic Republic. Under the pretext of fighting
against America . . . they placed themselves in the midst of God-
seeking revolutionaries of our country. At the same time, they were
laying the foundations of a long term plan so that through a creeping
coup d'état they could place their infiltrating agents in various
national organizations, and so that at the appropriate time they
could, according to their vain imaginings, control the levers of power
and drag the country in the direction they wished.[35]

The banning of the Tudeh was mostly for internal reasons, but it was
no less a function of Iran's relations with the Soviet Union. It was a
reaction to the renewed Soviet arms supplies to Iraq and Soviet intervention in Afghanistan. This was Iran's way of trying to 'punish' the
Soviet Union – it was a 'declaration of independence' from the USSR,
just as the seizure of American hostages was a similar declaration to the
United States.

The Kurds: A Policy Problem for Moscow

Fighting in Iranian Kordestan between the regime and the Kurds in revolt has continued with no settlement in sight. Khomeyni is opposed
to any compromise, because, if achieved, it might lead to a chain reaction of demands by other ethnic groups. The Soviet media have so far
avoided any comment on the Kurds and their struggle. A NVOI broadcast in January 1983 gave a clear view of the Soviet position on this
problem, saying, *inter alia*:

A specific wing of responsible individuals, whether in government
and security positions or in institutions, pursued an anti-Kurdish
policy . . . External elements and dependent groups in Kordestan
also fanned war and fratricide . . .
It should be said that without doubt an ethnic problem exists in
our country and it should not and cannot be ignored . . . Various
kinds of discriminatory policies have been pursued in Kordestan in
the past . . . The policy of . . . handing over self-rule or administrative
and cultural autonomy to the Kurdish people must be pursued . . .
The culture, religion, traditions, customs and language of the Kurdish

people must be respected . . . The Kurdish people must be given the permission and possibility to enjoy their indisputable and national rights within the framework of the Islamic Republic of Iran.[36]

Both the authorities and Kurdish 'extreme elements' were blamed here for the continuation of the fighting. But the main point was the call to meet Kurdish demands for self-rule or autonomy. It appears that the proximity of the Kurdish areas to the Soviet border makes it easy to maintain contact and probably provide some Soviet aid. The Soviets may not wish to lose Kurdish goodwill or completely break long-standing ties that have been so carefully developed. They wish to keep all their options open in order to be able to exploit the situation if it serves their interests or fits their objectives.[37]

Aims, Interests, Trends and Prospects

A revolution in Persia could become 'the key to a revolution in the whole East'. Just as Egypt and the Suez Canal were the key to British domination of the East, Persia is 'the "Suez Canal" of the revolution'. By 'turning the political centre of gravity of the revolution to Persia, the whole strategic value of the Suez Canal was lost'.[38]

Although these words were uttered by a Soviet writer in 1918 during the first days of the Soviet regime, they seem to be valid even today. Historically and geopolitically Iran was and has remained the key country in the region. In the East–West competition over Iran, the Soviet Union has the advantage of being a close neighbour. Iran has a 1,500 mile-long border with the Soviet Union. The shortest route to the open sea from the Soviet Central Asian and Transcaucasian republics passes through Iran. This gives the Soviets superiority both in communications and in the ability to provide military supplies. They can infiltrate their people, get to know the country and what is going on there. But there is also a large Muslim population in the Soviet Union, next door to Iran, which could be influenced by Iran's Islamic revival. The presence in Iran of forces of a great power hostile to the USSR could constitute a security threat to major Soviet areas and the Soviets are anxious to prevent such a situation.

Soviet aims in relation to Iran might be defined as follows:

Minimum:
(1) Working relations which are as good and correct as possible, main-

taining at least the bilateral ties that existed during the period of the
Shah's reign.

(2) The continuation of strained relations between Iran and the USA,
preventing an American 'comeback' in Iran.

Desired:

(1) The improvement of relations and increased influence.

(2) A regime friendly to the USSR, which maintains a neutralist foreign policy, but favours the Soviets.

(3) The maintenance of close ties with the USSR but strained ones
with the Western world.

(4) The co-ordination of foreign policy with the USSR, or at least,
taking Soviet desires and viewpoints into consideration.

The Soviets would undoubtedly wish for a Tehran government oriented toward them, but they can do little to bring this about as long as
the present situation continues. The lesson of Afghanistan has taught
them not to intervene if the time is not ripe. They see no chances for
success in a premature socialist revolution in Iran.

Will the Soviets intervene in Iran? The 24 Soviet divisions reported
to be based in the Caucasus region are able to reach the Gulf coast so
quickly that they could seize Iranian oilfields and threaten Saudi Arabia
and the other Gulf states without encountering any serious Iranian resistance, and even before other forces could arrive in the arena.

All this is possible, but in reality things are not quite as simple. Only
some of these reported 24 Soviet divisions are combat-ready, not all of
them are fighting units and only some are fully manned. Bringing them
up to strength might alert the Americans and others who would then
take suitable counter-action. From the Soviet border in the Transcaucasus region it is more than 1,200 miles to the Gulf of Oman, about
1,000 miles to the Strait of Hormuz and about 600 miles to the north
of the Gulf, and there are only a few roads in Iran over which Soviet
forces would be able to move. They would have to pass the Zagros
mountains where, apart from blocking roads, the Iranians would be
able to resist them, or at least slow their advance. The Iranians or the
Americans could bomb or mine these few passable roads, putting the
Soviets in an even more difficult position than that they faced in
Afghanistan;[39] this might make them think things over much more
carefully before taking any far-reaching decisions. Their behaviour towards Iran will depend to a considerable extent on the reactions they
expect not only from Iran, but from the entire region, the USA and the
Western world. The more resolute the expected reaction, the greater

will be their hesitation to intervene.

Such Soviet hesitation was evident in 1953 when the Tudeh Party came close to seizing power. At that time, the Tudeh held Tehran for a day or two, but the leadership hesitated, waiting for instructions from Moscow (which never arrived), and they lost their chance. In the 1980s the Soviets might be less hesitant, but they will only intervene if they feel sure of immediate success. Another condition is that they themselves should not be involved for long. They need assurance that there will be no real resistance and that the USA will not intervene except to protest.

As things stand at present, the Soviets are keeping all their options open. Their policy with regard to Iran is to watch and wait, not committing themselves to particular positions, while at the same time keeping a close eye on the outcome of internal struggles. This allows them greater flexibility of response as the situation develops.

Notes

1. Tehran radio, 3 January 1983. In FBIS, South Asia, 4 January 1983, pp. I5-I6.

2. Moscow radio in Persian to Iran, 6 January 1983. In FBIS, USSR, 10 January 1983, pp. H3-H4.

3. Moscow radio in Persian to Iran, 28 April 1983. In FBIS, USSR, 3 May 1983, p. H5.

4. Moscow radio in Persian to Iran, 31 January, 7 and 15 February 1983. In FBIS, USSR, 2 February 1983, pp. H3-H4; 9 February 1983, pp. H11-H12; 25 February 1983, p. H7.

5. Moscow radio in Persian to Iran, 4 December 1982. In FBIS, USSR, 9 December 1982, pp. H4-H5.

6. Richard Halloran, *International Herald Tribune*, 20 December 1982 (*New York Times*).

7. On 4 December 1982 the Paris-based Iranian opposition publication *Iran-e Azad* published the purported text of a secret military training agreement between Iran and the Soviet Union. Parts of it were published in the Paris magazine *L'Express*, 3 December 1982, p. 65.

8. Islamic Republic News Agency (IRNA), 8 April 1983. In FBIS, USSR, 11 April 1983, p. H1.

A report in the Kuwaiti *Al-Hadaf* said that Safranchuk presented a strongly worded memorandum calling for an end to the war with Iraq, and said that USSR-North Korean deliberations were underway to convince the latter to suspend its arms supplies to Iran. (Iraqi News Agency, 8 April 1983. In FBIS, USSR, 8 April 1983, p. H3.) The report of the memorandum was probably spread by Iraq as part of its psychological warfare, but it also indicates one of the indirect means of pressure that the Soviet Union can exert on Iran.

9. Moscow radio in Persian to Iran, 28 April 1983. In FBIS, USSR, 29 April 1983, p. H5.

10. *IHT*, 5 May 1983 (Reuters).

11. Amir Tahiri, *Al-Majallah*, 20-26 November 1982, pp. 13-15.

12. TASS in English, 1 October 1982. In FBIS, USSR, 4 October 1982, p. CC5.

13. V. Gudev, 'An Unnecessary and Dangerous Conflict', *Novoye Vremya*, no. 47 (19 November 1982), pp. 26-7.

14. Moscow Television, 23 April 1983. In FBIS, USSR, 25 April 1983, pp. CC19-CC20.

15. Saddam Husayn interview in *Al-Majallah*, 4-19 December 1982, pp. 14-21; Liz Thurgood, 'Russians Resume Arms Shipments to Iraq', *Guardian*, 27 September 1982; Monte Carlo radio in Arabic, 27 September 1982. In FBIS, Middle East, 28 September 1982, p. E1; Drew Middleton, *IHT*, 23 November 1982 (*New York Times*).

16. Aryeh Yodfat, 'Moscow and the Arab-Israeli Conflict', *Soviet Analyst*, vol. 12, no. 6 (23 March 1983), pp. 4-6.

17. John Bulloch, 'Soviet Arms for Iraq', *Daily Telegraph*, 11 January 1983; Muhammad Ma'tuq, 'Return of the Russians to the Middle East', *Al-Majallah*, 22-28 January 1983.

18. *Al-Majallah*, 16-22 October 1982, p. 11. Saddam Husayn denied that the release or any other treatment of the communists had anything to do with relations with the Soviet Union. (Ibid., 4-19 December 1982, pp. 14-21.)

19. Steven B. Kashkett, 'Iraq and the Pursuit of Nonalignment', *Orbis*, vol. 26, no. 2 (Summer 1982), pp. 477-94.

20. See Aryeh Yodfat, *The Soviet Union and the Arabian Peninsula* (Croom Helm, London and Canberra, and St. Martin's Press, New York, 1983).

21. Communiqué on the Summit, Manama Domestic Television, 11 November 1982. In FBIS, Middle East, 12 November 1982, pp. C1-C3; statement by the Saudi Interior Minister, Prince Nayif, to *Akhbar al-Khalij*, WAKH (Manama), 11 November 1982. In FBIS, Middle East, p. C3; *An-Nahar al-Arabi* (Beirut), 15 November 1982, *An-Nahar* (Beirut), 12 November 1982; Robin Wright, *The Times*, 14 November 1982.

22. Tehran radio, 26 December 1982. In FBIS, South Asia, 27 December 1982, p. I1.

23. *Pravda*, 28 December 1982; TASS, 27 December 1982. In BBC, SU/7218/A4/1, 30 December 1982; Robert Rand, 'Iran Criticizes Soviet Presence in Afghanistan', Radio Liberty Research (Munich), RL 3/83, 27 December 1982.

24. Richard Halloran, *IHT*, 15 November 1982 (*New York Times*).

25. Ali Nurizadeh, *Al-Dustur* (London), 22 November 1982, p. 84; Amir Taheri, 'Iran's Post-Khameini Therapy Has Already Started', *IHT*, 12 May 1983.

26. Dmitry Volsky, 'Iran: The Revolution at the Crossroads', *New Times*, no. 2, January 1983, pp. 13-15.

27. *Iran Press Service* (London), 20 January 1983.

28. Ehsan Tabari, 'The Role of Religion in our Revolution', *World Marxist Review*, no. 12 (December 1982), pp. 93-101; Nuraddin Kianuri, 'The Arduous Path of the Iranian Revolution', ibid., no. 3 (March 1983), pp. 40-8.

Tabari was considered to be the Tudeh ideologist. The Kianuri article was published after his arrest by the Iranian authorities.

29. *Ettela'at* and *Keyhan*, 7 February 1983; *Jomhuri-Ye Islami*, 7 February and 15 March 1983.

30. *Pravda*, 10 February 1983.

31. NVOI, 8 February 1983. In FBIS, South Asia, 9 February 1983, pp. I6-I7.

32. 'Against Iran's National Interests', *Pravda*, 19 February 1983.

33. Tudeh Party Central Committee statement on leader's arrest, NVOI, 23 and 24 March 1982. In FBIS, South Asia, 29 March 1983, pp. I1-I6; Tudeh Party 'open letter' to authorities, NVOI, 28 March 1983. In FBIS, South Asia, 31 March 1983, pp. I3-I4; Ali Khavari, Tudeh Politburo member, 'Against Repressions and

Persecution . . .', *World Marxist Review*, vol. 26, no. 4 (April 1983), pp. 104-5.

34. NVOI, 4 May 1983. In BBC, Middle East/7327/A/2, 7 May 1983. See also: 'Iranian Allegations a Malicious Provocation' and 'Trial by "confession"', *Soviet Weekly* (London), 14 May 1983, p. 6.

35. Tehran radio, 5 May 1983. In BBC, Middle East/7327/A/1, 7 May 1983.

36. NVOI, 17 January 1983. In FBIS, South Asia, 20 January 1983, pp. I6-I7.

37. Aryeh Yodfat, 'The Kurds; Policy Problem for Moscow', *Soviet Analyst*, vol. 11, no. 25 (22 December 1982), pp. 2-4; 'Kurds: The Mountains are Friendly', *The Economist*, 21 May 1983, pp. 58, 61.

38. Konstantin Troyanovski, *Vostok i Revolutsiya* (The East and the Revolution) (Moscow, 1918), pp. 47-8.

39. See 'Rapid Deployment Force. Will Europe Help America Help Europe?', *The Economist*, 11 December 1982, pp. 70-2.

SELECT BIBLIOGRAPHY

Books and Pamphlets

Abir, Mordechai, *Oil, Power and Politics. Conflict in Arabia, the Red Sea and the Gulf* (Frank Cass, London, 1974)

Abrahamian, Ervand, *Iran Between Two Revolutions* (Princeton University Press, Princeton, 1982)

Adamson, David, *The Kurdish War* (Allen & Unwin, London, 1964)

Adomeit, Hannes, *Soviet Risk-Taking and Crisis Behavior: A Theoretical and Empirical Analysis* (Allen & Unwin, Winchester, Mass., 1982)

Akhavi, Shahrough, *Religion and Politics in Contemporary Iran: Clergy-State Relations in the Pahlavi Period* (State University of New York Press, Albany, N.Y., 1980)

Alexander, Yonah and Alan Nanes (eds.), *The United States and Iran: A Documentary History* (Aletheia Books, University Publications of America, Frederick, Md., 1980)

Algar, Hamid, *Constitution of the Islamic Republic of Iran* (Mizan Press, Berkeley, Calif., 1980)

Amirie, Abbas (ed.), *The Persian Gulf and Indian Ocean in International Politics* (Institute for International Politics and Economic Studies (IIPES), Tehran, 1975)

—— and Hamilton A. Twitchell (eds.), *Iran in the 1980s* (IIPES, Tehran, 1978)

Amirsadeghi, Hossein (ed.), *The Security of the Persian Gulf* (Croom Helm, London, 1981)

Bakhash, Shaul, *The Politics of Oil and Revolution in Iran* (The Brookings Institution, Washington, D.C., 1982)

Bennigsen, Alexandre, *Islam in the Soviet Union* (Praeger, New York, and Pall Mall, London, in association with the Central Asian Research Centre, London, 1967)

—— and Marie Broxup, *The Islamic Threat to the Soviet State* (Croom Helm, London, and St. Martin's Press, New York, 1983)

Binder, Leonard, *Iran: Political Development in a Changing Society* (University of California Press, Berkeley and Los Angeles, 1962)

—— *Factors Influencing Iran's International Role* (Rand Corporation, Santa Monica, Calif., 1969)

—— *Revolution in Iran: Three Essays* (American Academic Association for Peace in the Middle East, New York, 1980)

Bonnie, Michael E. and Nikki R. Keddie, *Modern Iran: The Dialectics of Continuity and Change* (State University of New York Press, Albany, 1981)

Bradley, Paul C., *Recent United States Policy in the Persian Gulf (1971-82)* (Thompson & Rutter, Grantham, N.H., 1982)

Buchanan, George, *My Mission to Russia and other Diplomatic Memoirs* (Little, Brown & Co., Boston, 1923)

Buell, Floyd Clarence, *Communism in Iran* (School of Public and International

Affairs, George Washington University, Washington, D.C., 1968)

Burrell, R.M. and A.J. Cottrell, *Iran, Afghanistan, Pakistan: Tensions and Dilemmas* (Sage Publications, Beverly Hills, Calif., 1974)

Carter, Jimmy, *Keeping Faith: Memoirs of a President* (Collins, London, 1982)

Chaliand, Gerard (ed.), *People Without a Country: The Kurds and Kurdistan* (Zed Press, London, 1980)

Chubin, Shahram, *Soviet Policy Towards Iran and the Gulf* (International Institute for Strategic Studies (IISS), London, Adelphi Papers no. 157, Spring 1980)

—— and Mohammad Fard-Saidi, *Recent Trends in Middle East Politics and Iran's Foreign Policy Options* (Institute for International Politics and Economic Studies (IIPES), Tehran, 1975)

—— and Sepher Zabih, *The Foreign Relations of Iran: A Developing State in a Zone of Great-Power Conflict* (University of California Press, Berkeley and Los Angeles, 1974)

Cottam, Richard W., *Nationalism in Iran* (University of Pittsburgh Press, Pittsburgh, 1979)

Cottrell, Alvin I., *Iran's Quest for Security: U.S. Arms Transfers and the Nuclear Option* (Institute for Foreign Policy Analysis, New York, 1977)

—— and R.M. Burrell (eds.), *The Indian Ocean: Its Political, Economic and Military Importance* (Praeger, New York, 1979)

—— and Robert J. Hanks, Geoffrey Kemp and Thomas H. Moorer, *Seapower and Strategy in the Indian Ocean* (Sage Publications, London, 1981)

Cudsi, Alexander S. and Ali E. Hillal Dessouki, *Islam and Power* (Johns Hopkins University Press, Baltimore, Md., 1981)

Curzon, George N., *Persia and the Persian Question* (Longman, Green & Co., London, 1892; Frank Cass, London, 1966)

Degras, Jane (ed.), *Soviet Documents on Foreign Policy, 1917-1941* (Oxford University Press, London and New York, 1951-3)

Donahue, John J. and John L. Esposito, *Islam in Transition: Muslim Perspectives* (Oxford University Press, New York, 1982)

Eagleton, William, Jr., *The Kurdish Republic of 1946* (Oxford University Press, London, 1963)

Entner, Marvin L., *Russo-Persian Commercial Relations, 1828-1914* (University of Florida Press, Gainesville, Fla., 1965)

Eudin, Xenia Joukoff and Robert C. North, *Soviet Russia and the East, 1920-1927, A Documentary Survey* (Stanford University Press, Stanford, Calif., 1957)

Farid, A.M. (ed.), *Oil and Security in the Arabian Gulf* (Croom Helm, London, 1981)

Fatemi, Faramarz S., *The USSR in Iran* (Barnes & Co., New York, 1980)

Fatemi, Nasrollah S., *Diplomatic History of Persia, 1917-1923; Anglo-Russian Power Politics in Iran* (Russell F. Moore, New York, 1952)

—— *Oil Diplomacy; Powderkeg in Iran* (Whittier, New York, 1954)

Fisher, Louis, *The Soviets in World Affairs*, vol. I (1st edn, Jonathan Cape and H. Smith, New York, 1930; 2nd edn, Princeton University Press, Princeton, N.J., 1951)

Fisher, Michael M.J., *Iran: From Religious Dispute to Revolution* (Harvard University Press, Cambridge, Mass., 1980)

Forbis, William H., *Fall of the Peacock Throne: The Story of Iran* (Harper & Row, New York, 1980)

Fukuyama, Francis, *The Soviet Threat to the Persian Gulf* (Rand Corporation, Santa Monica, Calif., 1981)

Ghareeb, Edmund, *The Kurdish Question in Iraq* (Syracuse University Press, Syracuse, N.Y., 1981)

Graham, Robert, *Iran: The Illusion of Power* (Croom Helm, London, and St. Martin's Press, New York, 1978)

Grayson, Benson Lee, *United States–Iranian Relations* (University Press of America, Washington, D.C., 1981)

Greaves, Rose Louise, *Persia and the Defence of India, 1884-1892* (University of London, The Athlone Press, London, 1959)

Grumman, Stephen R., *The Iran–Iraq War: Islam Embattled* (Praeger, New York, with the Center for Strategic and International Studies, Georgetown University, The Washington Papers, no. 92, 1982)

Halliday, Fred, *Iran: Dictatorship and Development* (Penguin, London, 1978)

—— *Soviet Policy in the Arc of Crisis* (Institute for Policy Studies, Washington, D.C., 1981)

—— *Threat from the East? Soviet Policy from Afghanistan and Iran to the Horn of Africa* (Pelican, London, 1982)

Hamzawi, Abdol Hossain, *Persia and the Powers; An Account of Diplomatic Relations, 1941-1946* (Hutchinson, London, 1947)

Harrison, Selig S., *In Afghanistan's Shadow: Baluchi Nationalism and Soviet Temptations* (Carnegie Endowment for International Peace, Washington, D.C., 1981)

Heikal, Mohammed, *Iran: The Untold Story* (Pantheon, New York, 1982)

Helms, Cynthia, *An Ambassador's Wife in Iran* (Dodd, Mead & Co., New York, 1981)

Hickman, William F., *Ravaged and Reborn: The Iranian Army, 1982* (The Brookings Institution, Washington, D.C., 1983)

Hoveyda, Ferreydom, *The Fall of the Shah* (Weidenfeld & Nicolson, London, 1980)

Hunter, Robert E., *The Soviet Dilemma in the Middle East* (International Institute for Strategic Studies (IISS), London, Adelphi Papers, 1969: no. 59, Part I, The Problem of Commitment; no. 60, Part II, Oil and the Persian Gulf)

Hurewitz, Jacob C. (ed.), *Diplomacy in the Near and Middle East; A Documentary Record, 1914-1956* (2 vols., Van Nostrand, Princeton, N.J., 1956)

—— (ed.), *Soviet–American Rivalry in the Middle East* (Praeger, New York, 1969)

—— *The Persian Gulf After Iran's Revolution* (Foreign Policy Association, New York, 1979)

Ismael, Tareq Y., *The Iraq–Iran Conflict* (Canadian Institute of International Affairs, Toronto, 1981)

—— *Iraq and Iran: Roots of Conflict* (Syracuse University Press, Syracuse, New York, 1982)

Jabbari, Ahmad and Robert Olson (eds.), *Iran: Essays on a Revolution in the Making* (Mazda Publications, Lexington, Ky., 1981)

Jukes, Geoffrey, *The Indian Ocean in Soviet Naval Policy* (International Institute for Strategic Studies (IISS), London, Adelphi Papers no. 87, May 1972)

Katouzian, Hama, *The Political Economy of Modern Iran: Despotism and Pseudo-Modernism, 1926-1979* (New York University Press, New York, 1981)

Kattikas, Suzanne Jalicoeur, *The Arc of Socialist Revolutions: Angola to Afghanistan* (Shenkman Publishing Co., Cambridge, Mass., 1982)

Kazemi, Farhad, *Poverty and Revolution in Iran: The Migrant Poor, Urban Marginality and Politics* (New York University Press, New York and London, 1980)

Kazemzadeh, Firuz, *Russia and Britain in Persia, 1964-1914. A Study in Imperialism* (Yale University Press, New Haven and London, 1968)

Keddie, Nikki R., *Religion and Rebellion in Iran: the Tobacco Protest of 1891-1892* (Frank Cass, London, 1966)

—— *Iran: Religion, Politics and Society* (Frank Cass, London, 1980)

—— *Roots of Revolution. An Interpretive History of Modern Iran* (Yale University Press, New Haven and London, 1981)

—— and Cevic Hooglund (eds.), *The Iranian Revolution and the Islamic Republic: Conference Proceedings* (Middle East Institute, Washington, D.C., 1982)

Kedourie, Elie, *Islam in the Modern World* (Mansell, London, 1980)

—— and Sylvia G. Haim (eds.), *Towards a Modern Iran: Studies in Thought, Politics and Society* (Frank Cass, London, 1980)

Khomeyni, Ayatollah Ruhollah, *Islamic Government* (National Technical Information Service, Springfield, Va., 1979)

—— *Sayings of the Ayatollah Khomeini: Political, Philosophical, Social and Religious* (Bantam Books, New York, 1980)

—— *Islam and Revolution – Writings and Declarations of Imam Khomeini* (Mizan Press, Berkeley, Calif., 1981)

Klinghoffer, Arthur Jay, *The Soviet Union and International Oil Politics* (Columbia University Press, New York, 1977)

Kramer, Martin, *Political Islam* (Sage Publications, Beverly Hills, Calif., 1980)

Kumar, Ravinder, *India and the Persian Gulf Region, 1858-1909. A Study in British Imperial Policy* (Asia Publishing House, London, 1965)

Landis, Lincoln, *Politics and Oil: Moscow in the Middle East* (Dunellen Publishing Co., New York, 1973)

Laqueur, Walter Z., *The Soviet Union and the Middle East* (Routledge & Kegan Paul, London, and Praeger, New York, 1959)

Ledeen, Michael A. and William H. Lewis, *Debacle: The American Failure in Iran* (Alfred A. Knopf, New York, 1981)

Lenczowski, George, *Russia and the West in Iran, 1918-1948. A Study of Big-Power Rivalry* (Cornell University Press, Ithaca, N.Y., 1949)

—— *The Middle East in World Affairs* (Cornell University Press, Ithaca, N.Y., 1952)

—— *Soviet Advances in the Middle East* (American Enterprise Institute, Washington, D.C., 1974)

Lobanov-Rostovsky, A., *Russia and Asia* (George Wahr Publishing Co., Ann Arbor, Mich., 1965)

McLane, Charles B., *Soviet–Middle East Relations* (Central Asian Research Centre, London, 1973)

Moss, Robert, *The Campaign to Destabilize Iran* (Institute for the Study of Conflict, London, Conflict Studies no. 101, 1978)

Mossavar-Rahmani, Bijan, *Energy Policy in Iran: Domestic Choices and International Implications* (Pergamon Press, New York, 1981)

Motter, T.H. Vail, *The Persian Corridor and Aid to Russia* (Department of the Army, Office of the Chief of Military History, Washington, D.C., 1952)

Nakhleh, Emile E., *The Persian Gulf and American Policy* (Praeger, New York, 1982)

Nickbin, Saber, *Iran: The Unfolding Revolution* (Relgocrest, London, 1979)

Nollau, Gunther and Hans Jurgen Wieher, *Russia's South Flank: Soviet Operations in Iran, Turkey and Afghanistan* (Praeger, New York, 1963)

Noyes, James H., *The Clouded Lens: Persian Gulf Security and US Policy* (Hoover Institution Press, Stanford, Calif., 1979)

Pahlavi, Mohammad Reza Shah, *Mission For My Country* (McGraw Hill, New York, 1961)

—— *The White Revolution in Iran* (Imperial Pahlavi Library, Tehran, 1967)

Pranger, Robert J. and Dale R. Tahtinen, *American Policy Options in Iran and the Persian Gulf* (American Enterprise Institute, Washington, D.C., 1979)

Pryer, Melvyn, *A View from the 'Rimland': an Appraisal of Soviet Interests and Involvement in the Gulf* (University of Durham, Centre for Middle Eastern and Islamic Studies, Durham, 1981)

Ramazani, Rouhollah K., *The Foreign Policy of Iran, 1800-1941* (University Press of Virginia, Charlottesville, Va., 1966)

—— *The Northern Tier: Afghanistan, Iran and Turkey* (Van Nostrand, Princeton, N.J., 1966)

—— *The Persian Gulf: Iran's Role* (University Press of Virginia, Charlottesville, Va., 1972)

—— *The Persian Gulf and the Strait of Hormuz* (Sijthoff, Alphen van den Rijn, Netherlands, 1979)

—— *The United States and Iran: Patterns of Influence* (Praeger, New York, 1982)

Rawlinson, Sir Henry Creswicke, *England and Russia in the East. A series of papers on the political and geographical condition of Central Asia*, 2nd edn. (John Murray, London, 1875)

Rezun, Miran, *The Soviet Union and Iran: Soviet Policy in Iran from the Beginnings of the Pahlavi Dynasty until the Soviet Invasion of 1941* (Institut Universitaire de Hautes Etudes Internationales, Geneva; Sijthoff, Leiden, 1981)

Roosevelt, Kermit, *Countercoup: The Struggle for the Control of Iran* (McGraw Hill, New York, 1979)

Rubin, Barry, *Paved with Good Intentions: The American Experience and Iran* (Oxford University Press, New York, 1980)

Rubinstein, Alvin Z., *Soviet Foreign Policy Since World War II: Imperial and Global* (Winthrop Publishers, Cambridge, Mass., 1981)

—— *Soviet Policy Toward Turkey, Iran and Afghanistan* (Praeger, New York, 1982)

Rywkin, Michael, *Moscow's Muslim Challenge: Soviet Central Asia* (Sharpe, Armouk, New York, 1982)

Saikal, Amir, *The Rise and Fall of the Shah* (Angus & Robertson, London, 1980)

Salinger, Pierre, *America Held Hostage: The Secret Negotiations* (Doubleday & Co., Garden City, N.Y., 1981)

Shapiro, L. (ed.), *Soviet Treaty Series: A Collection of Bilateral Treaties, Agreements and Conventions, etc., concluded between the Soviet Union and Foreign Powers* (Georgetown University Press, Washington, D.C., 1950-1955)

Shari'ati, Ali, *Marxism and Other Western Fallacies: An Islamic Critique* (Mizan Press, Berkeley, Calif., 1980)

Shwadran, Benjamin, *Middle East. Oil and the Great Powers* (Praeger, New York, and Thames & Hudson, London, 1955)

Sim, Richard, *Kurdistan: The Search for Recognition* (Institute for the Study of

Conflict, London, Conflict Studies no. 127, 1981)

Spector, Ivar, *The Soviet Union and the Muslim World, 1917-1958* (University of Washington Press, Seattle, Wash., 1959)

Stempel, John D., *Inside the Iranian Revolution* (Indiana University Press, Bloomington, Ind., 1981)

Stoessinger, John G., *Why Nations Go to War*, 3rd edn. (St. Martin's Press, New York, 1982). (Includes a case-study on the Iran–Iraq war)

Sullivan, William H., *Mission to Iran* (Norton, New York, 1981)

Sykes, Percy, *A History of Persia*, 3rd edn. (Macmillan, London, 1930)

Tabataba'i, M.M., *Shi'ite Islam* (State University of New York Press, Albany, N.Y., 1975)

US Congress, 93rd Cong., 1st Sess., US House of Representatives, Committee on Foreign Affairs, Subcommittee on the Near East and East Asia, *New Perspectives in the Persian Gulf*, Hearings . . ., June, July and November 1973 (US Government Printing Office, Washington, D.C., 1973)

—— 93rd Cong., 2nd Sess., *idem, The Persian Gulf 1974: Money, Politics, Arms and Power*, Hearings, July-August 1974 (US Government Printing Office, Washington, D.C., 1975)

—— 94th Cong., 2nd Sess., US Senate, Committee on Foreign Relations, Subcommittee on Foreign Assistance, *US Military Sales to Iran*, A Staff Report . . ., July 1976 (US Government Printing Office, Washington, D.C., 1976)

—— 95th Cong., 1st Sess., US House of Representatives, Committee on International Relations, Subcommittee on International Organizations, *Human Rights in Iran*, Hearing . . ., 26 October 1977 (US Government Printing Office, Washington, D.C., 1977)

—— 96th Cong., 1st Sess., US House of Representatives, Subcommittee on Europe and the Middle East, *US Policy Toward Iran*, January 1979, Hearing . . . (US Government Printing Office, Washington, D.C., 1979)

Van Bruinessen, M.M., *Agha, Shaikh and State: On the Social and Political Organization of Kurdistan* (University of Utrecht, Utrecht, 1978)

Whighan, H.J., *The Persian Problem* (Scribner & Sons, New York, 1903)

Yeselson, Abraham, *United States–Persian Diplomatic Relations 1883-1921* (Rutgers University Press, New Brunswick, N.J., 1956)

Yodfat, Aryeh, *Arab Politics in the Soviet Mirror* (Halsted Press, John Wiley & Sons, New York and Toronto, 1973)

—— *Between Revolutionary Slogans and Pragmatism: The PRC and the Middle East* (Centre d'Etudes du Sud-Est Asiatique et de l'Extrême Orient, Brussels, 1979)

—— *The Soviet Union and the Arabian Peninsula: Soviet Policy Towards the Persian Gulf and Arabia* (Croom Helm, London and Canberra, and St. Martin's Press, New York, 1983)

—— and M. Abir, *In the Direction of the Gulf: The Soviet Union and the Persian Gulf* (Frank Cass, London, 1977)

—— and Yuval Arnon-Ohanna, *PLO. Strategy and Tactics* (Croom Helm, London, and St. Martin's Press, New York, 1981)

York, Valerie, *The Gulf in the 1980s* (Royal Institute of International Affairs, London, Chatham House Papers no. 6, 1980)

Zabih, Sepher, *The Communist Movement in Iran* (Univeristy of California Press, Los Angeles, 1966)

—— *Iran's Revolutionary Upheaval: an Interpretive Essay* (Alchemy Books, San Francisco, 1979)

—— *The Mosadegh Era: Roots of the Iranian Revolution* (Lake View Press, Chicago, 1982)

—— *Iran Since the Revolution* (Croom Helm, London, 1982)

Ziring, Lawrence, *Iran, Turkey and Afghanistan: A Political Chronology* (Praeger, New York, 1981)

Articles

Abidi, A.H.M., 'The Iranian Revolution, its origins and Dimensions', *International Studies* (New Delhi), vol. 18, no. 2 (April–June 1979), pp. 129-61

Abrahamian, Ervand, 'The Guerrilla Movement in Iran, 1965-1977', *MERIP Reports*, no. 86 (March–April 1980), pp. 3-15

—— 'Structural Cause of the Iranian Revolution', *MERIP Reports*, no. 87 (May 1980), pp. 21-6

—— ''Ali Shari'ati: Ideologue of the Iranian Revolution', *MERIP Reports*, no. 102 (vol. 12, no. 1, January 1982), pp. 24-8

Alpher, Joseph, 'The Khomeini International', *The Washington Quarterly*, vol. 3, no. 4 (Autumn 1980), pp. 54-74

Amirsadeghi, Hossein, 'With Russia and America: the Shah's Balanced Alignment', *New Middle East*, no. 38 (November 1971), pp. 7-11

Atkin, Muriel, 'The Kremlin and Khomeyni', *The Washington Quarterly*, vol. 4, no. 2 (Spring 1981), pp. 50-67

Avery, Peter, 'The Many Faces of Iran's Foreign Policy', *New Middle East*, no. 47 (August 1972), pp. 17-19

Bakhash, Shaul, 'The Day of the Mullahs', *The New Republic*, vol. 185, no. 18 (4 November 1981), pp. 15-18

Ballis, William B., 'Soviet–Iranian Relations during the Decade 1953-64', *Bulletin, Institute for the Study of the USSR* (Munich), vol. 12, no. 11 (November 1965), pp. 9-22

Baloch, Inayatullah, 'Afghanistan-Pashtunistan-Baluchistan', *Aussen Politik* (Hamburg–Stuttgart, English edn.), vol. 31, no. 3 (1980), pp. 283-301

Batatu, Hanna, 'Iraq's Underground Shi'a Movements: Characteristics, Causes and Prospects', *Middle East Journal*, vol. 35, no. 4 (1981), pp. 578-94

Bayat, Mangol, 'The Iranian Revolution of 1978-79: Fundamentalist or Modern?', *Middle East Journal*, vol. 37, no. 1 (1983), pp. 30-40

Beck, Lois, 'Revolutionary Iran and its Tribal Peoples', *MERIP Reports*, no. 87 (May 1980), pp. 14-20

Bill, James A., 'Iran and the Crisis of '78', *Foreign Affairs*, vol. 57, no. 2 (Winter 1978-9), pp. 323-42

—— 'Power and Religion in Revolutionary Iran', *Middle East Journal*, vol. 36, no. 1 (Winter 1982), pp. 22-47

Brewer, William D., 'Yesterday and Tomorrow in the Persian Gulf', *Middle East Journal*, vol. 23, no. 2 (Spring 1969), pp. 149-58

Burrell, R.M., 'Iranian Foreign Policy during the Last Decade', *Asian Affairs*, vol. 61, Part 1 (February 1974), pp. 7-15

—— 'Iranian Foreign Policy: Strategic Location, Economic Ambition, and Dynastic Determination', *Journal of International Affairs*, vol. 29 (Fall 1975), pp. 129-38

Burt, R., 'Power and the Peacock Throne: Iran's Growing Military Strength', *Round Table*, no. 260 (October 1975), pp. 349-56

Campbell, W.R. and Djamchid Darvich, 'Global Implications of the Islamic Revolution for the Status Quo in the Persian Gulf', *Journal of South Asian and Middle Eastern Studies*, vol. 5, no. 1 (Fall 1981), pp. 31-51

Catudal, Honore M., Jr., 'The War in Kurdistan: End of Nationalist Struggle', *International Relations* (London), vol. 5, no. 3 (May 1976), pp. 1024-44

Chubin, Shahram, 'Iran: Between the Arab West and the Asian East', *Survival* (July-August 1974), pp. 173-82

—— 'Iran's Security in the 1980s', *International Security* (Winter 1978), pp. 51-80

—— 'Local Soil, Foreign Plants', *Foreign Policy* (Spring 1979), pp. 20-3

—— 'Leftist Forces in Iran', *Problems of Communism*, vol. 29, no. 4 (July-August 1980), pp. 1-25

—— 'Gains for Soviet Policy in the Middle East', *International Security* (Spring 1982), pp. 122-52

—— 'The Soviet Union and Iran', *Foreign Affairs*, vol. 61, no. 4 (Spring 1983), pp. 921-49

Clementson, J., 'Diego Garcia', *RUSI*, vol. 126, no. 2 (June 1981), pp. 33-9

Cooley, John K., 'Iran, the Palestinians and the Gulf', *Foreign Affairs*, vol. 57, no. 3 (Summer 1979), pp. 1017-34

Cottam, Richard W., 'Goodbye to America's Shah', *Foreign Policy* (Spring 1979), pp. 3-14

—— 'American Policy and the Iranian Crisis', *Iranian Studies*, vol. 13, nos. 1-4 (1980), pp. 279-305

—— 'Revolutionary Iran and the War with Iraq', *Current History*, vol. 80 (January 1981), pp. 5-9, 38

Dawisha, Adeed J., 'Iraq: the West's Opportunity', *Foreign Policy*, vol. 41 (Winter 1980-81), pp. 134-53

—— 'Iraq and the Arab World: The Gulf War and After', *The World Today*, vol. 37, no. 5 (May 1981), pp. 188-94

Dawisha, Karen, 'Soviet Decision-Making and the Middle East: The 1973 October War and the 1980 Gulf War', *International Affairs* (London), vol. 57, no. 1 (1980-81), pp. 43-59

—— 'Moscow's Moves in the Direction of the Gulf – so Near and yet so Far', *Journal of International Affairs*, vol. 34, no. 2 (Fall/Winter 1980/81), pp. 219-33

—— 'Moscow and the Gulf War', *The World Today*, vol. 37, no. 1 (January 1981), pp. 8-14

Dowdy, W. III, 'Naval Warfare in the Gulf: Iraq versus Iran', *US Naval Institute Proceedings*, vol. 107, no. 6 (June 1981), pp. 114-17

Dunn, Keith A., 'Constraints on the USSR in Southwest Asia: a Military Analysis', *Orbis*, vol. 25, no. 3 (Fall 1981), pp. 607-29

Dupree, Louis, 'Afghanistan Under the Khalq', *Problems of Communism*, vol. 18, no. 4 (July-August 1979), pp. 34-50

Elwell-Sutton, L.P., 'Political Parties in Iran, 1941-1948', *Middle East Journal*, vol. 3, no. 1 (January 1949), pp. 45-62

—— 'Nationalism and Neutralism in Iran', *Middle East Journal*, vol. 12, no. 1 (Winter 1958), pp. 20-32

Epstein, Joshua M., 'Soviet Vulnerabilities in Iran and the RDF Deterrent', *International Security*, vol. 6, no. 2 (Fall 1981), pp. 126-58

Falk, Richard A., 'Khomeyni's Promise', *Foreign Policy* (Spring 1979), pp. 28-34

Fallaci, Oriana, 'Interview with Khomeyni', *New York Times Magazine* (7 October 1979), pp. 29-31

—— 'Iran Diary', *The New Republic*, vol. 182 (10 May 1980), pp. 9-13

Fatemi, Khosraw, 'Leadership by Distrust: The Shah's *Modus Operandi*', *Middle East Journal*, vol. 36, no. 1 (Winter 1982), pp. 48-61

Fukuyama, Francis, 'Nuclear Shadow-boxing: Soviet Intervention Threats in the Middle East', *Orbis*, vol. 25, no. 3 (Fall 1981), pp. 579-605

Graur, Mina, 'The Soviet Union versus Muslim Solidarity following the Invasion of Afghanistan', *Slavic and Soviet Series* (Russian and East European Research Centre, Tel Aviv University), vol. 4, nos. 1-2 (1979), pp. 74-89

Gunther, Michael M. and Stanford R. Silverburg, 'Violating the Inviolable: The Iranian Hostage Case and its Implications', *Journal of South Asian and Middle Eastern Studies*, vol. 5, no. 1 (Fall 1981), pp. 52-76

Halliday, Fred, 'The Arc of Revolutions: Iran, Afghanistan, South Yemen, Ethiopia', *Race and Class* (London), vol. 20, no. 4 (Spring 1979), pp. 373-90

—— 'The Iranian Revolution in International Affairs: Programme and Practice', *Millennium: Journal of International Studies*, vol. 9, no. 2 (1980), pp. 108-21

—— 'The Gulf Between Two Revolutions: 1958-1979', *MERIP Reports*, no. 85 (February 1980), pp. 6-15

—— 'Iran's Revolution: The First Year', *MERIP Reports*, no. 88 (June 1980), pp. 3-5

—— 'The Arc of Crisis and the New Cold War', *MERIP Reports*, nos. 100-101 (vol. 11, nos. 8-9, October-December 1981), pp. 14-25

Hammond, Thomas T., 'Afghanistan and the Persian Gulf', *Survey* (London, vol. 26, no. 2 (115) (Spring 1982), pp. 83-101

Helfgot, Leonard M., 'The Structural Foundations of the National Minority Problem in Revolutionary Iran', *Iranian Studies*, vol. 13, nos. 1-4 (1980), pp. 195-214

Hensel, Howard M., 'Soviet Policy Towards the Rebellion in Dhofar', *Asian Affairs*, vol. 13, Part 2 (June 1982), pp. 183-207

Hetherington, Norris S., 'Industrialization and Revolution in Iran: Forced Progress or Unmet Expectation?', *Middle East Journal*, vol. 36, no. 3 (1982), pp. 362-73

Hickman, W., 'Soviet Naval Policy in the Indian Ocean', *US Naval Institute Proceedings*, vol. 105, no. 8 (August 1979), pp. 42-52

Hirshfeld, Yair P., 'Moscow and Khomeyni: Soviet–Iranian Relations in Historical Perspective', *Orbis*, vol. 24, no. 2 (Summer 1980), pp. 219-40

Hottinger, Arnold, 'Tehran in its Fourth Post-Revolutionary Year', *Swiss Review of World Affairs*, vol. 32, no. 6 (September 1982), pp. 14-17

Irandoost, F.J., 'Soviet–Iran relations: some Long-term Considerations', *Mizan* (September-October 1969), pp. 255-7

Johnson, M., 'US Strategic Options in the Persian Gulf', *US Naval Institute Proceedings*, vol. 107, no. 2 (February 1981), pp. 53-9

Johnson, T. and R. Barrett, 'Mining the Strait of Ormuz', *US Naval Institute Proceedings*, vol. 107, no. 12 (December 1981), pp. 23-5

Jordan, R., 'Naval Diplomacy in the Persian Gulf', *US Naval Institute Proceedings*, vol. 107, no. 11 (November 1981), pp. 26-31

Kashkett, Steven B., 'Iraq and the Pursuit of Nonalignment', *Orbis*, vol. 26, no. 2 (Summer 1982), pp. 477-94

Kazemzadeh, Firuz, 'Russia and the Middle East' in Ivo J. Lederer (ed.), *Russia Foreign Policy, Essays in Historical Perspective* (Yale University Press, New Haven and London, 1962), pp. 489-530

—— 'Soviet–Iranian Relations: A Quarter-Century of Freeze and Thaw' in I.J. Lederer and W.S. Vucinich (eds.), *The Soviet Union and the Middle East: The Post World War II Era* (Hoover Institution Press, Stanford, Calif., 1974), pp. 55-77

Khalilzad, Zalmay, 'The Superpowers and the Northern Tier', *International Security* (Winter 1979-80), pp. 6-30

Kramer, Martin, 'New Ideals of an Islamic Order', *The Washington Quarterly*, vol. 3, no. 1 (Winter 1980), pp. 3-13

Laqueur, Walter, 'Why the Shah Fell', *Commentary*, vol. 67, no. 3 (March 1979), pp. 47-55

—— 'Is Khomeini a Neo-conservative?', *The New Republic*, 8 December 1979, pp. 9-12

Ledeen, Michael A. and William H. Lewis, 'Carter and the Fall of the Shah: The Inside Story', *The Washington Quarterly* (Spring 1980), pp. 3-40

Lee, Christopher D., 'The Soviet Contribution to Iran's Fourth Development Plan', *Mizan*, vol. XI, no. 5 (September-October 1969), pp. 237-47

Lenczowski, George, 'The Communist Movement in Iran', *Middle East Journal*, vol. 1, no. 1 (January 1947), pp. 29-45

—— 'The Soviet Union and the Persian Gulf: An Encircling Strategy', *International Journal* (Toronto), vol. 37, no. 2 (Spring 1982), pp. 307-27

Mansur, Abdul Kasim (pseud.), 'The Crisis in Iran: Why the US Ignored a Quarter Century of Warning', *Armed Forces Journal International* (January 1979), pp. 26-33

—— 'The Military Balance in the Persian Gulf: Who Will Guard the Gulf States From Their Guardians?', *Armed Forces Journal International* (November 1980), pp. 44-86

Marlowe, J., 'Arab–Persian Rivalry in the Persian Gulf', *Journal of the Royal Central Asian Society*, vol. 51 (January 1964), pp. 23-31

Melamid, Alexander, 'The Shatt al-Arab Boundary Dispute', *Middle East Journal*, vol. 20, no. 3 (Summer 1968), pp. 351-7

Menashri, David, 'Strange Bedfellows: The Khomeini Coalition', *Jerusalem Quarterly*, no. 12 (Summer 1979), pp. 34-48

—— 'Shi'ite Leadership: in the Shadow of Conflicting Ideologies', *Iranian Studies*, vol. 13, nos. 1-4 (1980), pp. 119-45

—— 'The Shah and Khomeyni: Conflicting Nationalisms', *Crossroads* (Jerusalem), vol. 8 (Winter-Spring 1982), pp. 53-79

Mottahedeh, Roy Parviz, 'Iran's Foreign Devils', *Foreign Policy* (Spring 1980), pp. 19-34

Nickel, Herman, 'The US Failure in Iran', *Fortune* (12 March 1979), pp. 94-106

Nikazmerd, Nicholas M., 'A Chronological Survey of the Iranian Revolution', *Iranian Studies*, vol. 13, nos. 1-4 (1980), pp. 327-68

O'Ballance, Edgar, 'The Kurdish Factor in the Gulf War', *Military Review*, vol. 61,

no. 6 (June 1981), pp. 13-20
—— 'The Iraq–Iran War', *Islamic World Defence* (London), issue 1 (Autumn 1981), pp. 15-18
Parvin, Manoucher, 'Political Economy of Soviet–Iranian Trade: An Overview of Theory and Practice', *Middle East Journal*, vol. 31, no. 1 (Winter 1977), pp. 31-44
Petrossian, Vahe, 'Iran's Crisis of Leadership', *The World Today*, vol. 37, no. 2 (February 1981), pp. 39-44
—— 'Iran: A Second Revolutionary Lesson', *The World Today*, vol 37, no. 10 (October 1981), pp. 363-6
Pipes, Daniel, '"This World is Political!!" The Islamic Revival of the Seventies', *Orbis*, vol. 24, no. 1 (Spring 1980), pp. 9-41
Price, David Lynn, 'Moscow and the Persian Gulf', *Problems of Communism*, vol. 18, no. 2 (March-April 1979), pp. 1-13
Ramazani, Rouhollah K., 'Iran's Changing Foreign Policy: A Preliminary Discussion', *Middle East Journal*, vol. 24, no. 4 (Autumn 1970), pp. 421-37
—— 'Iran's "White Revolution": a Study in Political Development', *International Journal of Middle East Studies*, vol. 5 (April 1974), pp. 124-39
—— 'Iran's Search for Regional Co-operation', *Middle East Journal*, vol. 30 (Spring 1976), pp. 173-86
—— 'Emerging Patterns of Regional Relations in Iranian Foreign Policy', *Orbis*, vol. 18, no. 4 (Winter 1979), pp. 1043-70
—— 'Iran's Revolution: Patterns, Problems and Prospects', *International Affairs* (London), vol. 56, no. 3 (Summer 1980), pp. 443-57
—— 'Who Lost America? The Case of Iran', *Middle East Journal*, vol. 36, no. 1 (1982), pp. 5-21
Rezun, Miran, 'A Note on the Religious Context of the Iranian Revolution', *Middle East Focus* (Toronto), vol. 5, no. 4 (November 1982), pp. 12-18
Richards, Guy, 'The Persian Gulf's Strait of Ormuz: A New Area of US–Soviet Conflict?', *East Europe* (New York), vol. 20, no. 1 (January 1971), pp. 8-15
Ricks, T., 'US Military Missions to Iran. 1943-1978: The Political Economy of Military Assistance', *Iranian Studies*, vol. 12, nos. 3-4 (1979), pp. 163-93
Roosevelt, Archie, Jr., 'The Kurdish Republic of Mahabad', *Middle East Journal*, vol. 1, no. 3 (July 1947), pp. 247-69
Ross, Dennis, 'Considering Soviet Threats to the Persian Gulf', *International Security*, vol. 6, no. 2 (October 1981), pp. 159-80
Rouleau, Eric, 'Khomeyni's Iran', *Foreign Affairs*, vol. 59, no. 1 (Fall 1980), pp. 1-20
Rubin, Barry, 'American Relations with the Islamic Republic of Iran, 1979-1981', *Iranian Studies*, vol. 13, nos. 1-4 (1980), pp. 307-26
Rubinstein, Alvin Z., 'Soviet Persian Gulf Policy', *Middle East Review*, vol. 10, no. 2 (Winter 1977-78), pp. 47-55
—— 'The Evolution of Soviet Strategy in the Middle East', *Orbis*, vol. 24, no. 2 (Summer 1980), pp. 332-7
—— 'The Soviet Presence in the Arab World', *Current History*, vol. 80, no. 468 (October 1981), pp. 313-16, 338-9
—— 'The Soviet Union and Iran under Khomeini', *International Affairs* (London), vol. 57, no. 4 (Autumn 1981), pp. 599-617
—— 'The Last Years of Peaceful Co-existence: Soviet–Afghan Relations 1963-1978', *Middle East Journal*, vol. 36, no. 2 (Spring 1982), pp. 165-83

—— 'Afghanistan Embraced by the Bear', *Orbis*, vol. 26, no. 1 (Spring 1982), pp. 135-53

Sale, Richard, 'Carter and Iran: From Idealism to Disaster', *The Washington Quarterly*, vol. 3, no. 4 (Autumn 1980), pp. 75-87

Sciolino, Elaine, 'Iran's Durable Revolution', *Foreign Affairs*, vol. 61, no. 4 (Spring 1983), pp. 893-920

Shmulevitz, Aryeh, 'The Iranian Revolution and the Iranian Marxists: Programme, Participation and Hopes', *Slavic and Soviet Series* (Russian and East European Research Centre, Tel Aviv University), vol. 4, nos. 1-2 (1979), pp. 59-73

Sicherman, Harvey, 'Reflections on "Iraq and Iran at War"', *Orbis*, vol. 24, no. 4 (Winter 1981), pp. 711-18

Smolansky, Bettie, and O.M. Smolansky, 'Soviet and Chinese Influence in the Persian Gulf' in Alvin Z. Rubinstein (ed.), *Soviet and Chinese Influence in the Third World* (Praeger, New York and London, 1975), pp. 131-53

Smolansky, O.M., 'Moscow and the Persian Gulf: an Analysis of Soviet Ambitions and Potential', *Orbis*, vol. 14, no. 1 (Spring 1970), pp. 92-108

—— 'Soviet Policy in Iran and Afghanistan', *Current History*, vol. 80, no. 468 (October 1981), pp. 321-4, 339

Steinbach, Udo, 'Iran – Half Time in the Islamic Revolution', *Aussen Politik* (English edn.), vol. 31, no. 1 (1980), pp. 52-68

Stork, Joe, 'Iraq and the War in the Gulf', *MERIP Reports*, no. 97 (June 1981), pp. 3-18

Sullivan, William H., 'Dateline Iran: The Road Not Taken', *Foreign Policy*, no. 40 (Fall 1980), pp. 175-86

Tekiner, Suleiman, 'Soviet–Iranian Relations over the Last Half Century', *Studies on the Soviet Union* (Munich), vol. 8, no. 4 (1969), pp. 36-44

Volodarsky, Mikhail and Yaacov Ro'i, 'Soviet–Iranian Relations During Two "Revolutions"', *Slavic and Soviet Series* (Russian and East European Research Centre, Tel Aviv University), vol. 4, nos. 1-2 (1979), pp. 33-58

Watt, D.C., 'The Persian Gulf – Cradle of Conflict', *Problems of Communism* (May-June 1972), pp. 32-40

Wheeler, Geoffrey, 'Soviet Interests in Iran, Iraq and Turkey', *The World Today* (May 1968), pp. 197-203

Wright, Claudia, 'Iraq – New Power in the Middle East', *Foreign Affairs*, vol. 58, no. 2 (Winter 1979-80), pp. 257-77

—— 'Behind Iraq's Bold Bid', *New York Times Magazine* (26 October 1980), pp. 43-117

—— 'Implications of the Iraq-Iran War', *Foreign Affairs*, vol. 59, no. 2 (Winter 1980-81), pp. 275-303

Wright, E.M., 'Iran as a Gateway to Russia', *Foreign Affairs*, vol. 20 (1941-42), pp. 367-71

Yodfat, Aryeh, 'Unpredictable Iraq Poses a Russian Problem', *New Middle East*, no. 13 (October 1969), pp. 17-20

—— 'Russia's Other Middle East Pasture – Iraq', *New Middle East*, no. 38 (November 1971), pp. 26-9

—— 'The People's Republic of China and the Middle East', *Asia Quarterly* (Brussels), Part I (1977/3), pp. 223-36; Part II (1978/1), pp. 67-78; Part III (1978/4), pp. 295-308

—— 'The USSR and the Persian Gulf Area', *Australian Outlook*, vol. 33, no. 1

(April 1979), pp. 60-72
——— 'Soviet–Iran Relations: Looking for Openings', *Soviet Analyst*, vol. 11, no. 3 (10 February 1982), pp. 3-5
——— 'Iraq–USSR: Between Friendship and Suspicion', *Soviet Analyst*, vol. 11, no. 10 (19 May 1982), pp. 1-3
Young, Cuyler T., 'Iran in Continuing Crisis', *Foreign Affairs*, vol. 40, no. 2 (January 1962), pp. 275-92
Zabih, Sepher, 'Communism in Iran', *Problems of Communism*, vol. 14, no. 5 (September-October 1965), pp. 46-55
——— 'Iran's International Posture: *de facto* Non-alignment within a pro-Western Alliance', *Middle East Journal*, vol. 24, no. 3 (Summer 1970), pp. 302-18

Periodicals and Newspapers

Abbreviations

L	–	London	P	–	Paris
M	–	Moscow	T	–	Tehran
NY	–	New York	W	–	Washington, D.C.

Arab-Asian Affairs (formerly *Afro-Asian Affairs*), L
Arab Report, L
Asia and Africa Today (English edn. of *Aziya i Afrika Segodniya*), M
Asian Affairs, L
Bakinsky Rabochy, Baku
Central Asian Survey, Oxford
Christian Science Monitor, Boston
Current History, Philadelphia, Pa.
Daily Report, Foreign Broadcast Information Service (FBIS), USA
Daily Telegraph, L
The Economist, L
[*Eight*] *8 Days*, L
Ettela'at, T
Events, L
Financial Times, L
Foreign Affairs, NY
Foreign Policy, NY and W
Horizont, East Berlin
L'Humanité, P
International Affairs, L
International Affairs, M
International Herald Tribune, P and Zurich
International Security, Cambridge, Mass.
Iranian Studies, Boston
Izvestia, M
Keyhan, T
Kommunist, M
Kommunist Tadzhikistana, Dushanbe

Krasnaya Zvezda, M
Literaturnaya Gazeta, M
MERIP (Middle East Research and Information Project) *Reports*, W
The Middle East, L
Middle East Focus, Toronto
Middle East International, L
Middle East Journal, W
The Middle East Newsletter, L
Middle East Review, NY
Middle Eastern Studies, L
Military Review, US Army
Mirovaya Ekonomika i Mezhdunarodniye Otnosheniya, M
Mizan, L
Monday Morning, Beirut
Le Monde, P
Moscow News, M
Narody Azii i Afriki, M
New Middle East, L
Newsweek, NY
New Times, M
New York Times, NY
Observer, L
Orbis, Philadelphia, Pa.
Peking (Beijing) Review, Beijing
Pravda, M
Problems of Communism, W
Radio Liberty Research, Munich
RIPEH (The Review of Iranian Political Economy and History), Georgetown University, W
RUSI (Journal of the Royal United Services Institute for Defence Studies), L
Soviet Analyst, L
Sovyetskaya Rossiya, M
Der Spiegel, Hamburg
SShA – Ekonomika, Politika, Ideologiya, M
Summary of World Broadcasts, British Broadcasting Corporation (BBC), L
Sunday Telegraph, L
Sunday Times, L
Survival, L
Swiss Review of World Affairs, Zurich
The Times, L
Trud, M
The Times, L
US News & World Report, W
Washington Post, W
The Washington Quarterly, W
World Marxist Review, Prague
The World Today, L
Za Rubezhom, M
Zarya Vostoka, Tbilisi

INDEX

Turkomans 57-9, 63
Tyrtov, P. 4

Union of Soviet Socialist Republics
(USSR): aims in relation to Iran
145-6; economic and technical
co-operation with Iran 16, 21, 22,
29, 30, 32, 34, 38-41, 46, 55, 59,
73-4, 100-2, 131; joint Soviet-
Iranian companies 18, 20, 21;
KGB in Iran 132, 142; military
co-operation, Soviet military supplies 30, 31, 33, 97-8, 131, 132,
147n7; rapprochement with Iran
27-31; Shah visits in the Soviet
Union 30, 32, 37, 39, 40; Soviets
and fall of Shah regime 44-52;
Soviets and internal Iranian
politics 82-4, 114-19; Soviet
attempts to attract Islamic Iran
54, 55, 93-7; Soviet criticism of
Islamic Iran 58-61, 102-5, 117-18;
Soviet involvement in Iran 47, 48,
50, 64, 71, 72; Soviet-Iranian
Intelligence co-operation 98-9;
Soviet-Persian Treaty of 1921
12-13, 26, 50, 65, 68, 72; Soviet-
Persian Treaty of 1927 13-14, 26;
'White Revolution', Soviet positions 29, 30, 41n16
United States of America (USA) 18,
20-2, 24n30, 25-8, 32-6, 38,
42n40, 44, 51, 52n12, 54, 61, 65,
66, 68-72, 77-80, 82, 83, 86, 94,
96, 103, 104, 107-9, 111-17, 119,
133, 136-8, 141, 146, 147;
seizure of American hostages 68,
70, 77, 78, 86, 113, 141; USA-
Iran Security Pact 1959 26
Universities in Iran, closure of 84,
115
Umm Qasr 39
Usmankhodzhayev, Inamadzhan 92
USSR, Muslims in 74-7, 89n34, 106,
108, 145

Vance, Cyrus 65
Velayati, 'Ali Akbar 99
Vinogradov, Vladimir 94, 95, 99
Volga 39, 73

Witte, S. 4, 7

Yazdi, Ibrahim 65, 99

Yemen, North 31, 109, 136
Yerevan 1, 2
Yugoslavia 102, 122, 131

Zagros mountains 146
Zahedi, Fazlollah 22
Zamyatin, Leonid M. 48, 49, 134